Toni Morrison

MANCHESTER
UNIVERSITY PRESS

CONTEMPORARY WORLD WRITERS

SERIES EDITOR   JOHN THIEME

Toni Morrison

JILL MATUS

Manchester University Press

Manchester and New York

distributed exclusively in the USA by St. Martin's Press

813.54
MORRISON

Published by Manchester University Press
Oxford Road, Manchester M13 9NR, UK
and Room 400, 175 Fifth Avenue, New York, NY 10010, USA

Distributed exclusively in the USA by
St. Martin's Press, Inc., 175 Fifth Avenue, New York, NY 10010, USA

Distributed exclusively in Canada by
UBC Press, University of British Columbia, 6344 Memorial Road, Vancouver, BC, Canada V6T 1Z2

British Library Cataloguing-in-Publication Data
A catalogue record for this book is available from the British Library

Library of Congress Cataloging-in-Publication Data applied for

ISBN 0 7190 4447 2 *hardback*
    0 7190 4448 0 *paperback*

First published 1998
05 04 03 02 01 00 99 98   10 9 8 7 6 5 4 3 2 1

Typeset in Aldus
by Koinonia, Manchester
Printed in Great Britain
by Bell & Bain Limited, Glasgow

SW/EST

For Geoff, Lauren
and Hayley

Contents

Acknowledgements

I thank first the students in courses I have taught on Morrison and other African American women novelists over the last five years at the University of Toronto, and in particular the members of my graduate seminar (1995–96). My focus on Morrison's engagement with questions of trauma, history and memory has been sharpened by the opportunity to think through these questions at every stage with perceptive and challenging readers.

The research for this project was funded by a grant from the Social Sciences and Humanities Research Council of Canada (SSHRCC) and a General Research Grant from the Department of English, University of Toronto. I thank also the Division of Humanities at Scarborough College, University of Toronto, for valuable release time. This project owes much to the labours of Jennifer Andrews and Heidi Tiedemann, my two indefatigable research assistants. Their industry and application have been inspirational.

I am very grateful to the many colleagues and friends who offered advice, suggestions, support and the opportunity to discuss my work. The Scarborough College theory group provided a stimulating forum for discussions on trauma. I am indebted also to the audiences who heard various parts of this project as conference presentations at The Learned Societies Conference, Montreal, Canada, 1995, and the 25th meeting of the International Comparative Literature Association, Leiden, Holland, 1997.

Finally, I would like to thank Matthew Frost, my editor at Manchester University Press, who made it possible for me to include a postscript on *Paradise*, which was published while this book was in press.

Note on the texts used

Unless otherwise specified, page references throughout the text refer to the Picador editions of Morrison's novels.

Series editor's foreword

Contemporary World Writers is an innovative series of authoritative introductions to a range of culturally diverse contemporary writers from outside Britain and the United States, or from 'minority' backgrounds within Britain or the United States. In addition to providing comprehensive general introductions, books in the series also argue stimulating original theses, often but not always related to contemporary debates in post-colonial studies.

The series locates individual writers within their specific cultural contexts, while recognising that such contexts are themselves invariably a complex mixture of hybridised influences. It aims to counter tendencies to appropriate the writers discussed into the canon of English or American literature or to regard them as 'other'.

Each volume includes a chronology of the writer's life, an introductory section on formative contexts and intertexts, discussion of all the writer's major works, a bibliography of primary and secondary works and an index. Issues of racial, national and cultural identity are explored, as are gender and sexuality. Books in the series also examine writers' use of genre, particularly ways in which Western genres are adapted or subverted and 'traditional' local forms are reworked in a contemporary context.

Contemporary World Writers aims to bring together the theoretical impulse which currently dominates post-colonial studies and closely argued readings of particular authors' works, and by so doing to avoid the danger of appropriating the specifics of particular texts into the hegemony of totalising theories.

Chronology

1931 Born 18 February in Lorain, Ohio to Ramah (Willis) and George Wofford. The second of four children, Morrison has an older sister and two younger brothers.

1949 Attended Howard University in Washington, DC; joined the Howard University Players.

1953 Graduated with a BA in English, minor in Classics.

Attended Cornell to pursue graduate studies in English.

1955 Graduated from Cornell with an MA in English; her thesis, submitted under the name of Chloe Ardellia Wofford, focuses on the treatment of the alienated in Faulkner and Woolf. Instructor in English at Texas Southern University, Houston from 1955–57.

1957 Returned to Howard as an instructor in English, 1957–64.

1958 Married Jamaican architect, Harold Morrison.

1964 Divorced Harold Morrison. Has custody of their two sons, Harold Ford and Slade Kevin.

1965 Lived with her parents in Lorain, Ohio; took a job as textbook editor for Random House in Syracuse, New York.

1968 Senior Editor, Random House, New York City; responsible for nurturing the careers of many African American writers, such as Gayl Jones, Toni Cade Bambara, Angela Davis and Andrew Young.

1970 *The Bluest Eye* published.

1971 Associate Professor, English, at SUNY, Purchase, NY (1971–72).

1973 *Sula* published.

1974 Edited *The Black Book*.

1975   Nominated for the National Book Award and Ohioana Book Award for *Sula*.

1976   Visiting lecturer at Yale University (1976–77)

1977   *Song of Solomon* published. (A Book-of-the-Month Club Selection.) Received National Book Critics Circle Award and the American Academy and Institute of Arts and Letters Award for *Song of Solomon*.

1980   Appointed to the National Council on the Arts by President Carter.

1981   *Tar Baby* published. Elected to the American Academy and Institute of Arts and Letters; appeared on the cover of *Newsweek*, the first African American woman since Zora Neale Hurston in 1943.

1984   Schweitzer Professor of the Humanities at State University of New York at Albany, 1984–89.

1986   Visiting Professor, Bard College (1986–88); 'Dreaming Emmett', a drama, produced in Albany, NY, on 4 January. Received New York State Governor's Art Award. The play remains unpublished.

1987   Published *Beloved*. Regent's Lecturer at University of California, Berkeley.

1988   Won Pulitzer Prize for fiction and Robert F. Kennedy Award for *Beloved*. Received Melcher Book Award and Before Columbus Foundation Award. Received Elizabeth Cady Stanton Award from National Organisation for Women.

1989   Robert Goheen Professor of Humanities at Princeton University; joint appointment in Creative Writing and African American Studies. Awarded Modern Language Association of America's Commonwealth Award in Literature.

1990   Awarded Chianti Ruffino Antico Fattore International Literary Prize.

1992   *Jazz* and *Playing in the Dark: Whiteness and the Literary Imagination* published. Edited *Race-ing Justice, En-Gendering Power: Essays on Anita Hill, Clarence Thomas, and the Construction of Social Reality*.

1993   Chicago premier of *Honey and Rue*, a cycle of songs performed by the soprano Kathleen Battle, composed by André Previn. Awarded the Nobel Prize for Literature, Stockholm, 7 December.

1994   *Nobel Lecture in Literature, 1993* published. Awarded Rhegium Julii Prize for Literature; Condorcet Medal, Paris; Pearl Buck Award. Held Condorcet Chair, Paris.

1996   Jefferson Lecturer. Awarded the National Book Foundation Medal for Distinguished Contribution to American Letters. *The Dancing Mind* published.

1997   Edited with Claudia Brodsky Lacour and introduced *Birth of a Nation'hood: Gaze, Script, and Spectacle in the O. J. Simpson Case.*

1998   *Paradise* published. Appeared on the cover of *Time*.

Contexts and intertexts

THE body of work that Toni Morrison has produced is power-fully engaged with questions of history, memory and trauma. This study explores the way in which Morrison's novels function as a form of cultural memory and how, in their engagement with the African American past, they testify to historical trauma.[1]

At the beginning of this century, the great African American scholar and writer, W. E. B. Du Bois, drew attention to the way American historical memory was functioning to exclude African Americans. Du Bois claimed that 'the black experience stood at the center of national history, at least for those who cared to look at conflict rather than only continuity'.[2] He described a 'swarthy spectre' sitting Banquo-like in 'its accustomed seat at the nation's feast', an image which underwrites his claim that the ghosts of the past have not been appeased or laid to rest. Du Bois was concerned to represent American historical memory as haunted so that Americans would pay attention to what had been excised or forgotten in American history. His entire career was dedicated to creating a 'counter-memory' of the past in black history that would challenge cherished American myths of a promised land, and revise the foundations on which narratives of American history were built.[3]

Writing in the last quarter of the twentieth century, Toni Morrison continues the tradition that Du Bois's vision of haunt-ed historical memory has bequeathed.

> The reclamation of the history of black people in this country is paramount in its importance because while you

can't really blame the conqueror for writing history his own way, you can certainly debate it. There is a great deal of obfuscation and distortion and erasure, so that the presence and the heartbeat of the black people has been systematically annihilated in many, many ways and the job of recovery is ours. It's a serious responsibility and one single human being can only do a very very tiny part of that, but it seems to me to be both secular and non-secular work for a writer. You have to stake out and identify those who have preceded you – resummoning them, acknowledging them is just one step in that process of reclamation – so that they are always there as the *confirmation* and the affirmation of the life that I personally have not lived but is the life of that organism to which I belong which is black people in this country.[4]

Toni Morrison's observations about the erasure of the past and the need to reclaim it signal a concern with history in all her work – essays, lectures, novels, interviews. If the African American writer's responsibility is to assume the task of recovering the 'presence and heartbeat of the black people' in America, her novels take that task of recovery seriously, involving a reconstruction, revisioning and revisiting of the past. Against the 'systematic annihilation' of the presence and heartbeat of black Americans, Morrison's novels constitute a resurrection of witnessing.[5] Staking out and identifying those who have come before is, as she says, just one part of the process, and it is a part with which Morrison's fiction is abidingly, even increasingly, occupied. Her later novels, *Beloved* (1987) and *Jazz* (1992), have been even more thoroughly focused on specific historical moments than her earlier ones, and, through their engagement with the history of slavery and early twentieth-century Harlem, have imagined and memorialised aspects of black history that have been forgotten or inadequately remembered. Bearing witness to the past, Morrison's novels can also be seen as ceremonies of proper burial, an opportunity to put painful events of the past in a place where they no longer haunt successive generations. There is also the possibility, however, that such narratives may not entirely quieten the spectral by locating and situating –

making past – the traumas of history. In revisiting and reactivating traumatic experiences, they may provoke readers to the vicarious experience of trauma and act as a means of transmission. The experience of Morrison's novels is never simply curative.

Morrison's expressed desire to represent the 'presence and heartbeat of the black people' seems initially to contain a totalising claim. Phrases such as 'the black community' or 'the black experience' suggest an essentialist vision that attempts to transcend time and history. But Morrison's writing is very attentive to historical specificity, which resists any monolithic categorisation of black identity. Indeed, one of the most interesting and compelling aspects of her work is the way it urges readers to see how identities are constructed temporally, relationally and socially.

Through her fictive narratives, Morrison offers ways of imagining the subject in history. By shaping cultural memory of the past, her novels offer readers different ways of relating to the past and the future and therefore of 'being in history'.[6] Morrison's novels (with the exception of *Tar Baby* (1981)) are set in the recent, or not so recent, past. By dwelling on what has been forgotten or deliberately erased from conventional historiography, they remind readers that there is a past to remember that is perhaps different from the records of the 'conquerors'. In so doing they challenge versions of the American past that have excluded or overlooked African American collective memory. If the concept of 'Americanness' – that is, the development of a national consciousness – has depended on parts of America's history being forgotten, then Morrison's novels form a challenge to cultural and political hegemony. Ernest Renan suggested in his late nineteenth-century essay on nationhood that 'forgetting, I would even go so far as to say historical error, is a crucial factor in the creation of a nation, which is why progress in historical studies often constitutes a danger for [principles of] nationality'.[7] As Morrison analyses in her essay *Playing in the Dark* (1992) – a discussion of whiteness in the American imagination – the concept of 'American' and the treasured aspects of nationhood with which that concept is associated often depend on the suppression or silencing of a dark, Africanist other. Similarly, the introduction to *Memory and Cultural Politics: New Approaches to American Ethnic Literatures* points out that 'the dominant group in any nation-state often resorts to nostalgia, to mental or cultural ellipses, and to general forgetfulness in search of meanings and definitions that serve its own ideological needs of the moment'.[8] When Morrison refers to the history written 'by the conqueror', she articulates her awareness both of historical record as a manifestation of power relations and of the possibility of subverting hegemonic narratives through alternative remembering and recording. Morrison makes clear that 'what becomes "known" as history, is not all there is to know'.[9]

I want now to turn to the political and historical context of Morrison's life and then to discuss the concepts of cultural memory, testimony and trauma which will illuminate her concern with history and politics and frame the readings of her novels in subsequent chapters.

Family history and the civil rights movement

Over the past twenty years Morrison has been interviewed many times. From her responses to a variety of questions in these conversations, we can reconstruct a quasi-autobiographical narrative dealing with her family and her formative years. Morrison's personal and familial history draws attention to significant aspects of the wider history of African American life since the mid-nineteenth century, from the days of emancipation and migration northward, to the civil rights movement. Morrison remembers her grandfather recalling his responses to emancipation. He was a boy of five when he heard that 'the Emancipation' was coming. Imagining it to be a terrible monster, he ran and hid under the bed.[10] Morrison's parents were part of the great wave of migration from the South in the early 1900s. Her mother's family left Greenville, Alabama around 1912; her father's parents came from Georgia. Morrison's great-grandmother was a North American Indian who had been given eighty-eight acres of land by the Government during Recon-struction. 'The land got legally entangled because of some debts my grandfather, who inherited it, owed – or, rather, didn't *know* he owed.... Those people didn't really understand what was happening. All they knew is that at one point they didn't own the land anymore and had to work for the person who did.'[11] In an interview with Jean Strouse, Morrison remembers the story of her grandparents' migration:

> They had lost their land, like a lot of black people at the turn of the century, and they were sharecroppers, which meant they were never able to get out of debt. My grand-father had left Greenville for Birmingham to earn money playing the violin. He sent money back. But my grand-mother began to get nervous, all alone in Greenville, because her daughters were reaching puberty and that was a dangerous business in the South, in the country, because white boys began to circle. So my grandmother decided to leave. She sent her husband an oral message: 'We're head-ing north on the midnight train. If you ever want to see us again, you'll be on that train.' She didn't know if he got the message, but with $18 to her name she packed up her six or seven children and got them all to the train in Birmingham... My grandfather was nowhere in sight. As the train left the station the children began to cry – then about an hour later, he showed up. He'd been there all along, hiding, for fear somebody would recognize him and stop them for owing money.[12]

In Kentucky her grandfather worked in a coal mine; her grandmother did washing and her mother and aunt attended a small school. The incentive that propelled her parents to Ohio to settle near Lake Erie, in the Midwestern industrial town of Lorain was the possibility of a better education for their children.[13] Morrison has frequently remarked on the curious position of Ohio in the spectrum of states known for racism and oppression: its northern part had underground railroad stations but the southern part was 'as much Kentucky as there is'.[14] In many ways, Ohio was 'a Mecca for black people', who came to the mills and plants because it offered 'the possibility of a good life';

it was 'neither plantation nor ghetto'.[15]

Morrison grew up in neighbourhoods where there was always 'a mix of races and nationalities'.[16] Lorain could not maintain strict segregation because the town attracted many kinds of immigrants seeking work. She recalls being the only black child in her class, and the only child who could read. (She had learned at the age of four.)[17] Exposure to the many different kinds of languages she heard among her classmates and in her neighbourhood, Morrison muses, made her listen carefully to, and appreciate, the language of her own family.

> In Lorain, Ohio, when I was a child, I went to school with and heard the stories of Mexicans, Italians and Greeks, and I listened. I remember their language, and a lot of it is marvellous. But when I think of things my mother or father or aunts used to say, it seems the most absolutely striking thing in the world. That's what I try to get into my fiction.[18]

Morrison talks in interviews about the rich cultural and imaginative life of her family. Each night they would settle down to tell ghost stories. Her father's were the most spine-chilling and the best. 'As a child I was brought up on ghost stories – part of the entertainment was storytelling. Also, I grew up with people who believed it.'[19] She explains that her 'grand-mother would ask about my dreams and, depending on the content of them, she would go to the dream book, which would translate dreams into a three-digit number. That was the number you played in the numbers game....'[20] The family's interest in dreams also taught Morrison not to hide the self that is often expressed in dream, 'the secret self, the unwashed self'.[21]

Growing up during the years of the Great Depression, she witnessed the family struggle for economic survival. Her father often worked at night and held a number of jobs in order to support his family, but there were nevertheless times when the family was reliant on welfare payments and her mother once wrote an indignant letter to President Roosevelt about the quality of food given to welfare recipients.[22] The family may have been poor, but they were clearly never demoralised. 'When I graduated from high school, it was a huge thing. My mother had graduated from high school, but not my father.'[23] Morrison was the first woman in her family to attend college and recounts how her mother took 'humiliating jobs' in order to send money regularly to her while she was in college at Howard University and graduate school at Cornell.[24]

Howard University in Washington DC was established in the post-Civil War years by both white and black educators; it had its first black president in 1926, and its faculty included 'some of the best minds in America'.[25] According to Vincent Harding, the Howard Law School of the 1930s had aimed at developing 'a cadre of lawyers' who would tackle the legal foundations supporting the segregation and racial discrimination prevalent in the United States. Kenneth Clark reported that '"there was a great ferment" at the University in those days' as people felt themselves participating in a burgeoning movement for civil rights.[26] But Morrison, who attended Howard from 1949 to 1953, does not remember it as a place that particularly stimulated her consciousness of black culture and politics. The highlight of her years there was her involvement with the Howard University Players, a repertory company whose productions took her on the road to the South and gave her a glimpse of what Southern black life was like in the early 1950s.[27] It was not so much her student days at Howard that stirred her consciousness as her experiences at the University of Texas where she held a lecturing post after graduating from Cornell.

> The consciousness of being Black I think happened when I left Cornell and went to teach at Texas Southern University. You see, I had never been in a Black school like that. I don't mean my awareness was all that intense, but even at Howard University where I went to school, I remember I asked once to do a paper in the English Department on Black Characters in Shakespeare, and they were very much alarmed by that … because Howard wasn't really like that. It was sort of middle class, sort of upwardly mobile and so on. But when I left Cornell and went to Houston, even though I was only there a year and a half, in the South they always had Negro History Week; I'd

never heard of it. We didn't have it in the North.... But then I began to think about all those books my mother always had in the house – J. A. Rodgers and all those people – and all those incredible conversations my grandfather had and all those arguments that would just hurt my head when I listened to them at the time suddenly had a different meaning. There was a difference between reading the *Call* and *Post* when it came or the *Pittsburgh Courier* and all the Black papers and then going someplace when there was something called the Black press. So I think it was as a novice teacher, and that was in 1957 or 1958, that I began to think about Black culture as a subject, as an idea, as a discipline.[28]

Morrison's account of her growing consciousness of black culture as an important subject resonates in the context of the civil rights and black cultural nationalist movements in the 1950s and 1960s. A brief survey of these movements will help to contextualise Morrison's life and work. In 1954, *Brown* v *the Board of Education*, a case often cited as a foundational moment in the history of civil rights, declared that classification based solely on race was in violation of the Fourteenth Amendment and effectively reversed the apartheid doctrine of the late nineteenth-century case *Plessy* v *Ferguson*.[29] Another crucial prelude to the civil rights movement occurred in 1955 with the brutal torture and death of fourteen-year-old Emmett Till, who had travelled from Chicago to Mississippi to visit relatives. Purportedly, he talked to a white woman, or perhaps whistled at her. His death and the subsequent acquittal of the two white men tried for the horrendous crime provoked protest and extensive media coverage. (Morrison mentions this incident in a number of her novels – *Song of Solomon* (1977), *Beloved* – and it formed the basis of her 1985 play, 'Dreaming Emmett'.)[30] The twelve-month bus boycott in Montgomery, Alabama from 1955–56 is another significant moment in civil rights history. Rather than ride in the back of segregated 'Jim Crow' buses, black residents walked or found other means of transport. The boycott followed an incident in which an NAACP (National Association for the Advancement of Colored People) organiser, Rosa

Parks, refused to give up her seat and stand so that a white man, who had climbed aboard after her, could sit down.[31] Also in 1955, Martin Luther King, Jr was elected president of the Montogmery Improvement Association, and addressed the boycott's first mass meeting.[32]

After leaving Texas Southern University, Morrison returned to Howard in 1957 and taught English there until 1964. She describes herself as a 'witness' of the early stages of the civil rights movement. Sit-in protests in 1960 (Greensboro, North Carolina) spread throughout the South; over seventy thousand students participated.

> Those kids, the first who were sitting in – many of them were in my classes. I was very young then. My son was born in 1961, and I think I was a little diverted from it. I know I always seem to be going into places backward. I was not in favor of integration. But I couldn't officially say that, because I knew the terror and the abuses of segregation. But integration also meant that we would not have a fine black college or fine black education.[33]

Morrison echoes here the view articulated by Zora Neale Hurston when she wrote to the editor of a Florida newspaper attacking the Supreme Court desegregation legislation after the decision in *Brown* v *the Board of Education* (1954) on the grounds that existing black institutions would be devalued. Similarly, on the subject of busing, Morrison wondered why the assumption ruled that 'black children were going to learn better if they were in the company of white children ... What I thought ought to happen was that the money should be there for the materials for education, for the fine faculty, and so on.'[34]

The mid-1960s was the time of the Freedom Rides, when volunteers from the North and South rode by bus through areas where segregation existed to test whether the Supreme Court rulings (taking place from 1956–59) had been implemented and to determine whether bus station facilities were segregated. At this time too, the SNCC (Student Nonviolent Coordinating Committee) was formed, but debates about the efficacy of non-violent methods of protest were also growing. In Birmingham in

1963 mass protests occurred against the wide range of discrimi-
nations African Americans encountered in everyday life. The
impact of the demonstrations was national; similar protests
against segregated facilities spread across the South. In August
1963, a march on Washington was organised to protest against
the lack of concern for economic hardships suffered by African
Americans.[35] The Mississippi Summer Project of 1964, an inter-
racial attempt to educate and register voters, drew attention to
the extent of oppression in the South. Both white and black
student volunteers were exposed to violent resistance on the
part of segregationists. Although the Civil Rights Acts of 1957
and 1960 had enshrined the right of Blacks to vote, many feared
to do so because of the discriminatory and intimidatory tactics of
white voter registrars.[36] The Civil Rights Act of 1964 and the
Voters Rights Act of 1965 followed protests in Selma, Alabama
and the Selma-to-Montgomery march.

By the middle of 1966, Stokely Carmichael emerged as the
radical new chair of SNCC. Morrison had taught him at Howard
and says that he was 'the kind of student you always want in a
class – smart, perceptive, funny and a bit of a rogue. He *never*
worked, and he stimulated all the others to think.'[37] Carmichael
graduated in 1964 and was going off to Mississippi to spend a
summer in the field, intending to enter Theological college in
the autumn.

The 'classic southern phase of the movement' gave way to a
black freedom movement geared more to the Northern cities
and social and economic problems there.[38] By the time Malcolm
X was assassinated in February 1965, the black nationalist
movement and the emergence of black power was well under
way. Although there had been divisive debates and differences
among King and other leaders, the assassination of Martin
Luther King Jr in 1968 galvanised tremendous energies for continued protest and change. Where the tone of the civil rights
movement had, Stokely Carmichael charged, 'been adapted to an
audience of liberal whites',[39] black power and the Black Panther
Party, with which it became associated, declared its frustration
and rage, producing much anxiety in white communities.

Black power advocates emphasised the importance of pride in racial identity; they urged the study of black history and demanded recognition of 'the need for black-controlled institutions'.[40] They also drew particularly on the works of Malcolm X and Frantz Fanon. Fanon was born in Martinique; his experiences as a psychoanalyst in Algeria gave rise to writings that continue to be extremely influential among post-colonial thinkers today. According to William Vandeburg, the effects of cultural colonisation were tantamount to 'serious psycho-affective trauma'. The movement 'undertook the task of promoting a therapy of collective identity for black America',[41] and was fuelled by a '*psychological* antidote to despair that spread a positive, empowering sense of pride throughout black America'.[42] Applying the critique of colonialism emerging from Fanon and others, black power militants drew attention to the fact that colonialism was not just content to exploit and dominate a people, but had also to distort and undermine their history and culture. If colonial rule succeeded, the colonised would become slaves of cultural imposition. In T*he Wretched of the Earth* Fanon asserted that colonisation was aimed at robbing the colonised of cultural memory and self-possession, thus drawing attention to the fact that culture was at the very core of the struggle for freedom.[43] Fanon recognised that subordinated peoples need to assert their indigenous cultural traditions and retrieve their repressed histories, but, as Homi Bhabha notes in his discussion of Fanon, 'he is far too aware of the dangers of the fixity and fetishism of identities within the calcification of colonial cultures to recommend that "roots" be struck in the celebratory romance of the past or by homogenizing the history of the present.'[44] Bhabha emphasises Fanon's understanding that there is 'no immediate access to an originary identity or a received tradition'. Rather than espouse the notion of an 'already authenticated cultural tradition' or a set of pre-given cultural or ethnic traits, Fanon recognises that the terms of cultural engagement are produced performatively.[45]

Although America itself can be seen as a post-colonial nation, it has been argued that 'postcolonial discourses compel us to remember America also as an imperialist nation'. It has been suggested, therefore, that the situation of African Americans and Native Americans in American society can be explained 'in terms of their treatment as internal colonial subjects'.[46] As early as the 1960s, black intellectuals 'began to speak of Afro-America as an internal colony at war with the forces of cultural degradation and assimilation'.[47] While obviously not exclusively cultural, then, the black power movement, Vandeburg rightly concludes, was 'essentially cultural'.[48] Black cultural nationalists formulated the programme that has become known as 'the Black Aesthetic'. As the 'cultural arm of black nationalism', it offered views and prescriptions about the function of black art.[49] The ideologies inscribed in the Black Aesthetic were in many ways inimical to women writers whose feminist consciousness reacted against its sexism. As recent studies have shown, the work of writers such as Morrison, Gayl Jones and Alice Walker demonstrates a complex ambivalence toward Black Aesthetic cultural and artistic prescriptions.[50] Yet it is also clear that Morrison's fiction can be usefully contextualised in terms of certain aspects of the Black Aesthetic – the cultural reclamation and anti-colonialism that forms its core.

Imagination and history

When asked by an interviewer if she was actively involved in current politics, Morrison affirmed her deep involvement, but not as a member of any organisation. 'I am active in terms of where I speak, and the things I write about.'[51] Morrison herself responds to political and social issues at times surprisingly, her opinions and perceptions often working against the grain of established opinion. As we have seen, she expressed reservations about desegregation in the 1950s. When discussing the question of teenage pregnancy with a recent interviewer, she rejected the standard view that young women should be persuaded to defer childbearing until they had job skills and a means of supporting themselves, arguing that teenage bodies were fit and ready to make babies. In 'What the Black Woman Thinks About Women's Lib', Morrison ironically applauded the segregationist label 'White Ladies/Colored Women' because 'women' were better than 'ladies'. While the former were associated with patriarchal propriety and class inequalities, the latter were identified as 'tough, capable, independent and immodest'. White feminists could thus be said to have stolen the roles of black women – 'shacking up' rather than marrying, taking on single parenthood, while also, in some cases, depending for their liberation on black women as child-minders and cleaners.[52] It is because Morrison often thinks against the grain that she arrives at the unusual, the profound. Refusing the tradition of protest fiction, refusing to subscribe to some of the tenets of the Black Aesthetic movement of the 1960s, refusing also any easy identification with the women's movement, Morrison's fiction is nevertheless decidedly political, aesthetic and feminist.

In what way is her art political? In a 1974 interview with Alice Childress (and again, more recently, in a television interview with Antonia Byatt) she was questioned on her views about the political nature of art and responded that 'all good art has always been political' and that no 'real artists have ever been non-political'. The artist 'bears witness' and in this way she cannot avoid being political.[53] The emphasis here on the political implications of bearing witness through art is often repeated in Morrison's articulations about her role as a novelist and the social power of art.

> I suppose all artists have either to bear witness or effect change – improvement – take cataracts off people's eyes in an accessible way. It may be soothing; it may be painful, but that's his job – to enlighten and to strengthen…. So now I think novels are important because they are socially responsible. I mean, for me a novel has to be socially responsible as well as very beautiful.[54]

Morrison has also said, 'I use this phrase "bear witness" to explain what my work is for. I have this creepy sensation … of loss. Like something is either lost, never to be retrieved, or something is about to be lost and will never be retrieved … [S]omebody has to tell somebody something.'[55]

Morrison's views about the power of art emerge in remarks she has made about some of the difficulties she faced when writing *Beloved*. She talks about the fear of not properly burying the people she has raised in imaginative recreation, her sense of 'the responsibility ... for the woman I'm calling Sethe, and for all these people; these unburied, or at least unceremoniously buried, people made literate in art'.[56]

> When I had problems, I thought: If they can live it, I can write about it. I refused to believe that that period, or that thing [slavery] is beyond art. Because the consequences of practically everything we do, art alone can stand up to. It's not the historians' job to do that – you know what I'm saying? You will get some truth out of it that is not just the province of the natural or social sciences. I said, then the slaveholders have won if this experience is beyond my imagination and my powers. It's like humor: You have to take the authority back; you realign where the power is. So I wanted to *take* the power. They were very inventive and imaginative with cruelty, so I have to take it back – in a way that I can tell it. And that is the satisfaction.[57]

What does it mean to say that 'art alone' can 'stand up to the consequences of practically everything that we do'? In contrasting the job of the historian to that of the artist and in distinguishing the truth of art from that of the natural or social sciences, Morrison draws attention to the special nature of literary testimony, which may have something to do with the fact that literature is able to explore the taboo, the psychic, as well as the historical. It can dwell on the imagined interior world and the formation of subjectivity. It is able to elicit powerful responses and urge ethical considerations.

Morrison observed in her *Nobel Lecture in Literature, 1993* that she has never regarded narrative as mere entertainment, but as one of the 'principal ways in which we absorb knowledge'. The tale she retells in that lecture concerns the power of language and the responsibility for using language properly. Language that lives has 'nuanced, complex, mid-wifery properties';[58] language that does not is 'dumb, predatory, sentimental,' exciting 'reverence in schoolchildren, providing shelter for despots, summoning false memories of stability, harmony among the public.[59] Morrison points to the dangers of 'memorializing language', which is needed to 'mask the pity and waste of needless death' and the dangers of the language of 'surveillance disguised as research; of politics and history calculated to render the sufferings of millions mute'.[60] Associating 'memorializing language' with the sentimentality and nostalgia needed for nation-building and forgetting, Morrison contrasts language that gives life, that assists with the birthing of new ideas and responses.[61] One question that can be put to her novels is whether language engaged in producing cultural memory can ever be exempt from the dangerous masks of memorialising she articulates here.

In bearing witness to what she has called the life of 'that organism ... which is black people in this country', to what sources does Morrison turn?[62] She says that when she first began to write she would do no research in the area because she distrusted 'the source of research, that is, the books that were available, whether they were religion or philosophy and so on. I would rely heavily and almost totally on my own recollections and, more important, on my own insight about those recollections.'[63] Morrison has also said that she cannot trust much research because the kind of information she wants is not written down: 'I mean I can't go to most history books. I can go to some now, I suppose, but certain kinds of things I have to either remember them or be reminded of them or something.'[64] Two rather unusual historical sources provided Morrison with the basis for her most recent novels: *The Black Book* and *The Harlem Book of the Dead*. When Morrison was an editor at Random House she helped produce *The Black Book*, a compendium of information – anecdotes, personal genealogies and histories, songs, newspaper clippings – that adumbrates a history of ante- and post-bellum black communities. It was from a newspaper report about the case of Margaret Garner, a slave woman who had killed her children rather than allow them to be taken back into slavery, that she found the germ of *Beloved*.

And in 1978, Morrison wrote the Foreword to *The Harlem Book of the Dead*, a collection of photographs and poems inspired by them, which was edited by Camille Billops. Here she saw the photograph of a young woman who was shot by her lover, which proved the inspiration for *Jazz*. What her Foreword to the book emphasises is the role of memory in historical recovery. To cherish remembrance is to allow memory to bring enlightenment:

> That this remarkable concert of Black subject, Black poet, Black photographer and Black artist focuses on the dead is significant for it is true what Africans say: 'The Ancestor lives as long as there are those who remember.' *The Harlem Book of the Dead* ... cherishes that remembrance and enlightens us as only memory can.[65]

Both history and the novel are discourses that depend on narrative but what distinguishes the novel is its acknowledgement and affirmation – even celebration – of the role of the imagination. Morrison's clearest articulation of the relation between cultural memory and imagination occurs in an essay, 'The Site of Memory', which appeared in *Inventing the Truth: The Art and Craft of the Memoir*, a volume of essays on autobiographical writing.[66] She begins by saying that her inclusion in a series of talks on autobiography is not 'a misalliance'. In the first place, an important part of her own literary heritage is the autobiography because the slave narrative, a form of autobiography, was an early form of African American writing. Many slave narratives were extremely popular and widely circulated, but because they were written expressly to further the abolitionist cause, they often excised the interior life of the writer and a veil was continually drawn over events too horrible to relate.

> For me – a writer in the last quarter of the twentieth century, not much more than a hundred years after Emancipation, a writer who is black and a woman – the exercise is very different. My job becomes how to rip that veil drawn over 'proceedings too terrible to relate.' The exercise is also critical for any person who is black, or who belongs to any marginalized category, for historically, we

were seldom invited to participate in the discourse even
when we were its topic.[67]

Morrison proceeds to claim a special status for the imagination
by showing how that faculty may penetrate areas that seem
erased from history. Memories are important, she concedes, but
'memories and recollections won't give me total access to the
unwritten interior life of these people. Only the act of the
imagination can help me.'[68] Elsewhere she notes that 'the vitali-
ty of language lies in its ability to limn the actual, imagined and
possible lives of its speakers, readers, writers.'[69] As we shall see
in the following chapters, Morrison's novels are not only an
exercise of imagination in history – an augmentation and creation
of memory – they also depend on her ability to imagine memories
and the feelings that accompany them. Since Morrison is
interested in the excised interior life, she dwells on the stuff of
subjective experience – memory, fantasy, desire, as well as
amnesia, trauma, denial. The process of remembering and coming to terms with memories of the past, evident pre-eminently
in *Beloved* and *Jazz* – the first two parts of a trilogy of novels
charting the history of African Americans – is also a concern in
her earliest work, *The Bluest Eye* (1970), whose narrator is
wrestling with her childhood memories and her implication in
the tragic fate of Pecola Breedlove. Through her emphasis on
memory, Morrison reveals an abiding interest in the presentness of the past and the ways in which collective memory can
become a powerful cultural authority. As Benedict Anderson
has famously observed, 'communities are to be distinguished not
only by their falsity/genuineness, but by the style in which they
are imagined'.[70] In 'Memory, Creation, and Writing', Morrison
lists the characteristics of African American aesthetic traditions,
including 'antiphony, the group nature of art, its functionality,
its improvisational nature, [and] its relationship to audience
performance'.[71] The text is like 'a map' which invites readerly
engagement; it must also 'bear witness and identify that which
is useful from the past and that which ought to be discarded'.[72]

    In Morrison's view, history is never over, never simply in
the past. Its repercussions and traumatic consequences generate

the effects of the present and continue to shape it.[73] Without knowledge of that history, the present can be only poorly understood. In order to illustrate the importance Morrison places on historical awareness, I want to turn briefly to two of her recent non-fiction publications, both of which insist on historicity and contextualisation, and draw attention to the consequences of denial or distortion. As editor of *Race-ing Justice and Engendering Power* (1992), a volume of essays on the confirmation of Clarence Thomas as a US Supreme Court Justice, Morrison contributed an introduction entitled 'Friday on the Potomac'. In it, she draws attention to the controversy surrounding the confirmation as it coalesced in the accusations of sexual harassment by Anita Hill. Her frame for the ensuing essays is an insistence on history and context: 'what is at stake during these hearings is history itself';[74] what we need, she says, is 'perspective, not attitudes; context, not anecdotes; analyses, not postures'. And if there is to be 'any kind of lasting illumination the focus must be on the history routinely ignored or played down or unknown'.[75] Morrison then goes some way to suggest that history by drawing an analogy between Clarence Thomas and the character Friday in Daniel Defoe's *Robinson Crusoe*. She focuses on the way Friday internalises Crusoe's language and its uses. But, she continues, 'being rescued into an adversarial culture can carry a huge debt'.[76] Once rescued, as it were, Thomas as Friday forgets from whence he has come:

> Both Friday and Clarence Thomas accompany their rescuers into the world of power and salvation. But the problem of rescue still exists: both men, black but unrecognizable at home or away, are condemned first to mimic, then to internalize and adore, but never to utter one single sentence understood to be beneficial to their original culture, whether the people of their culture are those who wanted to hurt them or those who loved them to death.[77]

Further, she asserts that the Clarence Thomas/Anita Hill case is not just about these two people, but can be seen as paradigmatic of the way race and gender routinely provide categories on to which the nation can project or displace its problems:

As in virtually all of this nation's great debates, nonwhites and women figure powerfully, although their presence may be disguised, denied, or obliterated. So it is perhaps predictable that this instance – where serious issues of male prerogative and sexual assault, the issues of racial justice and racial redress, the problematics of governing and controlling women's bodies, the alterations of work space into (sexually) domesticated space – be subsumed into the debate over the candidacy for the Supreme Court. That these issues should be worked out, on, and inscribed upon the canvas/flesh of black people should come as no surprise to anyone.[78]

Arguing that Thomas functions as a site for projection, she notes that 'in a society with a history of trying to accommodate both slavery and freedom, and a present that wishes both to exploit and deny the pervasiveness of racism, black people are rarely individualized'.[79] She herself moves from the individuals involved to analyse their situation in terms of a historical awareness of the way 'blackness' is socially constructed. 'The exorcism of critical national issues was situated in the miasma of black life and inscribed on the bodies of black people.'[80] Her emphasis on inscription here accords with the analysis in the lectures she gave at Harvard, later published as *Playing in the Dark: Whiteness and the Literary Imagination*, which focuses on the powerful, if often occluded, Africanist presence in American literature and therefore in the American imagination and construction of national identity. The first chapter of this short book, 'Black Matters', has been excerpted in anthologies of critical theory because very clearly and simply it articulates how the question of race ought necessarily to inform any reading of American literature. Here Morrison does for literature what Du Bois was trying to do for history in evoking the image of the 'swarthy spectre'. Drawing on post-structuralist theory of the last decade, especially the notion that meaning and identity are relational rather than essential or intrinsic, contingent rather than absolute, Morrison reveals how the opposition of 'white' and 'black' generates meanings which are mutually dependent. The meaning of what it is to be 'white' depends on, and is inextricably bound up with, the meanings associated with 'black'. She is not arguing here that we should read forgotten or unacclaimed texts by black writers, or even that black writers be admitted into the American canon. Rather, by showing us how the question of race has been eclipsed or erased from critical treatments of American literature, she reveals that, whether mentioned or not, whether absent or present in the literature, the Africanist presence was crucial to many generations' sense of their Americanness:

> One likely reason for the paucity of critical material on this large and compelling subject is that, in matters of race, silence and evasion have historically ruled literary discourse. Evasion has fostered another, substitute language, in which the issues are encoded, foreclosing open debate. The situation is aggravated by the tremor that breaks into discourse on race. It is further complicated by the fact that the habit of ignoring race is understood to be a graceful, even generous, liberal gesture. To notice is to recognize an already discredited difference. To enforce its invisibility through silence is to allow the black body a shadowless participation in the dominant cultural body.[81]

Talking of the 'ornamental vacuum' in literary discourse on the presence and influence of black subjects, Morrison argues that criticism needing 'to insist that literature is not only "universal" but also "race-free" risks lobotomizing that literature and the art and artist'.[82] She goes on to show that American literature could not help but be shaped by its encounter with racist ideology – in places it was complicit with racist thinking, in others it exploded and undermined it. The literary text that provides her with a test case is Willa Cather's unacclaimed novel, *Sapphira and the Slave Girl*. Cather attempts in the novel to address the interdependent working of power, race and sexuality in a white woman's battle for coherence. What Morrison shows is that the contradictions and problems in this text arise from racial questions and the way the identity of the white woman is dependent on her superiority and mastery of the black subjects around her.

> Nancy is not only the victim of Sapphira's evil whimsical scheming. She becomes the unconsulted, appropriated

ground of Cather's inquiry into what is of paramount
importance to the author: the reckless, unabated power of
a white woman gathering identity unto herself from the
wholly available and serviceable lives of Africanist
others.[83]

If Morrison's project in these lectures is to draw attention to
the Africanist presence in American literature and to show how
'whiteness' in the American literary imagination is dependent
on, and formed in relation to, 'blackness', her case study also
reveals that gender cannot be understood without inflections of
race. Who Sapphira is, and how the slave women are represented in the novel reveal that 'womanness' is not somehow held
fast while the variable of race is added – the combination is more
like a compound that changes the constitutive ingredients so
that they can no longer be considered separately. What Morrison urges is that we have to read Cather with attention to the
way identity is constituted through race and gender. But this
constitution takes place within time and history. The fact of
slavery – the imagination of a past under particular historical
conditions – is crucial to the story. So when we read a novel such
as Morrison's own *Beloved*, which deals with the formation and
deformation of identity under slavery, gender and race in history
will be primary concerns. Identity is relational, and white identity has in America been heavily dependent on the way it defines
itself implicitly and oppositionally to what it understands or
imagines as the black other.

In *Playing in the Dark*, Morrison considers that the 'cham-
pioned characteristics' of American literature, such as 'individu-
alism, masculinity, social engagement versus historical isolation;
acute and ambiguous moral problematics; the thematics of innocence coupled with an obsession with figurations of death and
hell', are probably 'responses to a dark, abiding, signing Africanist
presence'.[84] She continues:

Just as the formation of the nation necessitated coded
language and purposeful restriction to deal with the racial
disingenuousness and moral frailty at its heart, so too did
the literature, whose founding characteristics extend into

the twentieth century, reproduce the necessity of codes and restriction. Through significant and underscored omissions, startling contradictions, heavily nuanced conflicts, through the way writers peopled their work with the signs and bodies of this presence – one can see that a real or fabricated Africanist presence was crucial to their sense of Americanness.[85]

Both the introduction to *Race-ing Justice* and the thesis of *Playing in the Dark* historicise the way in which black people in the United States have constituted a site for constructing an other in order to produce and buoy up a superior white self. Both these works themselves are acts of bearing witness; they attest to the effects of racism that continue to shape identities in America and to reinforce the traumatic memories of slavery in successive generations of African Americans. Morrison claims that whether we are trying to understand the embroilments of race and gender in the Clarence Thomas controversy or interpreting the history of American literature, questions of black history are paramount.

In her introduction to the recently published book of essays *Birth of a Nation'hood* (1997), Morrison writes of O. J. Simpson as she did of Clarence Thomas – that his case is a site of projections and displacements. She argues that Simpson 'has become the whole race in need of correction, censoring, silencing; the race that needs its civil rights dissassembled'. The title of the essays draws attention to the repetition of history. *Birth of a Nation* (1915) was a film well received by the KKK (Ku Klux Klan) and responsible for an increase in vicious white racism. Writing in 1949, Ralph Ellison observed that with the release of this film 'the propagation of subhuman images of Negroes became financially and dramatically profitable. The Negro as scapegoat could be sold as entertainment, could even be exported. If the film became the main manipulator of the American dream, for Negroes, that dream contained a strong dose of such stuff as nightmares are made of.'[86] *Birth of a Nation'hood* invokes contemporary urban African American life through the addition of 'hood' and, in its allusion to the earlier title, calls attention to historical repetition in the resurgence of racism that attended the Simpson trial.

Memory, trauma and testimony

In a 1989 interview with Bonnie Angelo, Morrison talks about racism as it is taught, institutionalised and culturally reproduced. 'Everybody remembers the first time they were taught that part of the human race was Other. That's a trauma. It's as though I told you that your left hand is not part of your body.'[87] Her characterisation of racism as a trauma suggests a way to consider the project of her fiction. The testimony of Morrison's fiction, I will argue, is to the traumatic effects suffered not only in slavery, as represented in *Beloved*, but to the continuity, and indeed evolution, of those effects in a society that continues to be plagued by racial inequalities and structures of oppression despite the civil rights and black power movements. But if we are to consider the question of Morrison's fiction as testimony to the trauma of racism and to a history often erased or forgotten, we need to think about both the meaning of trauma and the special nature of literary testimony as opposed to, for example, testimony in a courtroom.

Usually we think of testimony as essentially historical; 'its function is to record events and to report the facts of a historical occurrence'. But, as Freudian psychoanalysis has shown, one does not have to '*own* the truth, in order to effectively *bear witness* to it'.[88] Speech itself is 'unwittingly testimonial' and the 'speaking subject constantly bears witness to a truth that nonetheless continues to escape him, a truth that is, essentially, *not available* to its own speaker'.[89] To some extent, as post-structuralist theory has emphasised, our speech is never quite in possession of its meanings. Speech is always the 'unwitting testimonial' never wholly in the grasp of the speaking subject. In the traumatised subject, however, this condition of speaking beyond consciousness and control is greatly heightened. As Cathy Caruth notes, while 'images of traumatic reenactment remain absolutely accurate and precise, they are largely inaccessible to conscious recall and control'.[90] Pondering the testimonies of survivors, psychoanalysts (for the most part) agree that what defines trauma is the very fact that an event or occurrence has not been assimilated; it is not available in the usual way to memory, interpretation, forgetting, distorting and so on. Trauma is therefore characterised as a 'disease of time'.[91] The past is not known *as* the past. Out of its place and time, it intrudes into the present, returning in exactness and literalness, pristine and ungrasped by memory.

When Freud wrote about the dreams of traumatised patients, he noticed that such dreams were not amenable to understanding in the usual terms; that is, the dreams of such patients literally returned the patients to the situations that caused them to fall ill. Unlike other dreams, the dreams of the traumatised were not interpretable in terms of unconscious wishes. Hence Cathy Caruth points out that PTSD (Post Traumatic Stress Disorder) must be understood as a pathological symptom, but not so much a symptom of the unconscious, as 'a symptom of history'.[92] It is a symptom of history presumably because the experience of the trauma has not yet been assimilated into the unconscious; it is still, in some miraculous way, a reproduction more faithful and pure, perhaps, than if it were assimilated, taken in and made the subject of memory and narrative. Yet if not made the subject of memory and narrative, the traumatic event cannot be possessed; it continues to possess the subject even though memory of it is unavailable to the consciousness.

Morrison's work is interested in 'the possessions of history', a phrase which signifies firstly the horrific events of the past that continue to possess those who were traumatised; secondly, Morrison's interest in hauntings and ghosts as manifestations of the power of that past; and thirdly, the importance Morrison places on cultural memory and historical knowledge. Steering between the poles of survival and loss, mourning and reintegration, remembering and forgetting, Morrison's fiction foregrounds memory as a crucial site for dealing with the complex negotiations of personal and communal identity.

A basic assumption (but one that is being increasingly problematised) in most work on trauma and memory is that 'the
determination and recuperation of the historical past has an
inherent ethico-political value'.[93] Theorists of trauma such as
Judith Herman observe that 'remembering and telling the truth
about terrible events are prerequisites both for the restoration of
the social order and for the healing of individual victims'.[94]
Following Pierre Janet's definition of traumatic as opposed to
narrative memory, Herman and others assert that traumatic
memory, which merely repeats the past without consciousness,
must be transformed into narrative memory, which narrates the
past as past. Once narrated, traumatic memory can be integrated
into the survivor's life story.[95]

> *Memory*, like belief, like all psychological phenomena, is
> an action; essentially it *is the action of telling a story*.
> Almost always we are concerned here with a linguistic
> operation.... The teller must not only know how to
> [narrate the event], but must also know how to associate
> the happening with the other events of his life, how to put
> it in its place in that life-history which each of us is perpet-
> ually building up and which for each of us is an essential
> element of his personality. A situation has not been satis-
> factorily liquidated, has not been fully assimilated, until
> we have achieved, not merely an outward reaction through
> our movements, but also an inward reaction through the
> words we address to ourselves, through the organization
> of the recital of the event to others and to ourselves, and
> through the putting of this recital in its place as one of the
> chapters in our personal history.[96]

It is perhaps disturbing to note that the orderly and co-
herent narrative that Herman (following Janet) posits as an
indication of cure bears a close resemblance to the 'classic' realist
narrative, whose conceptual framework includes the consistency
and continuity of the subject.[97] The traumatised subject is
'cured' by being able to position herself/himself as a transcendent and non-contradictory subject, the 'unified and unifying
subject' of her narrative's vision.[98] Characteristic of the realist

narrative is its will to coherence, the suppression of its discontinuous and disruptive elements, and its insistence on closure as the reinstatement of intelligible order. Along the same lines, one would want to remark the emphasis in accounts of trauma recovery on continuity and coherence, which overlooks the way the category of history and traditional narratives of history have been problematised by recent theorists. Writing in the late 1970s, Hayden White notes that

> [I]f the present generation needs anything at all it is a willingness to confront heroically the dynamic and disruptive forces in contemporary life. The historical serves no one well by constructing a specious continuity between the present world and that which preceded it. On the contrary, we require a history that will educate us to discontinuity more than ever before; for discontinuity, disruption, and chaos is our lot.[99]

Such post-structuralist discourse marks a turn to the acknowledgement of the unresolved, the discontinuous and the disruptive, which may call into question the emphasis in trauma theory and treatment on the continuous, sequential and integrated narrative of the self as a sign of health.

What is the relation of history and trauma to fiction? Current theorisings about trauma and the bearing of witness provide a suggestive frame for much of Morrison's fiction, whose narrative forms speak of the repressions, hallucinations and discontinuities associated with trauma and whose cast of characters includes many haunted by history, suffering from war trauma, memory dysfunction and unresolved losses. Although many critics have raised the question of trauma in relation to Morrison's representations of slavery and its effects in *Beloved*, the other novels also deserve close attention in this regard. One of the aims of the chapters that follow is to use current thinking about trauma and historical memory in readings of all Morrison's works. A potentially problematic aspect of regarding African American history as traumatic is the implied constitution of African Americans as victims, especially in the way that 'victim' connotes a pathology. When Zora Neale

Hurston declared herself 'nontragically Black', she wanted to emphasise that there was 'far too much spirituality, humor, and wisdom in the folk to view them as mere tragic victims'.[100] And bell hooks has observed that the presence of black victimisation is all too often welcomed by white liberals because victim status seems to exclude the possibility of activism or opposition. But even under traumatic circumstances – generations of slavery, oppression and racism – a rich culture of resistance, survival, heroism and celebration may exist. Nor is trauma uniformly experienced or passed on. As Morrison shows in *Song of Solomon*, even though the story of the flying African entails paternal loss and abandonment, it is also a celebratory and inspiring myth.[101] To acknowledge the traumatic effects of racism is therefore not necessarily to consign Blacks to a realm of passivity or lack of agency or to imply that victimisation is the basis of African American identity.

Another comment by bell hooks draws attention to the need to acknowledge the painful and traumatic in black history; she notes the 'envy black people have about the way the Jewish experience of the holocaust is increasingly documented – the way folks, especially in films, are made mindful and aware not only of this experience but the terrible damage to the psyches of survivors'.[102] Studies of the definition, manifestations and treatment of trauma deal most frequently with the Holocaust, the Vietnam war, the bombing of Hiroshima, and with cases of incest and rape. There is relatively little work on the experience of racism as traumatic, although some research has been undertaken to show that Vietnam war veterans experienced war traumas differently because of their different positions within American society. In 1985 Erwin Parson's research revealed the greater tendency amongst black veterans of the Vietnam war to post-traumatic stress disorders. He found that black soldiers showed a greater degree of identification with their Vietnamese victims than did other American soldiers; in addition, the experience of marginality and otherness within American society was seen as predisposing black soldiers to more serious war traumas.[103] Irving Allen has recently called for greater attention to the inflections of race in trauma research, since 'race permeates any subject related to trauma in American society: domestic violence against women, weapons control, health care....'[104]

Since trauma is often defined as an event beyond the range of normal human experience, it follows that traumatic experiences are conceived of as overwhelming events. The problem with focusing on '*an* overwhelming event' is that it excludes a range of behaviours and incidents not usually described as overwhelming and it precludes a consideration of duration and cumulation. Kai Erikson, a professor of Sociology and American Studies who has worked on responses to community catastrophes such as Three Mile Island, suggests that trauma must be understood as resulting from '*a constellation of life experiences* as well as from a discrete happening, from a *persisting condition* as well as from an acute event'. He also notes that the 'traumatic wounds inflicted on individuals can combine to create a mood, an ethos – a group culture, almost – that is different from (and more than) the sum of the private wounds that make it up. Trauma, that is, has a social dimension.'[105] Challenging the definitional status of the overwhelming event, feminist psychologists and therapists have been articulating the concept of 'insidious trauma', which refers to the 'traumatogenic effects of oppression that are not necessarily overtly violent or threatening to bodily well-being at the given moment but that do violence to the soul and spirit'.[106] As Laura Brown points out, '"real" trauma is often only that form of trauma in which the dominant group can participate as a victim rather than as the perpetrator or etiologist of the trauma. The private, secret, insidious traumas to which a feminist analysis draws attention are more often than not those events in which the dominant culture and its forms and institutions are expressed and perpetuated.'[107] Her analysis opens the way for exploring the experience of marginal groups constituted through ethnic and racial difference.[108]

If we cease to focus on an overwhelming event but look at the effects of a range of incidents, attitudes and behaviours which are cumulatively experienced by particular groups as oppressive and destructive, can we continue to speak of traumatised subjects? To claim that racial oppression should be viewed as productive of trauma is to move away from the emphasis on an overwhelming event that cannot be registered or recorded by the usual processes of memory in order to look at the local, habitual, everyday (therefore often unremarkable or invisible) forms of oppression. The scope of the term 'trauma' is further widened through the notion of trans-generational traumatic effects. Though usually thought to relate to an individual's direct experience, trauma can, according to some theorists, be experienced from one generation to the next. Maria Root observes:

> The effects of insidious trauma can be passed down trans-generationally through stories of atrocities about what has been done to those who have come before…. Over time, the nature of this type of trauma manifests itself in one's reactivity to certain environmental stimuli, as one carries not only one's own direct experiences, but also the unresolved traumatic experiences of those who went before. Given that the dynamics of domination by gender and race are similar, one's own experiences may easily make come alive the stories of those who went before.[109]

Both 'insidious' and 'trans-generational' trauma are important in considering the production of subjectivities in the context of race and gender oppressions.

In *Surviving Trauma*, David Aberbach notes that trauma can destroy a survivor's power to fantasise and thus greatly diminish spontaneity and individuality.[110] The defence against feelings that threaten to overwhelm is the cessation of feeling; survivors often deny whole sectors of emotion which are sealed off in response to trauma.[111] It is as if, bearing a freight of history, the traumatised patient is thoroughly overburdened. Among those overburdened with history in Morrison's canon are Pecola, Shadrack, Sethe, Violet and Joe, all of whom manifest symptoms of deep disturbance and disorders of memory or affect that direct attention to the personal and psychic effects of a wider history of racism and oppression. Characters who are *possessed* by the past allow Morrison to raise and mediate an unassimilated history. Indeed, Morrison's interest in the traumatised character is manifestly a sign of her own readiness to probe the horrors of the past: she restores history precisely by writing under the sign of trauma and denial. Though the question of trauma in Morrison's novels may be approached by looking at a range of characters who are to a greater or lesser degree possessed by history, the nature of the narrative itself (and the kinds of responses provoked in its readers) is often a way of inscribing trauma. The process of Morrison's novels is an imaginative re-envisioning of black history in order to allow her readers to re-experience the affect in relation to events that have not been collectively emotionally processed. Morrison's representation of trauma is an attempt to bring to consciousness what has been repressed and sealed off, both in literary and fictive representation and in historical narrative. Literature, then, becomes an important means of resurrecting the witness, an important form of cultural memory. As Shoshana Felman puts it, literature may become a witness, 'perhaps the only witness, to the crisis within history which precisely cannot be articulated, witnessed in the given categories of history itself'.[112]

Writing about *Beloved* a few years after its publication, Morrison characterised the book as a testament, a monument to those who lived and died in slavery:

> There is no place you or I can go, to think about or not think about, to summon the presences of, or recollect the absences of slaves; nothing that reminds us of the ones who made the journey and of those who did not make it. There is no suitable memorial or plaque or wreath or wall or park or skyscraper lobby. There's no 300-foot tower. There's no small bench by the road. There is not even a tree scored, an initial that I can visit, or you can visit in Charleston or Savannah or New York or Providence, or better still, on the banks of the Mississippi. And because such a place doesn't exist (that I know of), the book had to.[113]

Her equation of book and memorial serves to emphasise the way her work functions as testimony, but it does not take into account the interactive, dialogic possibilities that her narrative provides. *Beloved* may be likened to a 'bench by the road' – a physical or material monument – but it is also a powerful opportunity for working through and witnessing what has been traumatic and therefore unspeakable. Dori Laub, a psychoanalyst who has worked with Holocaust survivors, comments on the role of the listener in hearing the testimony of traumatised patients:

> While historical evidence to the event which constitutes the trauma may be abundant and documents in vast supply, the trauma – as a known event and not simply as an overwhelming shock – has not been truly witnessed yet, not been taken cognizance of. The emergence of the narrative which is being listened to – and heard – is, therefore, the process and the place wherein the cognizance, the 'knowing' of the event is given birth to. The listener, therefore, is a party to the creation of knowledge *de novo*. The testimony to the trauma thus includes its hearer, who is, so to speak, the blank screen on which the event comes to be inscribed for the first time. By extension, the listener to trauma comes to be a participant and a co-owner of the traumatic event; through his very listening, he comes to partially experience trauma in himself.[114]

Although, as Kali Tal points out in *Worlds of Hurt: Reading the Literatures of Trauma*, Laub's emphasis on the importance of the listener comes dangerously close to deflecting attention from the traumatised subject, there is generally agreement among clinicians and therapists that the opportunity to replay the past in the presence of a supportive other is very important in the way trauma patients come to terms with the past.[115] In his study of history, trauma and the Holocaust, Dominick LaCapra suggests that interviewers and analysts become secondary witnesses in a specific sense, that is, 'in and through a labor of listening and attending that exposes the self to empathetic understanding and hence to at least muted trauma. In other words, one would attempt to put oneself in the other's position without taking the other's place.'[116] Cathy Caruth summarises: 'The history of a trauma, in its inherent belatedness, can only take place through the listening of another'.[117]

   Critics have often remarked on the special power of Morrison's fiction to elicit an audience that crosses the boundary lines of class, race and gender.[118] Creating the reader as listener, as co-producer and participant in the testimony, the reader comes, as Laub says of the analyst, 'partially [to] experience trauma in himself'. Understanding that black Americans have not wanted to dwell on the horrors of the past, Morrison also understands the need now to witness and remember that past. 'There is a necessity for remembering the horror, but of course there's a necessity for remembering it in a manner in which it can be digested, in a manner in which the memory is not destructive. The act of writing the book, in a way, is a way of confronting it and making it possible to remember.'[119] Although the reader may in some respects be likened to the listener or witness, it is important to emphasise the variety of subject positions that the reader may occupy in relation to texts that represent trauma.[120] Indeed, the therapeutic situation in which a traumatised patient works to recover and process horrific memories with the help of a listener-therapist is seldom precisely replicated in fiction that bears witness to the past. Imaginative narratives have a variety of ways to represent, even reproduce, that basic situation. The positions of patient and listener may be dispersed and displaced, so that, for example, in *Beloved*, while Sethe remembers too much and too well, a fragmented and discontinuous narrative performs a repression of memory; memory may be represented as bodily so that the arrest of affect is figured as sensory deprivation; the reader may inhabit the subject position both of the victim, who reverberates with the effects of the unresolved past, and of the healing listener.

Morrison's focus on literature as a way of making the past available to memory recalls Freud's focus on the puzzling nature of dream work among the traumatised. In 'Beyond the Pleasure Principle' Freud comments that anxiety, fear and fright need to be distinguished. While anxiety denotes a state of expectation that something unpleasant may happen, and fear suggests a definite object of which to be afraid, fright alone conveys the 'state a person gets into when he has run into danger without being prepared for it'.[121] Freud recognised that his theory of the pleasure principle demanded alteration in the face of traumatic experience. In particular, the proposition that dreams are wish-fulfilments had to be amended. The dreams of patients suffering from traumatic neuroses or psychical traumas of childhood

> arise, rather, in obedience to the compulsion to repeat.... Thus it would seem that the function of dreams, which consists in setting aside any motives that might interrupt sleep, by fulfilling the wishes of the disturbing impulses, is not their *original* function. It would not be possible for them to perform that function until the whole of mental life had accepted the dominance of the pleasure principle.[122]

The difference between the dreams of traumatised patients and others is that during their waking time, the traumatised are not much occupied with the traumatic experience; indeed they do not seem to remember it at all. The function of dreaming is upset in this condition, for the dream is no longer an expression of unfulfilled wishes. 'These dreams are endeavouring to master the stimulus retrospectively, by developing the anxiety whose omission was the cause of the traumatic neurosis.'[123] This function does not contradict the pleasure principle, but it is, however, independent of it and 'seems to be more primitive than the purpose of gaining pleasure and avoiding unpleasure'.[124] The traumatic dream asks for the experience to be available to anxiety; ordinary dreams allay anxiety and allow sleep by addressing the anxiety and recasting it into fulfillment scenarios. It may be helpful to think of Morrison's novels in relation to both kinds of dream work. On the one hand, her line-up of grotesque characters and horrific situations suggests a witnessing of the unspeakable – the traumatic dream that provokes fright. In Morrison's fiction a mother pours gasoline on her son and sets him alight; a daughter watches her mother twitch and dance as she burns; a soldier in the First World War witnesses a headless comrade who keeps running even though his head has been blasted away, and in a woodshed a mother takes a knife to her own children, slitting one baby's throat and wounding two others.[125] On the other hand, however, Morrison's work is like the dream of wish-fulfillment, the dream that raises and allays anxieties. In re-enacting moments of personal and historical trauma, the novels make available to cultural memory that which has been occluded or unacknowledged; they also foreground experiences of guilt and processes of mourning which are always precluded in the traumatised subject. Morrison's texts function both as the dream work of the traumatised and as bearers of witness to those dreams. In English, the word 'trauma' is derived from the Greek 'trauma', a wound; the word 'dream' is derived from Old High German, 'troum', in modern German, 'traum'. The close relation of dream and wound is suggestive here of the way literature, as a kind of imaginative dreaming, may deal with the wounds of history.

If Morrison's novels are, as I am arguing, a form of historical and cultural memory, one issue that needs to be explored is the relation of aesthetics to memory and the representation of trauma. What are the implications of readerly response to work that gives pleasure while it represents horror and pain? An illuminating approach to the complexity of this issue is to be found in Barbara Johnson's 1993 essay on *Sula* (1973), where Johnson articulates the implications of Morrison's aestheticising of trauma:

> choosing to aestheticize a father's rape of his daughter, a mother's murder of her grown son, a daughter's watching her mother burn, and the scars on a slave woman's back, Morrison makes the aesthetic inextricable from trauma, taboo and violation. It is not a matter of choosing between politics and aesthetics but of recognizing the profoundly political nature of the inescapability of the aesthetic within personal, political, and historical life.[126]

Johnson is arguing that Morrison challenges the clear demarcations between the domains of the aesthetic and the political. By courting the risk of turning 'horror into pleasure, violence into beauty, mourning into nostalgia',[127] Morrison provokes her readers, forestalling the politically correct response, refusing to deliver her art into the realm of the predictable. In these and other ways, as the following chapters explore, Morrison engages questions about the role of fiction, art and beauty in the representation of historical trauma.

Although Morrison's novels focus on the reclamation of erased or occluded history, they avoid any easy sense of reparation for past losses and oppressions; indeed, they imply the impossibility of restoration or redemption. Dominick LaCapra observes that working through the past may require the 'recognition of loss that cannot be made good; scars that will not disappear and wounds that will not heal'.[128] He suggests that the work of 'memory and of mourning ... can never fully overcome the extremely destabilizing or radically fragmenting effects of trauma and the need to act them out. But this work may nonetheless more or less effectively engage them and enable, however, haltingly and incompletely, a limited renewal of life.'[129] Thus, at the end of *Beloved* Morrison allows Sethe and Paul D to move forward into a shared future, to put their stories next to one another, but while Beloved appears to have been exorcised, the novel does not allow us to banish her or consign her unproblematically to the past. As Sethe says near the beginning of the novel, alluding darkly to the death of Beloved: 'I will never run from another thing on this earth. I took one journey and I paid for the ticket' (25). But there are accounts and reckonings that never balance, that are simply irreparable. These are the aspects of the past that must be remembered even as they continue to trouble and give pain; they are never comfortably possessed and they can never be redeemed. 'There is a loneliness that can be rocked' concludes the narrator of *Beloved*. 'Then there is a loneliness that roams. No rocking can hold it down' (275). Similarly, Claudia's final focus in *The Bluest Eye* is on the collective guilt of the community for the madness of Pecola, and the narrative concludes with a reminder that Pecola's traumas of rejection and rape result in a hopeless and permanent splitting of the self. *Jazz* looks at the exodus from the South to the North and the great optimism that attends the growth of Harlem society in the 1920s, but it also refuses, as Craig Werner puts it, to 'disremember the price of the ticket'.[130] The price of Joe and Violet's ticket to a new accommodation with the past and each other is the teenage Dorcas, murdered by Joe and mutilated at her funeral by Violet. Thinking that they have left the past behind them to become 'new negroes' in New York, Joe and Violet have to discover the dangerous ways in which they are still possessed by their respective histories. And even though the ending of *Jazz* looks forward to the needle that can jump the groove and avoid repeated actings out of past hurts, we are never quite sure that the new threesome of Joe, Violet and Felice will not once again prove scandalous. 'Language', Morrison declares in the *Nobel Lecture in Literature*, must defer to the 'uncapturability of the life it mourns', must refuse to 'monumentalize' or claim the last word.[131] By gesturing always to the surplus, the excess that escapes the bounds of language, Morrison reiterates that language can never '"pin down" slavery, genocide, war. Nor should it yearn for the arrogance to be able to do. Its force, its felicity, is in its reach toward the ineffable.'[132] As much as Morrison's novels constitute a form of cultural memory, then, they also disclaim the possibility of entirely transforming painful, unassimilated history into satisfactorily integrated narrative.

Shame and anger in *The Bluest Eye*

> The trauma of racism is, for the racist and the victim, the
> severe fragmentation of the self.[1]

MORRISON has said that what prompted her to begin writing
her first novel was a sense of loss, a void. 'Things were moving
too fast in the early 1960–70s... it was exciting but it left me
bereft.... There were no books about me, I didn't exist in all the
literature I had read ... this person, this female, this black did
not exist center-self.'[2] Responding to a sense of absence and a
lack in representations, *The Bluest Eye* (1970) is an imagined
history of what it is to grow up black and female in the 1930s
and 1940s, but there is another important way in which it
responds to contemporary political movements – the way things
were moving too fast in the early 1960–70s. However self-
affirming assertions such as 'black is beautiful' were in the
1960s and 1970s, they were too simple to redress the complex
and long-prepared effects of valuations based on colour. Morrison commented on the movement's assertions of racial beauty:
'If the best thing happened in the world and it all came out per-
fectly in terms of what the gains and goals of the *Movement*
were, nevertheless nobody was going to get away with that; nobody was going to tell me that it had been that easy. That all I
needed was a slogan: "Black is Beautiful"'.[3] Focusing on the
complex formations of subjectivity in a racialised country,
Morrison's first novel implicitly takes on assertions of racial
pride – black is beautiful – and scrutinises the historical backlog
of self-devaluation that such assertions cannot magically erase.

At a time when the Black Aesthetic movement was calling for positive representations and role models, Morrison created troubled and traumatised characters. Her insistence on making the reader share through Pecola the trauma of racism's effects was a way of signalling the far-reaching range and insidious nature of those effects and their causes.

Perhaps the most telling anecdote concerning the genesis of *The Bluest Eye* is to be found in the 'Afterword' to a recent edition of the novel, where Morrison describes the anger she felt at a schoolfriend's wish for blue eyes: 'The sorrow in her voice seemed to call for sympathy, and I faked it for her, but, astonished by the desecration she proposed, I "got mad" at her instead.'[4] The sorrow in the other girl's voice may call for sympathy but the wish itself encodes shame. The girl signals that she does not think herself sufficient without blue eyes – a longstanding hallmark of beauty by white Western standards. She conveys her sense of deficiency as a black subject and potentially enlists all black subjects in feeling similarly ashamed. Resisting her own exposure and belittlement as she is pulled into the same shamed category, the younger Morrison, in this brief narrative, responds angrily. The anecdote articulates a relationship between the two main emotions with which Morrison's first novel is concerned – anger and shame.

The novel is built around two young women, Pecola Breedlove and Claudia MacTeer, and their respective families. Many parallels and points of comparison connect Claudia and Pecola: most significantly, Claudia matures to look back on the past and narrate some of the novel through her memories of childhood, while Pecola, in a state of permanent dissociation, is locked in a traumatised childhood and can remember nothing. Claudia's mother may be tough and often angry, but she nevertheless communicates a fierce and protective love; Pecola's mother is more protective of her white charge than her needy daughter. Whereas Claudia's father throws the child-molesting boarder out of their house, Pecola's father is the molester of his own child. Through the stories of Pecola and Claudia, Morrison examines how identity is constructed in young women, scrutinising in the process aspects of commodity and popular culture, pedagogical strategies and the knowledges they produce, and class and labour relations. Through Claudia and Pecola, Morrison attempts to analyse the processes of resistance and submission to a hierarchy of values enshrined in American culture. She does this by exploring the relationship of these girls-becoming-women to the culture and commodities that encode the superiority of whiteness. In the following section, I focus on the narrative's exploration of anger and shame. Anger, Claudia's childhood mode, produces resistance to cultural valuations of blackness; shame, which defines Pecola, ensures submission. Finally, I explore the passage from Claudia's angry younger self to the older, memorialising narrator. It is she who bears witness to Pecola's movement from a continually shamed and diminished self to the lost, traumatised and divided subject we see at the end of the novel.

To feel shame, according to psychological theorists, is to feel a violation of one's sense of dignity, an uncomfortable exposure; it is 'to feel *seen* in a painfully diminished sense'.[5] Profoundly interpersonal, the experience of shame is also therefore social and cultural. Shame is the result of feeling deficient, whether in relation to a parent, an admired school-friend or a more powerful social group. Psychologist Gershen Kaufman summarises: 'The significance of shame lies in its profound impact on personality, psychopathology, and interpersonal relations, as well as its role in minority group relations, minority identity development, national identity development, and international relations.'[6] Any denial of need which leaves the subject feeling belittled, marginalised or inappropriate in its desires is potentially a cause of shame. As Kaufman notes, 'contained in the experience of shame is the piercing awareness of the self as fundamentally deficient in some vital way as a human being ... Shame is an impotence-making experience because *it feels as though* there is no way to relieve the matter, no way to restore the balance of things. One has simply failed as a human being.'[7] This is precisely how Claudia feels when she is ill and her mother is angry:

She is not talking to me. She is talking to the puke, but she is calling it my name: Claudia. She wipes it up as best as she can and puts a scratchy towel over the large wet place.... My mother's anger humiliates me; her words chafe my cheeks and I am crying. I do not know that she is not angry with me but with my sickness. I believe she despises my weakness for letting the sickness 'take holt'.[8]

Only the narrator's present knowledge, which is implied in the sentence, 'I do not know that she is not angry with me', suggests that one day the young Claudia will understand the memory and offset it against the significant demonstrations of her mother's caring. Angry as Mrs MacTeer usually is, she is also capable of mending the disrupted interpersonal bridge that produces shame and humiliation in her daughters. On one occasion, Claudia's elder sister Frieda is whipped because it appears that she and Pecola are 'playing dirty', whereas Frieda is merely attempting to help Pecola deal with her first experience of menstruation: 'Frieda was destroyed. Whippings wounded and insulted her' (22). Eventually when Mrs MacTeer understands the situation, 'she pulled both of them toward her, their heads against her stomach. Her eyes were sorry. "All right, all right. Now, stop crying. I didn't know"' (22). That their mother is capable of making reparation, however slight, is important in allowing Frieda and Claudia to limit their internalisation of shame and to recover a sense of worth.

But Claudia, whose uninhibited responses to the world around her give her narrative its frankness and freshness of perception, is more often angry than shamed. The first paragraph of the novel introduces us to Claudia and her sister Frieda in the grip of a powerful desire to 'poke the arrogance' out of the eyes of their neighbour Rosemary Villanucci, who is taunting them from within her father's flashy Buick. They inhibit for the moment their urge to 'smash the ownership that curls her chewing mouth', but know that when she comes out of the car, they will beat her up, 'make red marks on her white skin, and she will cry and ask us do we want her to pull her pants down' (5). Rosemary's taunts, as well as her knowledge of self-abasement and submissive behaviour, suggest a familiar world of childish power struggles and retributions that seems to depend more at this point in the narrative on class and wealth than on race, although Morrison will go on to demonstrate the way these categories mutually inflect each other.

There are ample reasons why Claudia might well be angry, not only with Rosemary Villannucci lauding it over her less affluent neighbours, but, on a larger scale, with the pervasive marginalisation and devaluation of black subjects in American culture and society. The novel demonstrates the power of that devaluation in the opening chapter's emphasis on the normative white family of the Dick and Jane reading primer. There are also frequent references to icons of white beauty such as Shirley Temple and Jean Harlow, Heddy Lamar and Claudette Colbert – the white screen goddesses on whom Pauline and Maureen desire to model themselves – as well as the pretty faces that sell candies like 'Mary Janes'. Everywhere the message resounds in American culture that black cannot be beautiful; indeed, as the Breedloves' self-loathing demonstrates, the blacker, the less beautiful.

When unstifled, Claudia's anger and transgressive urges register a resistance to the indoctrination of the dominant culture's fantasies of beauty and worth. Her anger, however, is readily converted to shame because she does not really understand what makes her feel violent and aggressive.[9] Interested anger, the text implies, is appropriate, legitimate; disinterested anger cannot understand its provocation or bind itself to any rationale. The problem of appropriate anger is articulated as Claudia moves from confessing her destruction and dismembering of white baby dolls to her disturbing desire to perform the same rites of violence on white girls. As far as Claudia is concerned, her motivation is nothing more than curiosity. Like the child who dismantles a fascinating mechanism in order to see how it is put together, she wants to take apart little white girls in order to know the secret of how they work, what makes them beautiful and desirable: 'The indifference with which I could have axed them was shaken only by my desire to do so. To discover what eluded me: the secret of the magic they weaved on others' (15).

Offering curiosity as her motive, Claudia thus never fully confronts her punitive and destructive desires. Though she later refers to her urge for dismemberment as 'pristine sadism', the pleasure of vengeance visited on white baby dolls and little white girls is only implicit in her account of her violent tendencies:

> If I pinched them, their eyes – unlike the crazed glint of the baby doll's eyes – would fold in pain, and their cry would not be the sound of an icebox door, but a fascinating cry of pain. When I learned how repulsive this disinterested violence was, that it was repulsive because it was disinterested, my shame floundered about for refuge. (15–16)

The elder Claudia is suggesting that her violence is repulsive because it fails to take in the humanity of the other, for she approaches her subjects with a curiosity that finds even their pain 'fascinating'. Disinterestedness and objectivity are conditions to which the scientific investigator aspires, but in Claudia's case, wanting to know what makes white girls attractive cannot count as a laudatory scientific goal. The text registers some satisfaction, though, in Claudia's pursuits, which suggests that her response is in some ways legitimate, or at least understandable. To the extent that Claudia is disinterested, she might as well be taking a watch apart to see what makes it tick. But the desire to know is not her only motivation.

Disinterestedness suggests also impartiality; one does not stand to gain or lose from the outcome of an act or investigation. Is Claudia's violence interested or disinterested? Though she does not gain anything from the dismemberment of white girls, she would find it of benefit, she thinks, to know the secret of their charms. Is the implication then that, had Claudia been acting openly out of political or other interests, her violence would possibly have been righteous or at least justifiable? Does Claudia's hindsight as she narrates her memories contain the recognition that she would have been less shamed by her impulses had she known that she felt murderous and enraged rather than merely curious? Or perhaps the novel suggests that by confusing curiosity and anger, she displaces the objects of her interested violence. Morrison's text stops short of acknowledging that Claudia may be less disinterested than she protests, but that that interestedness may make her violence less, not more, repulsive.

In her essay on consumer culture in *The Bluest Eye*, Susan Willis reads this passage in the following way: 'By demonstrating that violence against whites runs the risk of being "disinterested violence", Morrison suggests that white people are little more than abstractions'.[10] The point is surely not so much that whites are 'to some extent reified subjects against which it is impossible to mount passionate, self-affirming resistance or retaliation'.[11] It is rather, as Claudia later understands, that dolls, little white girls, or even 'high yellow' girls in Claudia's community are not the 'Enemy' because they are not the sources of power; they are only vessels into which power flows. No doubt dismembering white girls would have revealed as little of their secret power as had dismembering the dolls that Claudia reduced to their sawdust, gauze and metal constituents. As she admits later, when reflecting on how she hates and envies Maureen Peal, an infuriatingly self-assured, light-skinned schoolmate, 'all the time we knew that Maureen Peal was not the Enemy and not worthy of such intense hatred. The *Thing* to fear was the *Thing* that made *her* beautiful, and not us' (58). But if a '*Thing*' is behind the hierarchy of beauty and worth that Claudia is discovering, then in what forms does it manifest itself as an appropriate target for anger? As Claudia and her sister Frieda shout insults at the retreating Maureen Peal, their 'angry faces knotted like dark cauliflowers', they at least keep the 'Thing' outside of themselves. In contrast, Pecola stands apart in pain, folded into herself like a 'pleated wing'. The vulnerability of Pecola provokes Claudia's anger here just as, in the rape scene later, it will enrage her father. Pecola reminds these others of their own vulnerabilities and the perilous weakness of their defences. That perilous weakness is indicated in the incident where Cholly turns his anger on his young girlfriend rather than feel the impotence of anger against the goading white men who interrupt his first sexual experience. So Claudia is irked by Pecola's collapse in the face of Maureen Peal's insults. Whereas she and Frieda maintain a sense of their own worth by conjuring insults and creatively cursing the powerful Peal, Pecola subsides, having absorbed the slurs and teasing. Claudia reacts by wanting 'to open her [Pecola] up, crisp her edges, ram a stick down that hunched and curving spine, stand erect and spit the misery out on the streets. But she held it in where it could lap up into her eyes' (57).

Claudia's anger, directed outward, protects her sense of self. The difference then between Claudia and Pecola is that Pecola internalises the world's actions and judgements, whereas Claudia is able to defend her vulnerability by keeping devaluation external. In so far as it allows her to 'spit the misery out onto the street', her anger is salutory but, as the narrating Claudia will later admit, while anger may protect the self, it may also project itself on to a target selected because it is poorly defended and vulnerable. In that case, anger merely participates in transferring blame – a process that leads to tragic scapegoating.

Pecola's woundability – her tendency to absorb and internalise – is demonstrated in a series of shamings and rejections: the boys' taunting of her at school; the contempt of Geraldine, the mother of one of those boys; her mother's wrath and rejection when Pecola upsets the blueberry cobbler. In each case, Pecola responds to ridicule or castigation in silence, simply absorbing the censure and humiliation. Cholly's rape of his daughter is only the last, and most graphic and literal, instance of the way in which Pecola internalises the incursions of the outside. When Mr Green, the boarder who has been allowed inside the MacTeer's family home, molests Frieda, her parents forcibly expel him from the house as soon as he comes 'up on the porch'. Claudia's father hurls a tricycle at his head and her mother hits him with a broom. In contrast, there is no one to defend the boundaries of Pecola's home (and internal spaces) as her father staggers in drunk and sees her washing dishes.

But while distinctions between inside and outside may tentatively hold in the material cases of the body or the home, they

are unstable fictions when negotiating the conceptual boundaries of self and other. As we have seen, Morrison noted that the
reclamation of racial beauty in the 1960s made her think about
why such slogans as 'black is beautiful' were necessary. Even if
reviled by others, why could 'this beauty not be taken for granted within the community?'[12] As *The Bluest Eye* reveals, the
community is permeated by standards, aspirations and self-
valuations derived not only from the commodity culture which
it consumes, but inherent in the structuring of labour relations
and class positions, both heavily inflected by race. The project of
the novel is to reveal the difficulty in maintaining a strong
'inside' whether of self or community against the insidious pervasiveness of racial devaluations.

If anger helps to maintain distinctions between what belongs
to the self and what must be kept outside it, shame disturbs
those distinctions by distorting responsibility and encouraging
self-blame. In so doing it prevents interested and appropriate
anger. The culture of shame displaces the focus on external causes
or forces. Instead of feeling angry at something, one feels
ashamed of the self for something. As a means of producing self-
regulating and conforming subjects, the inculcation of shame
secures dominant interests, converting and perverting anger in
order eventually to breed false loves and desires. So shamed is
Claudia by her propensities for violence toward white girls, violence apparently unprovoked and without cause, that she opts
for the assuagement of discomforting anger in hypocritical
friendships. Her 'shame flounders about for refuge' and finds it
in shamming.

Shame displaces anger more thoroughly in Pecola's negotiations with the world. The one occasion in the text during which
Pecola experiences feelings of anger is illustrative. Not only is
her anger displaced from an appropriate target, but it hardly
rises before it subsides under shame. Feeling a storekeeper's distaste for her blackness when she pays him for the precious Mary
Jane candies she is buying, Pecola is shamed by his reluctance to
touch her hand as he takes her pennies. On leaving the store, she
is roused to a transferred anger as she trips on a sidewalk crack:

Anger stirs and wakes in her; it opens its mouth, and like a hot-mouthed puppy, laps up the dredges of her shame. Anger is better. There is a sense of being in anger. A reality and presence. An awareness of worth. It is a lovely surging. Her thoughts fall back to Mr. Yacobowski's eyes, his phlegmy voice. The anger will not hold; the puppy is too easily surfeited. Its thirst too quickly quenched, it sleeps. The shame wells up again, its muddy rivulets seeping into her eyes. (38)

The relationship between anger and shame, raised earlier in relation to Claudia's feelings towards white dolls and white girls, is made even clearer, therefore, in the case of Pecola. Anger feels better than shame because it empowers her; shame is a crippling emotion that leaves her merely humiliated, disempowered. But brief 'lovely surges' subside easily not only because the power of the other's distaste is strong, but because the anger itself is displaced. Pecola never actually feels angry with Mr Yacobowski. She is angry because she trips in the sidewalk crack. In both Pecola and Claudia, anger does not identify its appropriate object because neither Pecola nor Claudia is sufficiently aware of what causes their anger in the first place. Claudia implies that the process of growing up has, for her, included a shaming away of anger. Shame swallows anger then itself takes refuge in 'fraudulent love'. As a child, Claudia has hated baths and experienced the absence of dirt as humiliating (22); she suggests further that anger belongs to the dark, unwashed self, but the inevitable effect of being socialised means learning to love Shirley Temple and learning to love cleanliness. The linkage between fraudulent love and cleanliness suggests the sanitising, whitening process of enculturation, experienced in retrospect as a loss, or at best, 'adjustment without improvement'. Pecola's passage in the novel is from repeated shaming and humiliation to dissociation and madness. Claudia's passage is from anger to the fraudulent love which replaces anger and shame, and beyond that, through her memorialising narrative, to a recognition of the community's internalisation of self-hatred and its scapegoating techniques.

Claudia's narrative bears witness not only to the trauma of the incest and rape that Pecola experiences, but to the trauma of pervasive racism. As I outlined in the previous chapter, Laura Brown has recently argued that prevailing definitions of trauma need to be revised to accommodate the trauma that women and girls experience because of their vulnerability to rape and molestation. While trauma is usually defined as an experience of overwhelming or unusual proportions, an event 'outside the range of human experience', the work of Brown suggests that such definitions disqualify those who suffer experiences that are not, statistically speaking, beyond the range of human experience.[13] Brown objects to the way 'normal' traumatic events are defined. 'War and genocide, which are the work of men and male-dominated culture, are agreed-upon traumas; so are natural disasters, vehicle crashes, boats sinking in the freezing ocean.'[14] By defining trauma as the extraordinary, Brown argues, we delude ourselves into believing that ordinary life is safe and manageable. But ordinary life is hardly safe for incest victims or for victims of rape and molestation. She argues that there is a 'constant presence and threat of trauma in the lives of girls and women of all colors, men of color in the United States, lesbian and gay people, people in poverty, and people with disabilities'. What does it mean, she asks 'if we admit that our culture is a factory for the production of so many walking wounded?'[15] Her metaphor – factory and production – does the same work as Claudia's metaphor in the opening chapters of the novel of the unyielding earth and the seeds that fail to come to fruition. Brown's analysis of insidious trauma draws attention to the everyday occurrences that may prove traumatic for marginalised groups in a society. Brown notes too that, while mainstream trauma theory has recognised that post-traumatic symptoms can be inter-generational, as in the case of children of survivors of the Holocaust, it has yet to explore the ways 'trauma can be spread laterally throughout an oppressed social group as well, when membership in that group means a constant lifetime risk of exposure to certain trauma'.[16] Although Brown's analysis focuses largely on gender, it is also clearly applicable to race, and potentially illuminating, therefore, of Morrison's concerns in *The Bluest Eye*, a novel that represents both the traumatogenic effects of living in a racialised society as well the trauma of incest.

Brown's analysis demands that we reconsider the defining condition of Freudian trauma. Do unpreparedness, shock and fright continue to be important elements in insidious trauma? Fright itself, it could be argued, is produced not only in response to cannons firing, ships sinking or natural disasters, but also in response to the quiet opening of the bedroom door or the embrace of a male relative that is sexual under the guise of being protective. Incest may be accompanied by complex feelings that are overwhelming but may go beyond fright, covering a wide range from pain and powerlessness to guilt and pleasure. How are these to be accommodated into traditional definitions of trauma?

Morrison allows Pecola to bear witness to her suffering in her conversations with her imagined friend, but the dialogue of the split self in no way approximates a therapeutic dialogue in which teller and listener share the burden of the sufferer's history. Laub's emphasis on the listener in any testimony to trauma shows the need for sharing, participation and transmission[17] but Pecola's remains a story incapable of transmission; she cannot tell it in the 'real' world. There is, therefore, no reclamation of the past in a way that allows Pecola to assimilate and process what has happened to her.

The function of bearing witness falls to Claudia, who mediates Pecola's story, enlisting the reader as 'listener' and ultimate co-owner of the trauma. When Morrison says in an 'Afterword' that she thinks she failed in the novel because readers pity Pecola rather than find themselves moved by her, she signals her desire to have implicated the reader in Pecola's trauma. Is it possible for Claudia to 'infect' the reader with Pecola's suffering? Can the bearing of witness be delegated, as it were, to an agent?[18] Pecola is almost entirely silent throughout the novel as she sustains blow after blow of rejection and devaluation; her final dialogue as a split self is her most expressive moment. Paradoxically,

Morrison articulates Pecola's suffering most powerfully by making her a silent victim.

The nature of Pecola's silence is particularly important in the rape scene, controversially narrated largely from the father-rapist's point of view. In his discussion of the novel, Michael Awkward compares Morrison's handling of this incident to an earlier treatment of rape in the Trueblood episode of Ralph Ellison's *Invisible Man*.[19] Awkward argues that Matty Lou, Trueblood's daughter, is marginalised in a way that Pecola is not. He sees Morrison as rewriting Ellison, taking him to task for the 'phallocentric nature of his representation of incest'.[20] But Ellison's Trueblood episode is surely parodying racist stereotypes of Blacks as lacking in self-control and ruled by animal lust, an aspect of the representation that complicates Awkward's charge of phallocentricism. In his discussion of *Invisible Man*, Awkward claims that 'never in the sharecropper's rendering of the story are Matty Lou's feelings in the foreground or even actually shared with the reader'.[21] In fact, Trueblood does render his daughter's feelings, although the feelings he represents would underscore Awkward's charge of phallocentricism. Trueblood describes her initially as protesting against the rape but then responding to his presence inside her by moving rhythmically: 'Then if that ain' bad enough, Matty Lou can't hold out no longer and gits to movin' herself.... She didn't want me to go then – and to tell the honest-to-God truth I found out that I din't want to go neither.'[22] Trueblood's narrative of his daughter's physical response is admittedly self-serving since it conveniently absolves him from the blame of initiating copulatory movements, but it does go on to include the outrage of his wife and daughter and their banishment of him from the home. In contrast to what he sees as the absence of Matty Lou's feelings from Ellison's text, Awkward finds that Morrison's narrative of Pecola's response to her father's penetration of her body includes her feelings and responses. Though we are following Cholly's thoughts and successive emotional responses to Pecola – rage, revulsion, hate, love, tenderness, lust – Pecola is present through descriptions of her intake of breath – 'a hollow suck of air at the back of her throat' (128) – and the description of Cholly's painful attempt to remove himself from her dry vagina. Pecola's feelings are not represented in this scene at all, but the description of her physical state, presumably from the point of view of the omniscient narrator, suggests her feelings through descriptions of her bodily state. What Awkward does not take into account, however, is that later, in Pecola's dialogue with 'her friend', there is some close questioning about how horrible it was to have Cholly 'coming at her'. The friend quizzes her: 'The second time too?' (159). Pecola's dialogue is an internal debate in which she accuses herself of having in some way enjoyed the attentions of Cholly. Although the incest scenes are narrated very differently, both Ellison and Morrison raise the question of the daughter's response, both drawing some attention to the horror of possibly pleasurable feelings arising from an illicit and violating source. Furthermore, at the end of her novel, Morrison provocatively has Claudia recognise that Cholly loved his daughter enough to 'touch her, envelop her, give something of himself to her' (163). She recognises too that the love of a 'free man' – a man without self-imposed obligations and responsibilities – is 'never safe. There is no gift for the beloved. The lover alone possesses his gift of love. The loved one is shorn, neutralized, frozen in the glare of the lover's inward eye' (163).

The references to Pecola's rigid, 'shocked body', the silence of her 'stunned throat', the 'hollow suck of air in the back of her throat' may tell us something about her responses to the rape, but such details are signifiers of Pecola's shock, not accounts of her emotions and responses. The narrator observes that Cholly becomes conscious of her wet soapy hands on his wrists, 'but whether her grip was from a hopeless but stubborn struggle to be free, or from some other emotion, he could not tell' (128). Neither can the reader. Morrison does not, it seems, write Pecola's feelings into the scene, but rather represents through their absence the collapse of witnessing that the rape effects. The scene is narrated as if a slow-motion camera were taking in its details. It has been noted that, in moments of disclosure, incest patients are able to recall great detail and deliver accounts of the process as if it took place in slow motion.[23] What is typically absent from narration of the scene is how the victim felt. The trauma is therefore an 'event without a witness', because the witness is blocked from remembering herself or himself as a participant in the event.[24] The collapse of witnessing does not mean that the traumatised subject remembers nothing; on the contrary, what is missing from the remarkable verisimilitude of the account is only the presence of the victim. That is, commonly in trauma cases, the victim can only recount the scene by removing the consciousness or memory of self and participation. This illustrates why trauma precipitates a crisis in witnessing. The witness cannot know herself or himself as a participant in a scene of horror. If trauma occasions the excision of the self from memory, memory of one's participation and feelings, however painful, is presumed to be a sign of health. Either one possesses the past, or one is possessed by it. The emphasis on memory and remembering as a condition of health and growth in *The Bluest Eye* takes on new significance in this light. For as much as the novel is about Pecola, it is also about Claudia, whose ability to remember and bear witness, is its most hopeful aspect.

Indeed, Claudia's narrative relishes and cherishes its capacity to remember. The elder narrating Claudia has a sympathetic connection to and understanding of her younger self, whom she re-experiences as able to discern adult emotions even if she cannot comprehend the actual conversation: 'The edge, the curl, the thrust of their emotions is always clear to Frieda and me. We do not, cannot, know the meanings of all their words, for we are nine and ten years old. So we watch their faces, their hands, their feet, and listen for truth in timbre' (15). Remembering her father, Claudia recalls: 'My Daddy's face is a study. Winter moves into it and presides there. His eyes become a cliff of snow threatening to avalanche … And he will not unrazor his lips until spring' (47). Although this description does not seem to include the feelings of the younger Claudia, they are communicated indirectly in the childlike possessive, 'my daddy', and in the extended simile of his stern, wintry visage. Now Claudia understands the burdens and pressures her parents faced during the

Depression; then she simply experienced him as remote and cold. In a Proustian moment, Claudia conveys her reminiscences of summer: 'I have only to break into the tightness of a strawberry and I see summer – its dust and lowering skies' (147). 'But', she continues, self-consciously investigating the nature of memory,

> my memory is uncertain; I recall a summer storm in the town where we lived and imagine a summer my mother knew in 1929. There was a tornado that year, she said that blew away half of south Lorain. I mix up her summer with my own. Biting the strawberry, thinking of storms, I see her. A slim young girl in a pink crepe dress ... So much for memory. Public fact becomes private reality, and the seasons of a Midwestern town become the *Moirai* of our small lives. (147)

Claudia's musings here about the adaptive and absorptive nature of memory signal the difference between the mind that is constantly creative and porous and that which is indelibly imprinted but sealed off from conscious recall. Yet Claudia's reflections seem at first to undercut the power of memory to tell the truth, since memory mixes together imagination, public knowledge, and remembered affective associations. Memory's power to tell the truth, however, goes beyond accuracy of reportage. Its power is to create a past, to make narrative, to put things in time:

> The brain is an enchanted loom where millions of flashing shuttles weave a dissolving pattern. Since the mind recreates reality from the abstractions of sense impressions, it can equally well simulate reality by recall and fantasy. The brain invents stories and runs imagined and remembered events back and forth through time.[25]

Claudia's interrogation of memory late in her narrative brings the recognition that her oppositional stance toward 'everything and everybody' has bred a habit of mind that resists and critiques all around it. One the one hand, this habit of mind, like anger, is a form of salvation; on the other, it has produced an unreal valuation of self-efficacy.

We remembered Mrs. Breedlove knocking Pecola down and soothing the pink tears of the frozen doll baby that sounded like the door of our icebox. We remembered the knuckled eyes of schoolchildren under the gaze of Meringue Pie and the eyes of these same children when they looked at Pecola. Or maybe we didn't remember; we just knew. We had defended ourselves since memory against everything and everybody, considered all speech a code to be broken by us, and all gestures subject to careful analysis; we had become headstrong, devious, and arrogant. (150)

As Claudia's attention focuses on the state in which Pecola remains frozen, her own narrative becomes more self-conscious about the processes of memory, allowing an interrogation of herself and her own motives in the community's responsibility for Pecola's fate.

When we leave Claudia at the end of her meditation on anger and its accommodation in fraudulent love, we may wonder how she grows from that point to become the mature memorialising narrator who looks back on Pecola's life in the final section of the novel and reflects on Pecola's fate and the way identities are formed relationally. 'The damage done was total', she tells us (162). By this point, Claudia recognises the extent to which Pecola's vulnerability has been exploited by others. We felt 'so wholesome after we cleaned ourselves on her. We were so beautiful when we stood astride her ugliness ... We honed our egos on her, padded our characters with her frailty and yawned in the fantasy of our own strength' (163). Claudia also recognises that strength was really only aggression. Her closing litany of the accommodations and falsifications that she and others have perpetrated articulates an understanding both of why Pecola stepped into madness and the terms on which she, Claudia, survived. The honesty and self-scrutiny of the last paragraphs of the novel suggest a Claudia who can see without fraudulent accommodations, can shoulder responsibility without succumbing to the conformist culture of shame. As Claudia's narrative merges with that of the omniscient narrator, whose voice was previously more markedly distinct from Claudia's at the beginning of each seasonal section, the reader measures the extent of Claudia's growth. Whereas it is the omniscient narrator who recounts the scene of the rape – 'So it was on a Saturday afternoon, in the thin light of spring, he staggered home reeling drunk and saw his daughter in the kitchen' (127) – it is clearly Claudia who comments on the tragic fulfillment of Pecola's desire for blue eyes. 'So it was. A little black girl yearns for the blue eyes of a little white girl, and the horror at the heart of her yearning is exceeded only by the evil of fulfillment' (162). An omniscient narrator is necessary because logically Claudia cannot know and tell of the histories of Cholly and Pauline, Soaphead Church, the three whores and Geraldine; nor is she in a position to describe the rape of Pecola. Yet the closeness of their voices and vision by the end of the novel suggests that the wisdom of this all-knowing narrator is also Claudia's. What defines her, and replaces the anger and aggression of childhood, is ultimately an imaginative understanding, discernible earlier in the quality of her memories and mode of expression, but more explicit in the closing paragraphs of the novel as she comments on the fatal nature of Cholly's love and the sad infertility of the cultural climate for a thriving African American psyche.

The self-recrimination in Claudia's confession of the responsibility she and others bear for Pecola's demise is the cost of her survival. She experiences remorse and self-recrimination; she mourns. The states of emotion that Claudia feels, unpleasant as they may be, underscore the contrast between her and Pecola, who, in her dissociated state, is beyond guilt and grief.

Sula: war and Peace traumas

IN 1920, when Freud returned to exploring the concept of trauma, his theorising grew out of observations about soldiers who had suffered overwhelming experiences in World War I. Freud's attention to war neuroses provided him with opportunity for further reflection on the nature of unconscious desire and its manifestation in dreams. He noticed that the dreams of the traumatised repeatedly drew the patient back to the situation of the trauma and repeated his frightful experience of it.[1] If, as Cathy Caruth has argued, the traumatised carry 'an impossible history within them', it is because they are unable to possess their history.[2] It works on them instead of their working on it by submitting it to the processes of memory, response and assimilation.

Like Freud, Morrison begins her exploration of unassimilated history with the experiences of the young soldier, Shadrack, whose exposure to the horror of war in 1919 traumatises him for life. Shadrack witnesses a blasted comrade's face fly off; the man's body continues to run while the helmet slides down, an inverted soup bowl over brains that have liquified. In this graphic and horrifying visual image, the narrator compels the reader to imagine what shock Shadrack must have registered. When Shadrack awakes in the hospital he is phobic about the possible chaos of the world and his body. Morrison describes his reactions to the food he is served – rice, meat and stewed tomatoes – in a way that enables us to understand his continuing trauma. Only when things are kept apart and compartmentalised are they manageable. The tray with three triangular areas keeps separate the lumpy whiteness of the rice, the quivering blood tomatoes and the greyish-brown meat. Thus described, the dinner recalls the human stew that Shadrack witnessed, but his rising horror is checked because the food is contained in its triangles. The balance soothes him and transfers its equilibrium to him. Such containment does not, however, extend to his own body, which refuses to keep its usual shape. He is relieved to be bound into a straitjacket, for confinement ensures his fingers will be kept under control. The laces of his straitjacket contrast with his unlaced mind. After discharge from the institution which, by alienating him from himself and his home, has, if anything, perpetuated his trauma, he recovers some sense of control over his body. He sees his black face and finds it reassuring; even his hands remain courteous. Retiring to the shack near the river that belonged to his grandfather, he institutes National Suicide Day, an attempt to structure human chaos in the same way as his food is divided on the plate. The opposition must be maintained between life and death, order and disorder, survival and suicide. National Suicide Day makes a disorderly world orderly; because of the possibility on this day of killing oneself, one can live other days without feeling the need to do so. National Suicide Day acknowledges the overwhelming trauma of loss and despair and the desire for self-annihilation. It is, one might say, the institutionalisation and commemoration, but also the containment, of the death drive. Once the community gets to know Shadrack's madness, they are also able to fit him into the scheme of things (15). The folks in the Bottom may think they pay no attention to Shadrack, but National Suicide Day becomes a 'lieu de memoire' – a place of memory, a landmark in time and a point of reference.[3]

The war experiences of Shadrack introduce the notion of trauma and the madness of trying to keep order in a world of incalculable loss and death. But Shadrack's is not simply the generic trauma case. The specific historical circumstances of his experience are significant: he is a black soldier serving in the armed forces in World War I. The returned soldiers on the train that Helene Wright takes to New Orleans, as well as Sula's regressed and drug-addicted uncle Plum, are all reminders of the presence of black soldiers in this war. Written round the time of increasing US involvement in Vietnam, where America was waging a war in which African American soldiers made up a disproportionate number of the casualties, *Sula* (1973) registers the injustice that when it comes to giving their lives for their country, black people suffer no exclusions.[4] But, as we see from Helene's journey, black servicemen have still to travel on Jim Crow cars. Later, in describing the growing anger felt by the Bottom community at the job exclusions black men experience, the narrator refers to the draining of hope that 'kept them excited about other people's wars … kept them convinced that some magic "government" was going to lift them up, out and away from that dirt, those beans, those wars' (160).[5] The issue of black servicemen crops up repeatedly in Morrison's work as an example of the duplicity of American race relations: in *Song of Solomon* the members of the Seven Days vengeance group talk about their service in the war and the hostility that black veterans encountered on their return; in *Jazz*, Joe witnesses the Fifth Avenue parade of the three-sixty-nine, a black regiment that served in World War I.

Though the world of the Bottom seems remote, it is hardly impervious to, or separated from, the outside world. Morrison has pointed out that so much of African American life is lived in towns like Medallion, on the outskirts, rather than in exotic big cities like New York. Remote Medallion may be, but if Shadrack is allowed to constitute a powerful example, World War I and its terrors are right there psychically in the Bottom's back yard. Morrison brings the war trauma of Shadrack home to historicise and contextualise the position of African Americans in 1919.

If the first chapter begins by showing the blasted life of one black American soldier, it closes with a chapter containing Nel's blues-like rhapsody to the beautiful young men of the neighbourhood:

> Jesus, there were some beautiful boys in 1921! Look like the whole world was bursting at the seams with them.

> Thirteen, fourteen, fifteen years old. Jesus, they were fine.
> … They hung out of attic windows, rode on car fenders,
> delivered the coal, moved into Medallion and moved out,
> visited cousins, plowed, hoisted, lounged on the church
> steps, careened on the pool playground. (163–4)

The praise of the neighbourhood's young men recalls them as the objects of Nel and Sula's adolescent desire, but it also records the waste and loss of a generation full of promise and beauty yet denied rights and opportunities to work. When Shadrack, a latter-day Pied Piper, leads the community to the tunnel that eventually collapses on them, the text draws attention to the vengeance in the hearts of the people for the exclusion of their men from good work and good pay. 'They didn't mean to go in, to actually go down into the lip of the tunnel, but in their need to kill it all, all of it, to wipe from the face of the earth the work of the thin-armed Virginia boys, the bull-necked Greeks and the knife-faced men who waved the leaf-dead promise, they went too deep, too far…' (161–2).

Recklessness, despair and rage result in the apocalyptic collapse of the tunnel and the death of many of the Bottom's number. The exclusions from work and economic opportunity faced by African Americans recall the preface to the novel, which tells of the adult pain that a sensitive observer may read in the community and links it to the history and inception of the Bottom. The narrator registers a note of nostalgia about the passing of a community, a neighbourhood. Listing the places that will be demolished so that the Medallion Golf Course can be built, she bears witness to the life that dwelt in Irene's palace of cosmetology, Reba's Grill, the Time and a Half Pool Hall. Metonymies signify the materiality of the people and their moment in history – tan shoes stand for the men who tap their feet at the Pool Hall; Nu-Nile and hair soaping index aspirations to current standards of beauty; a hat worn always by the cook at Reba's Grill guarantees memory of the recipes and suggests a one-of-a-kind community restaurant, no link in a chain of fast food outlets. All this is going to make way for the Medallion Golf club. A series of words and phrases that suggest demolition follow –

'level', 'raze', 'knock', 'pry loose' – as the obliteration of the Bottom is predicted. The novel's concern with loss and pain is written into its first paragraphs as the community about to be chronicled in the ensuing chapters is already under erasure.

The narrator imagines a visitor from the valley in order to show us a scene of everyday life in which pleasure and pain mingle indistinguishably. The valley man might miss the pain under the eyelids, in the head rags or soft felt hats, or behind the frayed lapels. Only in exposing himself to the voice or the touch of singers or carvers could the visitor detect it. The emphasis here, on pain as an easily undetected signature of this neighbourhood, prompts the reader to wonder about its nature and source. The ensuing account of the neighbourhood's genesis goes some way to explain it in political and historical terms.

Land is at stake in the anecdote of how the Bottom began. A slave who has performed difficult chores is promised his freedom and a piece of good land. The farmer has no problem with freedom in the abstract, but incurring economic loss by parting with valuable fertile land is more difficult, and so the promise is reinterpreted and the slave hoodwinked into taking infertile hilly land at the 'bottom of heaven' rather than in the valley. Future generations tell this so-called joke of origins, but it means different things in different communities. Whites tell it when they are looking to find a little comfort 'somewhere' and Blacks tell it when they are looking to find a little comfort 'somehow'. The distinction between 'somewhere' and 'somehow', between place and modality, is illuminating. In the first instance comfort comes from outside, elsewhere, because the joke is on 'them'. In the second instance, from the point of view of 'colored folks', the joke is on 'us' and without seeking to lay blame elsewhere, the community looks for a way to tell their misfortune that makes it less painful. The contrast between the social use and significance of the joke explains the narrator's view of the relative positions of these communities: humour provides a boost for the sense of superiority on which the white self depends in one case; in the other, humour works as self-deprecation, expressing the pain and pathos of a history of victimisation that continues beyond slavery and the founding of the Bottom, beyond the destruction of the tunnel and the demise of the community so that a golf course can be built. Both the origin and the ending of the Bottom reflect the primacy of white interests and the concomitant marginalisation of black ones.

The preface and first chapter introduce a novel that will continue to explore a wide spectrum of trauma and loss, for *Sula* is undeniably a novel filled with traumatic events, the fate of Shadrack's comrade being only the first in a long list that includes the amputation of Eva's leg – people suspect she has done it to herself so that she can collect insurance; the sudden, accidental drowning of Chicken Little; Eva's setting alight of her son Plum; Sula's self-mutilation when threatened by white boys; the horrible burning of Hannah Peace; and the apocalyptic collapse of the tunnel which is tantamount to a community suicide.

At first glance, Sula appears to be the only one in the novel who can look upon trauma and pain with disinterest. In the creation of Sula, Morrison experiments with anti-conventionalism – the woman who will not nurture, mother, or take her place in the heterosexual social order that defines women like Helene Wright and her daughter Nel. She is in part a feminist experiment in that Morrison tries to imagine a self-creation, rebelling from, and at odds with, all previous prescription. Morrison has said that she wanted to take a woman other than the one she often writes about, who prepares herself for marriage and home-making and folds away many parts of herself. She describes this woman in *The Bluest Eye* (Geraldine) and in *Sula* (Nel's mother, Helene Wright and Nel). In Sula, Morrison imagines a woman who, intent on opening up all parts of herself rather than folding them away, flouts convention and received morality.[6]

In cutting Sula loose from the responsibilities, pieties and proprieties of conventional womanhood, Morrison appears also to cut her loose from feeling, to give her detachment and distance and to make her in many ways shockingly evil. Thus, Sula callously disposes of her grandmother Eva, putting her out of her own home and into a less than satisfactory place for old people;

in the community's mythology, a host of signs link her with evil and the devil. Morrison has said in a number of interviews that she is interested in the way black communities tolerate evil, learning to live and survive in its presence rather than responding anxiously and aggressively to exorcise or banish it. More than simply tolerating it, however, the community helps to constitute in Sula the evil that it sees and even needs. Sula becomes for the community members a challenge to find their best selves. The sense of relief and hope that follows her death is short-lived: 'Without her mockery, affection for others sank into flaccid disrepair' (153). If Pecola in *The Bluest Eye* functioned as the deficient and ugly other on whom the community could 'dump their garbage', leaving themselves cleansed, Sula is similarly a site of projection, though one constituted not through shame and a sense of rejection, but through her own glorious defiance and self-isolation: '[M]y lonely is *mine*' (143), she proclaims triumphantly.

The question of the individual's relationship to community is, as very many critics have noted, compelling in all Morrison's works. Detachment and isolation versus connection and involvement is a subject that has long interested her and it was the topic of her MA thesis (Cornell 1953).[7] Concluding her analysis of *Mrs Dalloway*, *The Sound and the Fury* and *Absalom, Absalom!*, Morrison writes: 'Mrs. Woolf champions the honesty of her Clarissa Dalloway and believes that her isolation has provided the means for acute self-analysis. Conversely, William Faulkner's Quentin Compson never attains self-knowledge because he is alienated and Thomas Sutpen is blinded by isolation to the point of not even recognizing his own evil.'[8] What interests Morrison in these two writers is the accounting of alienation – the relative costs and gains. *Sula*, too, is an assessment of isolation and connection, and how these states inflect identity. Like all Morrison's works it is about the negotiations and relationship between the inside and the outside.

One of the paradoxes of identity is that we can only know ourselves as selves if we have a sense of separateness, but at the same time we can only know ourselves in relation to others.

Critics have often wondered why Sula returns to Medallion after she has been to college and travelled around for the ten years that remain an unexamined lacuna in the text between parts 'I' and 'II'. Just as Sula needs to be isolated from the Medallion community in order to create and contemplate herself, so she also needs to know herself in relation to it. Sula's identity depends on her defiant alienation from the community; yet that identity also depends, as does the community's sense of itself, on comparison and relationship.

As many commentators have noticed, Sula's 'delicious disinterestedness' associates her with the figure of the artist as one who must be able to contemplate life aesthetically, creating from the disturbances of life the orderliness of art. Sula does indeed assume a detachment after she 'exorcises her sense of responsibility' and learns that she can count on neither her mother nor herself. She lives an experimental life, we are told, and personifies curiosity. She provokes unease in her admission that she thrilled to see her mother burn and in her recognition that it is just as well Ajax has left her, for she would have liked to tear the flesh from his face to get to the secret of his blackness and beauty.

What does the narrator mean by describing Sula as an artist without an art form? Though Morrison seems to be suggesting that had Sula found a creative medium for her energies she would have been less restless and more satisfied, the point is not so much an outlet for Sula's energies, but a focus on the costs of aesthetic curiosity and self-scrutiny without the consolations of creativity. On the face of it, the novel seems implicitly to probe the question: 'At what price disinterestedness?'[9] In Sula's case, caring feelings, empathy and vulnerability seem to have been sacrificed – her treatment of Eva, her seduction of Nel's husband Jake – suggest a profound lack of, or disregard for, feeling. Determining to live one's life on one's own terms, as Sula does, means disregarding the usual constraints that socialisation involves. But although Sula seems to accomplish her disregard for convention without cost, the novel (especially in its last chapters) is explicit about the pain and suffering that Sula, disinterested as she seems, has not managed to leave behind. Despite her desire to be 'free of the possibility of distraction' she is haunted, not by guilt or self-recrimination, but simply by sorrow and pain. Indeed, by the second part of the novel, Sula seems to have become a repository of pain – personal, local and cosmic. For Sula the act of lovemaking is, somewhat surprisingly, not an opportunity ultimately for sensuous and carnal pleasures, but for 'misery and the ability to feel deep sorrow' (122). Seeking out the 'eye of sorrow in the midst of all that hurricane rage of joy', she finds at the centre of 'that silence … the death of time and a loneliness so profound the word itself had no meaning' (123). It is then that Sula can weep for 'the deaths of the littlest things: the castaway shoes of children; broken stems of marsh grass battered and drowned by the sea; prom photographs of dead women she never knew; wedding rings in pawnshop windows; the tiny bodies of Cornish hens in a nest of rice' (123). Despite the generality of these references, the last, which summons an image of the death of little chickens, associates her cosmic grief with a specific trauma of her past, the death of Chicken Little.

The death of Chicken Little is the novel's central symbol of loss or lack. One moment he is there, laughing as Sula swings him, holding him by the wrists; the next he is gone: 'The water darkened and closed quickly over the place where Chicken Little sank' (61). Chicken Little's sky falls in, recalling the hapless chicken of the barnyard fable who thought the sky was coming down on his head when he was hit by an acorn.[10] The narrator refers to the effect of Chicken's death as 'something newly missing' (61). What is newly missing, what dies with Chicken Little, is clearly different for every person at the funeral, but the text does emphasise how the women mourners relate to the event by identifying with the child as 'innocent victim', the child in themselves whom the world has hurt. They are reminded of the 'oldest and most devastating pain there is: not the pain of childhood but the remembrance of it' (65). The funeral foregrounds childhood as a time of vulnerabilities, pain and loss, just as, we might say, Chicken Little's death is a symbol of Sula's own childhood hurt and loss.

Shortly before she and Nel go swimming, Sula overhears her mother's conversation with friends about the problems of child rearing. Robert Grant warns that too much significance should not be placed on this conversation: 'Too often Hannah's comment is interpreted as a determining factor in Sula's personality formation, as if this one remark betokened a socio-behavioral pattern and "key" – that is, maternal neglect or insensitivity.'[11] Grant does not deny, however, that the comment does affect Sula by clarifying her independence. The moment functions as a turning point for Sula, which the text itself emphasises in a subsequent retrospective of key moments in Sula's life:

> As willing to feel pain as to give pain, to feel pleasure as to give pleasure, hers was an experimental life – ever since her mother's remarks sent her flying up those stairs, ever since her one major feeling of responsibility had been exorcised on the bank of a river with a closed place in the middle. The first experience taught her that there was no other that you could count on; the second that there was no self to count on either. She had no center, no speck around which to grow. (118–19)

What Hannah says is that children are a nuisance. Her friends agree – they may love their children but they do not like them. Hearing her mother's pronouncements, Sula is stung, immersed in 'dark thoughts' until Nel calls to her to go swimming. Chicken Little, then, may be seen as the childhood that slips from Sula's grasp that day. Chicken Little's death may represent the pain of losing innocence and childhood, but it also represents, through Shadrack's promise to Sula, the permanence of childhood captured and secured by death. When Sula runs to Shadrack's shack after Chicken Little has disappeared in the water, she hears the one word he utters, 'always', as a consolation. The drowned boy's long sleep of water is permanent peace, a notion that Sula returns to shortly before her own death. She dies in considerable pain, with the feeling of 'being completely alone – where she had always wanted to be – free of the possibility of distraction' (148). Thus free she might draw her legs up to her chest, close her eyes, put her thumb in her mouth and float over and down the tunnels … until she met a rain scent and would know the water was near, and she would curl into its heavy softness and it would envelop her, carry her, and wash her tired flesh always. Always. Who said that? She tried hard to think. Who was it that had promised her a sleep of water always? (149)

In Shadrack's remembrance of his exchange with Sula, he promises her not ostensibly the sleep of water, but a stay against change and the 'falling away of skin, the drip and slide of blood. He had said "always" to convince her, assure her, of permanency' (157). Shadrack's 'always' undertakes to banish death and change, so that when he sees Sula's corpse after her death and realises that yet another whose face he knew has died, the hope preserved in his sense of 'always' vanishes. He is then propelled to despair and doubts that his suicide day has helped to keep order in the universe. Sula's death therefore sets off the chain of circumstances that leads to the tunnel's collapse and the deaths of many of Bottom's community members.

We are never told the exact nature of Sula's illness. In the chapter entitled '1939', Sula's experiences with Ajax are described; the next chapter, '1940', would suggest that the loss of Ajax is the reason for her mysterious demise. Whatever the nature of her ailment she avoids discussing it with Nel, leaving us with the impression that 'all the songs have been sung' and she is now content to go 'down like one of those red-woods' (143). What becomes clear in her final conversations with Nel is that having lived life on her own terms, she has not avoided pain or denied feeling, but refused merely to school or order her feelings to suit conventional practices. As she says to Nel, the cult of womanhood that urges, prescribes and proscribes emotions and behaviours is not worth following: 'Being good to somebody is just like being mean to somebody. Risky. You don't get nothing for it' (144–5). Similarly, Sula's shocking (and much-quoted) speech imagining the time when the world will love her is really a speech about iconoclasm, taboo breaking and the shattering of social and sexual conventions:

After all the old women have lain with the teen-agers; when all the younger girls have slept with their drunken old uncles; after all the black men fuck all the white ones; when all the white women kiss all the black ones ...' (145).

The death of Chicken Little is not the only traumatic incident that returns to Sula as she lies dying. One of the most horrifying incidents in the novel is the death by burning of Sula's mother, Hannah Peace. At this point, more than any other, the reader is convinced of Sula's strangeness, the terrible inappropriateness of her response. Sula enjoys the spectacle. While some may think that shock has transfixed the girl, she later admits 'I stood there watching her burn and was thrilled. I wanted her to keep on jerking like that, to keep on dancing' (147). She confirms what Eva has known, that Sula was not just 'paralyzed' as was 'natural', but was interested. But just before her admission of being thrilled, Sula says, 'I didn't mean anything. I never meant anything' (147). These lines are surely ambiguous, but one way to interpret them is to see Sula declaring her innocence: her looking was pure curiosity, not spiteful pleasure or unfeeling callousness. Sula defends the capacity simply to contemplate. Interest and curiosity do not rule out the pain but rather merely mask it and the loss that return to haunt Sula in her dreams. After Nel has visited her for the last time, the narrator describes Sula's death, the agonising pain she suffers and her last thoughts about her life. Immediately after Sula admits that she watched her mother burn and was thrilled, she experiences a recurrent nightmare:

'I wanted her to keep on jerking like that, to keep on dancing.' Then she had the dream again. The Clabber Girl Baking Powder lady was smiling and beckoning to her, one hand under her apron. When Sula came near she disintegrated into white dust, which Sula was hurriedly trying to stuff into the pockets of her blue-flannel house-coat. The disintegration was awful to see, but worse was the feel of the powder – its starchy slipperiness as she tried to collect it by handfuls. The more she scooped, the more it billowed. At last it covered her, filled her eyes, her nose, her throat, and she woke gagging and overwhelmed with the smell of smoke. (147–8)

Symptoms common to those who have suffered trauma include delayed reaction and haunting dreams. In dreaming of the Clabber Girl Baking Powder lady who disintegrates into white dust, Sula relives her mother's death, completing in dream-form the transformation from the burning flesh she witnessed to the white ashes, symbolised in the baking powder and the smell of smoke that choke her.[12] She may have thrilled to watch her mother burn, but that does not mean she did not experience Hannah's death as deeply traumatic. If anything, Sula's artistic sensibility – the interestedness, curiosity, aesthetic wonder – leaves her more vulnerable to pain than others who see more restrictedly and conventionally.

Eva contrasts illuminatingly with Sula. As the abandoned wife and mother who survives, she faces, and overcomes, enormous obstacles. Mother-love as desperate effort is evident in the scene where she literally 'unplugs' the constipated Plum, and again when she hurls her one-legged self through an upper-storey window to try to save her burning daughter. But mother-love as supreme arbiter of the children's fate is also evident in her decision to burn the war-wasted, infantile Plum. Eva is a woman of action. She *does*, while Sula observes. One of the final scenes in the novel concerns Eva, now in her nineties and senile, talking with Nel. As she questions Nel about how Sula killed Chicken Little, her own guilty, self-justifying memories become evident. First she assumes that Nel and Sula *meant* to throw Chicken Little in the water; then she accuses Nel of watching. 'You watched, didn't you? Me, I never would've watched' (168). It is true that when Eva doused Plum with petrol and set him alight, she did indeed close the door behind her and go to sit quietly in her room. Eva acted but preferred not to watch; Sula and Nel simply witnessed. Her further comment suggests a need to absolve herself of Plum's death by insisting that the method she chose was better than the one Sula and Nel selected: 'It's awful cold in the water. Fire is warm' (168). And when Nel asks her who has been telling her these things about the death of

Chicken Little, Eva answers 'Plum. Sweet Plum. He tells me things' (169), thereby revealing her own haunting rather than Nel's guilt. And yet, the encounter does alert Nel to feelings she had while she witnessed the loss of Chicken Little. It urges her to tell the truth to herself, to be honest about feelings, sensations and impressions long buried. Once she has done that, she is also able to realise and admit that it is Sula she has been missing rather than her husband Jude. By owning her unspeakable feelings – the enjoyment of watching something that has horrifying and tragic consequences – she is released from the script that disallowed her mourning the loss of Sula. Admission of aesthetic pleasure facilitates further admissions. Aesthetic pleasure comes to stand for the truth of response beyond inhibition, moral censorship and so becomes a key that unlocks further feeling. Nel can therefore dispense with the script she has been following that says she should have missed Jude. Through the feelings that memory now accesses, she undergoes a complete reconfiguration of self after Sula's death.

As these and other incidents reveal, *Sula* is a novel bound up with delayed reactions, dissociations, repressed memories and the 'psychic discontinuity' of event and affect.[13] That discontinuity is evident in Shadrack's response to the experiences of the battlefield, Nel's reponse to discovering her husband Jude committing adultery with her best friend Sula, and Sula's response to the drowning of Chicken Little. Many characters experience the disjunction between the immediate event and the registration of its psychic consequences. Eva is a good case in point: for some time after Boyboy leaves her Eva does not know what she feels and then it strikes her that she hates him: 'It hit her like a sledge hammer and it was then that she knew what to feel. A liquid trail of hate flooded her chest' (36). This is one of many delayed effects that accumulate to form a structural principle in the novel. Barbara Johnson comments: 'While the chapter headings promise chronological linearity, the text demonstrates that lived time is anything but continuous, that things don't happen when they happen, that neither intentionality nor reaction can naturalize trauma into consecutive narrative.'[14] The highly wrought, 'quasipalindromic' structure of the novel, so astutely described by Robert Grant, is further testimony to its concern with delayed effects. '*Sula* divides precisely into two equal parts ("I" and "II" contain almost exactly the same number of pages), and characters introduced and developed in "I" are brought back in "II" in inverse sequence. The novel begins in memory and concludes with Nel's crucial remembrance of Sula.'[15] More importantly, the novel foregrounds the act of remembering. 'A bright space opened in her head and memory seeped into it' (168). Confronted with Eva Peace's indictment of her 'watching' the death of Chicken Little, Nel reconfigures a number of long-held memories. 'All these years ... now' becomes the novel's refrain at this point.

At the close of the novel, Morrison invokes the image of the concentric circles in the cries of sorrow that Nel emits for Sula as she discovers in a delayed reaction the loss of her girlhood friendship – her other half. The concentric circles recall an earlier image of loss in the water that closes over the head of Chicken Little.

Nel is not the only one whose life is profoundly shaken by Sula's death. After Sula's funeral, Shadrack and Nel pass each other on the road: 'The distance between them increased as they both remembered gone things' (174). Sula's death triggers a revisiting of Shadrack's original trauma. In addition to Shadrack's ritual activities, the symbolic meaning of Sula has kept disorder at bay, her visit to his shack and his promise to her 'always' representing a stay against confusion and death. When he sees her on the slab at the mortuary, he is dismayed: 'She lay on a table there. It was surely the same one. The same little-girl face, same tadpole over the eye. So he had been wrong. Terribly wrong. No "always" at all. Another dying away of someone whose face he knew' (158). This year, instead of inviting the populace to end their lives 'neatly and sweetly', which was always a way of helping them, he does not have his heart in National Suicide Day. Everything is reversed. Whereas in the past Shadrack has cared and the community has shut the door in his face, this year he does not care and they follow him delightedly to their destruction.

The wider political significance of delayed memories and recurring losses is manifest in the gap between the closing chapter, '1965', and the opening of the novel sometime later, when the threatened demise of the community has become an actuality. Melissa Walker sees the novel's structure reminding contemporary (1970s) readers of the need to understand and measure the past against social and political developments of the present: 'By ending Sula in 1965, some years before the time of the beginning passage of the novel, Morrison invites readers to come full circle and begin again, to re-experience the narrative in terms of Nel's final question about whether the Bottom and in particular the "the black people" in general had ever been a community at all.'[16] Nel decides that even if it was not a community, it was a place and 'now there weren't any places left' (166). The opening sentence of the novel recalls and anticipates that view: 'In that place' the narrator begins, 'where they tore the nightshade and blackberry patches from their roots ... there was once a neighborhood' (3). *Sula* is an invitation to the reader to consider the following questions: what was community and what did it mean personally, collectively? How can it be remembered? How can its erasure and the loss of it be re-experienced? *Sula* is a novel that battles nostalgia while exploring the pain of missing something that did not seem valuable enough to ever be missed at the time when you had it. Against the compounding pain of delayed reaction – you don't know what you've got till it's gone – stands Morrison's dedication to the novel, an expression of anticipated reaction: 'It is sheer good fortune to miss somebody long before they leave you. This book is for Ford and Slade, whom I miss although they have not left me.' To miss someone before he or she leaves is good fortune, the dedication suggests, because the missing signifies knowledge of the value of what is temporally present. Morrison's dedication tends to the proleptic; knowing that her sons will leave her, she represents them as already gone, although they are still with her. Presence is given meaning by impending absence. Invoking a neighbourhood, and not an idealised community, Morrison probes what it means to miss the lives lived in small, rural communities, when all along the value of that way of life was never discernible to its inhabitants.[17] Morrison's novel is revivalist in the sense that it seeks to provoke and rekindle emotions and responses toward something as simple, everyday and unmissed as the Bottom neighbourhood. Like the short-lived butterflies that appear repeatedly in the novel – when Chicken Little is lowered into his grave, for example, or when Ajax releases a jar of them in Sula's bedroom – there is something ephemeral and evanescent about that past.[18] The Bottom is important because it is an instance of the forgotten, a part of the fabric of an unremembered past, which, if not memorialised in its limitations and shortcomings, remains an unassimilated history and an impediment to a historicised narrative of African American experience and therefore to future envisionings of community.

Song of Solomon: raising Dead fathers

The fathers may soar and the children may know their
names

SONG *of Solomon* (1977) is a novel about fathers, or more
specifically, the loss of fathers.[1] At its heart are two revelatory
incidents of traumatic loss which govern the novel's investigation of the history and future of African American men in
relation to society and their own families. A brother and sister,
Pilate and Macon Dead (the second), witness their father being
shot to death by greedy white neighbours who resent his pros-
perity and covet his land. But this father himself experienced the
traumatic loss of his father, who, legend has it, decided to fly
away from America and his condition of enslavement. He
attempted to take his baby son Jake with him, but dropped the
child a few moments after he took off in flight back to Africa.
His bereft wife lost her mind through grief and the child was
reared by others. Knowledge of the second of these traumas,
withheld almost to the close of the novel, explains not only the
riddle on which the novel turns, but reveals the generational
transmission of traumatic effects that hampers all the Dead men,
descendants of Jake, who is also known as the first Macon Dead.
The multivalent meanings of Solomon's flight in the novel
allow Morrison to celebrate an early and marvellous escape from
slavery, while also registering the trauma of those who must
function without the father. Though Solomon's flight may offer
inspiration as a version of the celebratory legend of the Flying
African, the novel also emphasises the grief and mourning of

those who were abandoned.

The trauma of the father's abandonment or death infects the descendants of Solomon – as it does the text – with a series of distortions in memory and obstacles to interpretation. Among these, for example, is the cryptic admonition that Pilate's father utters when he appears to her on a number of occasions after his death. Guiltily, she interprets his saying that you can't just fly off and leave a body as an injunction to return to the bones of the man she and Macon left dead in the cave. When we later learn the history of Jake, we understand that his poignant refrain relates repeatedly the central loss of his own childhood – the fact that he was the body left when his father flew off. Another example is the name of Macon Dead, created by a slip of the pen. Failing to fill the information in the correct boxes, the Yankee clerk at the Freedmen's Bureau takes the place of origin as the first name, writing the condition of the father in the box for the surname. Though one point about this history of naming is that a careless drunk official has the power to change the name of a family, another, and more significant, point is that the new name further emphasises the death of the father. Like the riddle of the children's song, which tells the story of Solomon's flight but cannot be understood until Milkman can hear it properly, the name 'Dead' is a riddle, which also draws attention to the question of the father's survival. In Milkman's world, the 1930s to the 1960s, the father is 'already Dead'. Milkman tells his friend Guitar about the naming:

> 'Say, you know how my old man's daddy got his name?'
> 'Uh uh. How?'
> 'Cracker gave it to him.'
> 'Sho 'nough?'
> 'Yep. And he took it. Like a fuckin sheep. Somebody should have shot him.'
> 'What for? He was already Dead.'[2]

In the genealogy of the Deads, the trauma of paternal loss reveals one father who flew away and one who died violently at the hands of whites while trying to make good in America. The two instances record different responses to life in racist America, each of which entails traumatic consequences – Solomon miraculously flies off, becoming a symbol of transcendence and escape, but bequeathing also a legacy of bereavement, loss and forgetting; Jake stands his ground but is cut down, leaving his family similarly bereft. Both modes raise the question of how black men in America survive and how they position themselves in relation to dominant social and political structures. In confronting the loss of the father, Morrison's novel looks at the ways in which the history of its consequences might be rewritten.

The extent to which the novel is focused on the traumatic loss of the father may be gauged in the narrator's accounts of Macon Dead's death. Early in the novel, after Milkman has returned from talking with his strange aunt Pilate, whom his father has forbidden him to visit, Milkman raises the question of his grandfather's death. In the course of this clandestine visit, Pilate has given Milkman her account of her father's violent death and now Macon is moved to remember and talk about the event:

> His son's questions had shifted the scenery. He was seeing himself at twelve, standing in Milkman's shoes and feeling what he himself had felt for his own father. The numbness that had settled on him when he saw the man he loved and admired fall off the fence; something wild ran through him when he watched the body twitching violently in the dirt. (50–1)

The death of the first Macon Dead affects not only his son, but, as Milkman later learns, an entire community of men who took Macon as an exemplum of success and self-improvement. Talking to the men of his father's generation in Danville, Pennsylvania, Milkman functions as

> the ignition that gunned their memories. The good times, the hard times, things that changed, things that stayed the same – and head and shoulders above all of it was the tall, magnificent Macon Dead, whose death, it seemed to him, was the beginning of their own dying even though they

were young boys at the time. Macon Dead was the farmer they wanted to be, the clever irrigator, the peach-tree grower, the hog slaughterer. ... (235)

Macon Dead seems to preach to them in the same style in which Baby Suggs in *Beloved* will speak to the freed slaves. Whereas she tells black folk that they have to love themselves because no one else is going to love their flesh, Macon's farm and attitude to life speak of helping oneself:

We live here. On this planet, in this nation, in this country right here. *No*where else! ... Grab it. Grab this land. Take it, hold it, my brothers, make it, my brothers, shake it, squeeze it, turn it, twist it, beat it, kick it, whip it, stomp it, dig it, plow it, seed it, reap it, rent it, buy it, sell it, own it, build it, multiply it, and pass it on – can you hear me? Pass it on! (235)

But, the narrator continues, 'they shot the top of his head off and ate his fine Georgia peaches. And even as boys these men began to die and were dying still' (235).

Macon Dead (the second) takes to heart that injunction to 'rent it, buy it, sell it, own it' by becoming a heartless landlord. Setting great store by the symbols of power and success – the keys in his pocket, the big Packard in which he takes the family for a joyless Sunday ride – he relentlessly pursues the bourgeois dream. Only his visit to Pilate, secretly at night in order to hear her sing with her daughter and granddaughter, suggests the vestigeal remains of an emotional life. 'As Macon felt himself softening under the weight of memory and music, the song died down' (30). For the most part, Macon Dead has spent his life suffering from a dissociation of feeling. Milkman meditates on his father's life:

And his father. An old man now, who acquired things and used people to acquire more things. As the son of Macon Dead the first, he paid homage to his own father's life and death by loving what that father had loved: property, good solid property, the bountifulness of life. He loved these things to excess because he loved his father to excess.

> Owning, building, acquiring – that was his life, his future,
> his present, and all the history he knew. That he distorted
> life, bent it, for the sake of gain, was a measure of his loss
> at his father's death. (300)

The loss of the father as a central concern of the novel is also expressed in the case of Guitar Bains – 'my father died when I was four. That was the first leaving and the hardest' (307). Bains's father dies from traumatic amputation – his body is sawn in half in an accident that exposes the exploitation of 'coloured' workers in unsafe working conditions. The children are given a sack of 'Divinity' – candy to recompense them for the loss of their father, and forever afterwards Guitar is sick to his stomach at the thought, let alone the taste, of sweet things. However, he confesses later in the novel that it was not really the candy that made him sick but his mother's smiling gratitude for the four ten-dollar bills that the foreman gave her. Guitar recalls the horrific sight of his father, lying in the coffin, his body sliced vertically in two halves, and the fact that his mother bought the children peppermint rock with some of the money the sawmill owner gave her (224–5). In Guitar's reckoning there are no blandishments, no sweet things capable of buying off black claim and rage. 'Don't let them Kennedys fool you' is the warning that concludes this account of his father (225). His desire for the gold that Milkman believes now hangs in a sack in Pilate's house is not cupidity but vengeance – he wants it to fund the Seven Days' reprisal activities.

The quest motif in the novel, to which critics have drawn much attention,[3] is specifically a quest to understand the father's trauma and the genealogy of the paternal line. By following the trail that brings him to understand the fate of his grandfather and great-grandfather, Milkman feels 'on his own skin', as it were, the inextricability of personal and public history.[4] To understand the trauma of the lost father in the Dead genealogy is to recognise the forces of history that have produced that trauma. If history is 'precisely the way we are implicated in each other's traumas'[5] then the personal, quotidian, mythological history of Milkman's family is not just Dead history; it implicates a wide range of others and it is relevant not only in the context of the novel, but also to the 1990s. Morrison engages Milkman in his people's collective history by sending him on a quest for his own familial, paternal past. It is indeed a quest to raise the Dead fathers. When Milkman is alone in the forest during the night of hunting, it is as if he is protected and aided by a mothering grandfather: 'Down either side of his thighs he felt the sweet gum's surface roots cradling him like the rough but maternal hands of a grandfather' (279). The quest functions as quests traditionally do, and Milkman predictably recovers pride in his heritage, wisdom to face difficult tasks, and a newly crystallising sense of identity. '"My great granddaddy could fly! Goddam! … He didn't need no airplane. Didn't need no fuckin tee double you ay. He could fly his own self!"' (328).

Milkman was born, we recall, to discover the meanings of flight. His mother went into labour at the time that Robert Smith leapt from the top of a building in what appears initially to be a suicidal imitation of Icarus. Smith's cryptic note, 'I will take off from Mercy and fly away on my own wings. Please forgive me. I loved you all' (3) cannot be decoded until much later in the novel when we understand his involvement with the Seven Days, but it serves usefully at the outset of the novel to raise questions about flying, and in particular, flying away. Milkman's governing desire as a child is to fly, to the extent that when he learns humans are not fitted for it, he is profoundly disappointed: 'To live without that single gift saddened him and left his imagination so bereft that he appeared dull even to the women who did not hate his mother' (9). Flight, however, as Morrison gradually reveals in the novel, is not always what it seems. Whereas Robert Smith looked like a 'nutwagon', an Insurance Agent who had flipped out, he turns out to be a member of the Seven Days, strained to the point of suicide because he is unable to deal with the pressures of his commitment. The Seven Days is a group that responds in kind to racial violence, representing the 'fight' rather than 'flight' alternative to oppression and persecution. Milkman's grandfather, Solomon, represents the alternative of 'flight'. The alternatives of flight and fight come together in the final scene of the novel as Milkman leaps into the air to grapple with Guitar – an act of confronting, surrendering and soaring.

Yet even as Morrison allows Milkman to experience elevation and pride in the legends of his flying ancestor, the text does not lose sight of the loss on the other side of celebration. For every joyous escape, every transcendent flyer, there is a grounded wife and mother. For every Leap there is a Gulch, a Ryna for a Solomon. The quintessential 'blue note' in the Solomon myth is Ryna, whose weeping and wailing symbolises the distress of those left behind. Morrison therefore uses the myth of the flying African both to celebrate and to mourn. As Milkman discovers that he is the successor of his flying forebear, the reader begins to see the hapless Hagar as a latter-day incarnation of her ancestor, Ryna. When Milkman hears the song the children are singing in the playground, his recriminations about Hagar are associated with the line that bemoans Solomon's leaving: 'And she stood there like a puppet strung up by a puppet master who had gone off to some other hobby. *O Solomon don't leave me here*' (301). And when Susan Byrd is telling Milkman the history of Solomon and Ryna she remarks,

> You don't hear of women like that anymore, but there used to be more – the kind of woman who couldn't live without a particular man. And when the man left they lost their minds, or died or something. Love, I guess, but I always thought it was trying to take care of the children by themselves, you know what I mean? (323).

Hagar is the price of Milkman's ticket to self-understanding and maturation, just as Ryna and her children were the price of Solomon's triumphant flight.

In the light of ongoing debates about fatherlessness in relation to African American families (debates initiated to a large extent by the Moynihan report of the 1960s and manifested in the 1990s in Louis Farrakhan's orchestration of a 'million man march' on Washington)[6] Morrison's novel speaks to concerns about male commitment and responsibility. In some ways, *Song of Solomon* can be characterised as a mythologising of desertion. Solomon gives leaving a good name because his reasons for escape are inarguable and his mode of leaving is spectacular enough to command awe, inspiration and celebration. Rather than pathologise the father who leaves, Morrison recovers the history of good reasons for taking flight. The flying African myth also functions here as a consolatory myth – men leave, but they do so in response to intolerable pressures and constraints.

In its multiple versions, the myth of the flying African does not necessarily focus on the father. There are many myths dealing with escape from slavery: the Ibo version is that the people who arrived in America took one look at what life would be like there and simply turned round and walked back over the water to Africa. Paule Marshall's *Praisesong for the Widow* draws on this version. Virginia Hamilton's *The People Could Fly: American Black Folktales* has a tale about the power of flight in which a young slave woman successfully flies away with her baby. With the magic words, '*Kum ... yali, kum buba tambe*' she takes to the air and escapes the cruelty of the overseer.[7] Morrison's particular deployment of this well-known escape myth is therefore significant. She *chooses* to make her flying African the father of twenty-one sons, who leaves his wife and family. Instead of invoking only the familiar blues theme – a woman bemoaning her abandonment; a man leaving a woman – Morrison puts a new and favourable spin on the history of male peripateticism.

At the same time, however, that Morrison's version of the myth places emphasis on the man's miraculous flight and on the woman's loyalty and love, she also draws attention to the fact that women are left to bear the brunt of the desertion. Though Susan Byrd affirms that women who die of grief for their men are few and far between – 'You don't hear of women like that anymore, but there used to be more' – she certainly has a point in her initial understanding of the grief and madness of women like Ryna: 'I always thought it was trying to take care of the children by themselves, you know what I mean?' (323). The myth of the flyaway father offers a grand drama of male escape and female pining, but in more quotidian terms, whatever the provocation to escape, Solomon does leave Ryna holding the baby – twenty-one of them, in fact.

Once in touch with his history, Milkman's pride in his flying ancestor alerts him now to the significance of the place names: 'He read the signs with interest now, wondering what lay beneath the names. The Algonquins had named the territory he lived in Great Water, *michi gami*. How many dead lives and fading memories were buried in and beneath the names of the places in this country' (329).[8] He can now make sense and knowledge of the random facts he knows: 'He closed his eyes and thought of the black men in Shalimar, Roanoke, Petersburg, Newport, News, Danville, in the Blood Bank, on Darling Street, in the pool halls, the barbershops. Their names. Names they got from yearnings, gestures, flaws, events, mistakes, weaknesses. Names that bore witness' (330). Possessing some history, and aware of how much more awaits excavation, Milkman is newly and appropriately empowered. It is as if the rekindling of memory, fading but embedded in oral histories, has animated those dead lives and consequently the Dead fathers come to life in Milkman's possession. He now presents the strongest contrast to his increasingly desperate friend Guitar, who is also struggling to memorialise a dead father and to vindicate the dead, the casualties of racism.

As Melissa Walker and others have shown, *Song of Solomon* is a novel whose dense and precise historical texture cannot be overlooked.[9] In casual references and conversation, characters gesture to a wider public history taking place from the 1930s, when Milkman is born, to the 1950s and 1960s and the early stages of the civil rights movement. Events such as the death of Emmett Till (1954) and the Birmingham bombing (1963) offer occasions for the articulation of the Seven Days' policies of revenge. The death of Till is being broadcast over the radio and causes the listeners to speculate how the papers will report it. Guitar bursts out: 'A kid is stomped and you standin round fussin about whether some cracker put it in the paper. He stomped ain't he? Dead, ain't he?' (81). Guitar's response to 'the

Dead' – African Americans who have died as a result of racial terror – is to become the Sunday man for the Seven Days. Murders or outrages against blacks committed on a Sunday will fall to him to avenge. When Guitar's turn comes around, he is responsible for righting the balance after the Birmingham church bombing that killed four little girls. On Milkman's way back from Shalimar, he knows that Guitar will be waiting for him, determined to kill him because Milkman has, Guitar mistakenly believes, cheated him of the gold meant to finance his revenge activities. The situation is rather clumsily rigged to provide a suitably dramatic ending; it strains the reader's credulity to have to see Guitar as suddenly deranged and bent on murdering his erstwhile friend:

> Either Guitar's disappointment with the gold that was not there was so deep it had deranged him, or his 'work' had done it. Or maybe he simply allowed himself to feel about Milkman what he had always felt about Macon Dead … The Sunday-school girls deserved better than to be avenged by the hawk-headed raven-skinned Sunday man who included in his blood sweep four innocent white girls and one innocent black man. (331)

Ultimately, there is no mistaking the narratorial judgement on the eye-for-an-eye policy of the Seven Days. Figured as predatory and hawk-like, Guitar's revenge against an outrage is itself an outrage. Once before, when Milkman surrendered to the earth while Guitar was attempting to strangle him, he found new energy and power to resist. Now, at the close of the novel, as Milkman leaps into the 'killing arms of his brother' for a freeze-frame closure, there is every possibility that his surrender to the air will enable him to ride it. A latter-day incarnation of his flying ancestor, Milkman represents the raising of the Dead, and the final face-off between Guitar and Milkman allows Morrison to contrast different ways of dealing with the history of death and Dead history.

As an incarnation of his flying ancestor, Milkman is like Solomon in that the cost of his freedom and flight is a woman's sanity and life. The fate of Hagar and Ryna calls attention to the position and representation of women in relation to fathers and the paternal law – Lena and Corinthians, Milkman's sisters, his mother, Ruth Foster, and Pilate, his aunt. Since the epigraph of the novel is 'the fathers may soar/and the children may know their names' we need to ask also about the response of women in the novel to soaring, flying, leaving fathers.

If Milkman's understanding of his father's obsession with money and property involves recognising that Macon Dead (the second) loved his father 'to excess', his understanding of his mother ought also to take in the excessive nature of her daughterly love. Part of the propulsion towards self-definition in Milkman's case is the conflicting and irreconcilable versions of the past that he hears from each of his parents. According to his father, the essential rift between Macon and Ruth stems from his interpretation of her excessive and incestuous love for her father. Seeing Ruth in what he regards as a necrophiliac embrace with her dead father, he turns away from her in permanent disgust. On the occasion of her marriage, Ruth has been handed over from father to husband with some relief: 'Fond as he was of his only child, useful as she was in his house since his wife had died, lately he had begun to chafe under her devotion' (23).

Ruth's version when Milkman asks her, '"Were you in bed with your father when he was dead. Naked?"' is that she was not naked; she had her slip on and she was simply kissing his fingers, the only part of him that was recognisable and unbloated (126). Ruth's account of herself as someone 'pressed small' by propriety and socialisation so that her father seemed always big and safe and caring is a familiar account of the daughter bred to service and dependency, who takes her identity entirely from her position in relation to a powerful and respected father. Holding on to a 'cared for feeling', Ruth clings to her father as she will later prolong her son's nursing. Fiercely protective of her son when his life is being threatened by Hagar, she nevertheless does little to prevent her daughters being pressed as small as she was.

Lena and Corinthians, inhibited and diminished by their father, exist to show the overwhelming effects of the combination of powerfully repressive forces such as black patriarchy and white racism. Educated at a fine college, Bryn Mawr, Corinthians is nevertheless destined to be a lady's maid rather than an amanuensis and the best she can do for herself is to take the love of a troubled, rough, Southside man like Henry Porter. Corinthians has a brief moment of narrative limelight in Chapter 9, when she emerges from a depression in a last desperate bid for love and relationship at the age of forty-two. Despite her education at Bryn Mawr and in France, despite her father's money and her mother's status as the daughter of Doctor Foster, she has proved no attractive prize for a professional man of colour. An early incident symbolises not only Milkman's relation to his sisters but more generally that of men to women in this novel: as a small boy Milkman interrupts a family drive because he urgently needs to pee. Lena, who has to take her young brother into a field to relieve himself, finds herself caught in his arc as he turns round before he has finished urinating. Later the long-aggrieved Lena reminds him of the incident in a tirade about his masculine self-absorption in his disregard for women: 'After you peed on me, I wanted to kill you' (213). 'There are all kinds of ways to pee on people,' accuses Lena, referring especially to his most recent betrayal of the secret of his sister Corinthians's relationship with Henry Porter. Although Corinthians finds some happiness with Porter,[10] he too is someone who has 'peed' on women. In another early incident, Porter, drunk and suicidal, is perched in an attic window. Pulling out his penis, he pees 'in a high arc over the heads of the women, making them scream and run in a panic that the shotgun had not been able to create' (25).

When Milkman returns from the quest that has presumably altered his relationship to his history, his family and himself, we learn that his mother is thankful that he is unhurt, and Lena, 'though unforgiving as ever, was civil enough to him since Corinthians had moved to a small house in Southside, which she shared with Porter' (334). Although Milkman returns from his quest having experienced a wonderful reciprocal relationship with Sweet, his new-found awareness of female needs and entitlements seems superficial. He berates himself for the death of Hagar and realises that the women in his life have done so much for him and that he has never so much as made them a cup of coffee, but there is not much to suggest that the situation of women is altered. The law of the father – even, of course, the Dead father – is that women serve, love, wait and suffer abuse or abandonment.

Unsurprisingly, mothers are marginally significant in this novel about fathers: Ruth's father is her only important parent; Pilate's mother dies giving birth and is little remembered by her elder brother, Macon Dead. Her only significance is her name 'Sing' and her Native American status, which allows Morrison (through Susan Byrd and her friend Grace Long) to give a condensed account of hybridity and intermixing in African American genealogy. Pilate is an exception in the novel as a free-standing woman, whose knowledge and way of seeing the world provides a contrast to the bourgeois values Macon has adopted, and who represents a matrilineal line. Although there is something free and exciting about her household of women, its nutritional and other eccentricities, wonderful singing, and hand-to-mouth existence, Pilate's line neither thrives nor survives. Her descendants become less independent and self-possessed. Her daughter Reba, who shares many qualities with Hannah Peace in *Sula*, lives for pleasure, and although wonderful, winning and generous, is never quite an adult. As she lies dying, Pilate enjoins Milkman to look after her daughter. And whether we see Hagar as constrained by a crude determinism in the novel that constitutes her as an incarnation of her grieving, mind-tossed maternal ancestor, Ryna, or whether we see her as a version of Pecola in her absorption of white consumer culture, she too is an increasingly pathetic, doomed woman. Whereas Milkman's quest serves to raise the Dead fathers through possession of paternal history, the mothers, daughters and wives associated with the Dead are yet to be raised. The ways of Pilate, who could fly without leaving the ground, are an inspiration for Milkman – 'There's got to be at least one more woman like you' (337) – but in the world of the novel, there are no others like her; nor does she have female descendants who will raise and possess her for their futures.[11]

Tar Baby: a message mailed from under the sink

AT a climactic moment in *Tar Baby* (1981), we learn that Michael, the long-awaited but always-absent son of Margaret and Valerian Street, was abused by his young mother who burned him with cigarette tips and pricked him with pins. Margaret's maternal shortcomings are only hinted at during the course of the novel, causing the reader to wonder uneasily about her relationship with her son: 'When he was an infant he seemed to want everything of her, and she didn't know what to give. She loved him even then. But no one would believe it. They would think she was one of those mothers in the *National Enquirer*' (58). Now nearly fifty, Margaret herself continues to suffer from bouts of aphasia and perception disorder when she forgets 'the names and uses of things' (58; 84): she can mistake a stick of celery for a knife or pour water from her glass instead of gravy over the prime ribs (61).[1] Although neither Michael nor his mother is Morrison's primary focus in this novel, the secret of his excruciating childhood experiences and the reasons for her forgetfulness have wider significance in relation to the novel's central concerns. Everyone in the novel is somehow implicated in Michael's trauma by keeping the secret, bearing the knowledge, or staying ignorant. Michael's trauma also involves others because the paradigm of his abuse and the relations it structures articulate the novel's concern with 'parenting' in its wider collective and cultural, rather than narrowly personal, sense. While the narrative enters very vividly and compellingly, but briefly, into the imagined pain of the small boy, whose 'delicious' skin is periodically pierced and burnt by his mother, Morrison is more interested in Michael's trauma as a way of exposing power relations in the Street household – and in the larger culture – than she is in probing the nature of childhood trauma itself.

Trauma is about remembering and forgetting. The novel's engagement with these questions and with nurture and betrayal begins in a small space with a little boy under the sink and widens from there. The child's father does not want to confront the familial history and secrets he has avoided knowing, just as he does not want to face the implications of his larger capitalist, colonialist and patriarchal history. Questions of remembering, forgetting and facing history are also paramount in relation to Jadine and Son and inform their contentions about African American values, tradition, attachments and assimilation.

While Michael never appears, never speaks, his absence and his silence are pivotal. The action revolves very clearly around his anticipated arrival at Christmas, the disruptive memories and desires that the prospect of his visit kindles, and the explosive disappointment of his non-arrival. Valerian invites the interloper, Son, to stay at his home expressly because he has been thinking about his son and knows that Michael would have liked him to have welcomed Son: Michael seemed to be 'smiling at him last night … [a]nd Valerian believed that was part of the reason he invited the black man to have a seat, the forepresence of Michael in the dining room. His face smiling at him from the bowl of peaches was the winsome two-year-old under the sink and the thirty-year-old Socialist.' (144). Earlier Valerian and Jadine have been discussing Michael and his shortcomings as an adult. According to Valerian, Michael is always complaining, 'mewing' about the problems of the oppressed, the dispossessed or the environment. Michael has made a career out of other people's pain; a 'cultural orphan', he has 'sought other cultures he could love without risk or pain' (145). Valerian is close to the truth he avoids knowing, but Michael is not so much a cultural orphan as a survivor of childhood trauma, who may indeed seek to love where there is neither risk nor pain or who may identify with those who have experienced pain and betrayal of trust.

Michael never testifies to his traumatic childhood experiences; it is through his shocked father's imagination of the events that the trauma is witnessed:

> I have to cry blood tears for his wounds. But I will need several lives, life after life after life after life, one for each wound, one for every trickle of blood, for every burn. I will need a lifetime of blood tears for each one of them. And then more. Lives upon lives upon lives for the the the the the. Hurt. The deep-down eternal little boy hurt. The not knowing when, the never knowing why, and never being able to shape the tongue to speak, let alone the mind to cogitate how the one person in the world upon whom he was totally, completely dependent – the one person he could not even choose not to love – could do that to him. (236)[2]

Although Valerian remembers a feeling of having 'rescued' Michael from under the sink, he recognises that he has done little to address Michael's betrayal. For Valerian, the new-found knowledge of his son's ordeal is shattering, not simply because he empathises with and inhabits Michael's pain, but because his own history of not knowing is suddenly clarified. Michael's trauma is Morrison's means of implicating his father, whose ignorance of the childhood abuse is revealed to be a guilty and hideous innocence: 'He had not known because he had not taken the trouble to know … [He] had chosen not to know the real message that his son had mailed him from underneath the sink … Was there anything so loathsome as a wilfully innocent man? … No man should live without absorbing the sins of his kind.' (245).

Michael's impending visit creates a climate of reliving and retrieving memory. Valerian wonders why he has 'rattled' on to his servants' niece; Margaret suffers from bouts of forgetfulness; Valerian is 'visited' in his greenhouse by figures from the past – his first wife, his son, the washerwoman who helped him cope with bereavement. Remembering Michael as a child, Valerian muses about his son's need for 'soft' in the darkness:

When he was just a little thing I came home one day and went into the bathroom. I was standing there and I heard this humming – singing – coming from somewhere in the room. I looked around and then I found it. In the cabinet. Under the sink. He was crouched in there singing … When I'd pull him out, ask him what he was doing here, he'd say he liked the soft. He was two, I think, two years old, looking in the dark for something – soft. Now imagine how many soft, cuddly things he had in his room (74).

Sinks and laundries have a particular symbolic resonance in this novel as spaces associated with safety or relief. If Michael finds comfort in the 'soft' under the bathroom sink, Valerian in his childhood found solace in doing the laundry. Just before Valerian invites Son to stay in his home, he has been musing about a traumatic experience in his own childhood: 'Valerian was in his greenhouse staring out of the one glass window imagining what was not so: that the woman in the washhouse was bending over a scrub board rubbing pillow slips with a bar of orange Octagon soap' (140). He is, in fact, remembering the day his father died and the way the washerwoman saved him from drowning in the realisation of his father's permanent absence by putting him to work to scrub the pillowslips. Valerian's sense of loss is likened to a 'bottomless bucket of time into which his little boy legs were sinking and his little boy hands were floundering' (142). By making him scrub with her, the washerwoman enables him to 'tread the black water in the bucket that had no bottom' (140). The washerwoman is later fired for using him to do her work, but he commemmorates her and his struggle by building a separate washhouse on the island, though the present-day, local washerwoman remains anonymous and unimportant to him. When Valerian is berating himself for his loathsome innocence of Michael's abuse, the narrative draws again on the image of the bucket: 'He was satisfied with what he did know. Knowing more was inconvenient and frightening. Like a bucket of water with no bottom. If you know how to tread, bottomlessness need not concern you' (245). In part, Valerian's sensitivity to painful and overwhelming knowledge explains his avoidance of knowing that his child was being abused by his wife, but we see too that the early lesson Valerian learned from the washerwoman has not stood him in good stead for plumbing the depths of his son's pain.

Valerian's capacity for remembering some things makes all the more culpable his failure to know and remember others. Just as he has failed to hear the message mailed to him from the small boy underneath the sink, so he has been wilfully unknowing about his relationship to his servants, Ondine and Sydney, his patronage of their niece Jadine, his treatment of his 'trophy wife', the effects and consequences of his business empire, his Caribbean home and its connection to a history of colonialist enterprises. Valerian's sin of omission is weighed against Margaret's of commission; her unconscionable 'marking' of her child's 'creamy and delicious' flesh implicates the political and social practices that uphold and perpetuate gender, class and race relations under capitalism and patriarchy. Through Margaret, the novel raises the question of how, under these circumstances, a woman can be good enough – 'good enough for a child; good enough for a man – good enough even for the respect of other women' (283).[3]

Margaret married when she was little more than a girl, after Valerian saw her float by, a beauty queen in a pageant. Removed from the trailer home, which she always found cosy rather than cramped, to the palatial dwelling of the Candy King, she is the lonely and ornamental young wife of an older, wealthy and dictatorial man. When her socialising with the servants, Sydney and Ondine, is discouraged, she vents her frustration and powerlessness on her young son – the only being less powerful than herself.

Margaret may not have been a 'woman good enough for a child' but, as Ondine recognises, Valerian contributed to her failure by keeping her 'stupid and idle' (281). Margaret, the novel suggests rather stereotypically, is a prisoner in the institution of motherhood shaped by patriarchy, and in hurting her baby son she lashes out at Valerian's control; the child becomes also a metonymy for her own fragmented and objectified body.[4]

Ondine has silently condemned Margaret for years even while she kept her secret – it was woman's stuff – and eventually she comes to understand that Margaret stuck pins in *his* baby; *hers* she loved (281). Although such a conclusion seems a little pat in the light of Margaret's own understanding of her behaviour and the emotional horror that attends the situation, it serves to situate maternal abuse within a context of power relations rather than merely demonising or pathologising the aberrant mother.

The excruciating pain that Valerian experiences when this secret is revealed is part of a series of punishments that seem to strip him of his power and confer it on those he has patronised, employed, and married, which is to say that the diminishment of the patriarch is one of the structural movements of the novel. As soldier ants invade his precious greenhouse on the Isle des Chevaliers, the (fictive) West Indian island on which he has a remarkable home, and as his butler begins to dominate and control him, Valerian, named after an imperial Roman ruler, feels his imperial sway weaken. His wife, newly invigorated by her confession, also turns her energies to organising, manipulating and infantilising him. Yet, as Ondine points out, whether master, patient or baby, he is still the centre of things (281). Imperial and patriarchal power may look shaken and enfeebled at the end of this novel, but it is by no means dislodged.

The Roman imperial power invoked by Valerian's name looks forward to a more recent form of imperial power, which is responsible for shaping the history of the Isle des Chevaliers. The labour demands of the sugar industry established in the colonies was a primary reason for the importing of slaves to the Caribbean islands. In Son's reckoning, Valerian's imperial profile betokens imperial interests; his business empire is intimately linked with the West Indies:

> Son's mouth went dry as he watched Valerian chewing a piece of ham, his head-of-a-coin profile content … although he had been able to dismiss with a flutter of the fingers the people whose sugar and cocoa had allowed him to grow old in regal comfort; although he had taken the sugar and the cocoa and paid for it as though it had no value … but he

turned it into candy … and made a fortune in order to move near, but not in the midst of, the jungle where the sugar came from … (203–4)

Morrison's introductory description of the island makes clear its association with slavery and settlement: it is this island that 'three hundred years ago, had struck slaves blind the moment they saw it' (6). At the beginning of its colonial history, when the land was cleared by labourers imported from Haiti, the landscape experienced the apocalyptic trauma of human interference:

> clouds and fish were convinced that the world was over, that the sea-green green of the sea and the sky-blue blue of the sky were no longer permanent … Only the champion daisy trees were serene. After all, they were part of a rain forest already two thousand years old and scheduled for eternity, so they ignored the men … It took the river to persuade them that indeed the world was altered. That never again would the rain be equal, and by the time they realized it and had run their roots deeper, clutching the earth like lost boys found, it was too late. The men had already folded the earth where there had been no fold and hollowed her where there had been no hollow. (7)

A once proud river was broken and insulted and became a demented stream: 'Now it sat in one place like a grandmother and became a swamp … And witch's tit it was: a shrivelled fogbound oval seeping with a thick black substance that even mosquitoes could not live near' (8). Verbs such as 'evicted', 'forced', and adjectives 'exhausted', 'ill' and 'grieving' define the river and the subjugation of the landscape. Today, the inhabitants are wealthy men like Valerian Street, who own winter houses on the island – men like Dr Michelin, the dentist, who 'had been run out of Algeria' (13). The dentist recalls the French colonial context – although expelled from Algeria in its resistance to colonial domination, he finds comfortable exile on the Isle des Chevaliers, close to Haiti, but apparently not independent since reference is made to the French colonial taxes Valerian must pay. When toothache drives Valerian to his neighbour, the pounding on his door makes Dr Michelin, who lives with the coloniser's fear, think he is being 'assaulted by local Blacks – whose teeth he would not repair'.[5]

The choice of a French colonial island setting for this novel allows Morrison to import her American characters to a 'here' in order to see more sharply what they bring with them from 'there'. It also allows her to move beyond the boundaries of the United States to explore 'the cultural divisions that exist within the Diaspora', and to suggest the parallel pasts which have shaped African American and Caribbean peoples and the shared characteristics of different national colonisations.[6] The island, which functions as a place where histories are confronted, is the destination of a variety of fugitives. The opening chapter of the novel emphasises the fugitive status of Son, stowed away on Margaret's boat. Flight from a problematic present is especially evident in the case of Jadine, who has fame, success and three marriage offers in Paris – one from an exciting European unmysteriously named Ryk ('rich'). The narrator poses the question of why she would suddenly leave: 'A lucky girl – why leave the show? cable to old relatives? Write a cheery request-type, offer-type letter to a rich old pushover and split to Dominique on whatever Air France had to offer when everything on her shopping list was right there in Paris?' (44).

Set in the early 1980s, *Tar Baby* attempts to take stock of African American tradition and history by putting into competition demands that arise from a feminist manifesto (largely blind to economic and race relations) and claims that arise from the perspective of economic and race relations (largely blind to feminism). It takes as one of its driving questions what black women need to remember and preserve in the traditions of their foremothers as they define themselves in relation to prevailing feminist critiques of patriarchal constructions of gender. The dedication, epigraph and title of the novel are three introductory strategies that enable Morrison to raise the question of a female tradition. Firstly, the novel is dedicated to the women of Morrison's family – mother, grandmothers, aunts – 'all of whom knew their true and ancient properties'. The phrase 'true and ancient properties' is repeated like a mantra throughout the novel, although a thorough scrutiny of its content is never offered. Secondly, the novel's epigraph is from *I Corinthians*; the biblical context is Paul's first letter to the Corinthians in which he addresses the divisions in the Church and appeals to all brothers and sisters that 'there be no divisions among you, but that you be united in the same mind and the same purpose' (I Corinthians 1.3). It is a plea for unity in the face of division. Morrison once again evokes her own family through the allusion to 'the house of Chloe': 'For it hath been declared unto me of you, my brethren, by them which are of the house of Chloe, that there are contentions among you.' Morrison's birth name is Chloe Anthony Wofford. The quotation suggests therefore that the members of Chloe's house detect and report on the quarrels within the community. Since the dedication has listed the members of the house of Chloe, the dedication and epigraph produce a sense that the house preserving its true and ancient properties is in a position to assess and report on the community contentions.

Thirdly, the title of the novel invokes the old African American folktale of the tar baby created by Brer Fox to trick Brer Rabbit into capture.[7] Instead of a scarecrow, the rabbit's opponent creates an effigy of tar, which, of course, remains silent when Brer Rabbit addresses it. Feeling snubbed and insulted, Brer Rabbit eventually strikes the tar baby and finds himself stuck to its sticky surface. He outwits his captor by begging him not to throw him (Brer Rabbit) into the briar patch, his preferred habitat, and escapes, running 'lickety-split, lickety-split'. In the light of this tale, Son, who finds himself running 'lickety-split' at the end of the novel, occupies the position of the wily rabbit stuck for a time on the tar baby – a woman whose beauty seduces him but who has lost touch with her true and ancient properties. There are other possible meanings of 'tar baby' and tar, however, that complicate this assignment of roles. A tar baby was at one time a very pejorative label for black children, black girls especially, as Morrison explains in an interview: '"Tar baby" is also a name, like nigger, that white people call black children, black girls, I recall.'[8] Jadine Childs is a world-famous model whose face, her aunt says, 'made those white girls disappear. Just disappear right off the page' (37). Her beauty and success reclaim the insulting label 'tar baby' with proof that black is beautiful. But at the moment that Ondine is puffing with pride about her niece's success, she is stirring milk into chocolate paste, an image suggestive perhaps of Jadine's unemphatic blackness. Is she successful as a black model only because she is 'beige' rather than black?[9] Jadine, who is repeatedly described as light-skinned, 'yalla' and 'whitened' by her education, material privilege and aspirations, may be moving so far from her racial roots that the label 'tar baby' ironically calls attention to her deracination rather than her blackness.[10] Morrison's way of staging Jadine's dilemma of identity and choice is to present her with a number of alternatives that question her authenticity and recall her to past traditions. Yet the alternatives presented are by no means unambiguous, and, as we shall see, Jadine is never simply the erring child who needs to be reclaimed by an unquestionably sustaining set of past practices. In addition to the story of the tar baby and the connotations of the label 'tar baby', Morrison also draws on other associations of tar:

> I found that there is a tar baby in African mythology. I started thinking about tar. At one point, a tar pit was a holy place, at least an important place, because tar was used to build things. It came naturally out of the earth; it held together things like Moses's little boat and the pyramids. For me, the tar baby came to mean the black woman who can hold things together.[11]

Although the novel announces its concern with Jadine and the nature of the 'new black woman' in a variety of ways, Jadine's dilemma is inextricably linked to that of Son. The narrator comments: 'One had a past, the other a future and each one bore the culture to save the race in his hands' (272). Critics often quote the question relating to Jadine – 'Culture bearing black woman whose culture are you bearing?' – but it should not be read without its corresponding half, the question that relates to Son: 'Mama-spoiled black man, will you mature with me?' (272).[12] It is not, however, difficult to understand why critics often overlook the problems ascribed to Son and why, within the text, Jadine's complaint about Son lacks bite. Although Morrison rehearses lengthy debates between the lovers about the 'condition our condition is in', the text tolerates, and ultimately supports, his position, leaving Jadine not only orphaned *in* the text, but also orphaned *by* the text.

Despite his numerous aliases for official purposes, Son has a strong loyalty to a sustaining past and a solid sense of identity. He is the generic son, a position confirmed by the fact that his father is known simply as Old Man. And he is the novel's chosen son, ensured escape from whatever constrains or hampers him: the novel opens with his jumping ship and closes with his running, presumably, to join the chevaliers. Morrison used the myth of the flying African in *Song of Solomon* to invigorate Milkman's sense of his paternal history; she now draws on the Afro-Caribbean myth of the blind horsemen, who have been galloping apace for centuries from repression and containment. The novel delivers him to a future, admittedly open-ended, but surely in the line of resistance to the forces with which Jadine is complicit. Contentions in *Tar Baby* therefore amount to a feminism tainted with capitalist consumer values that is pitted against an anti-capitalist anti-colonialism, which, however naive and chauvinistic in its 'respect for fraternity', is still judged preferable.

I want now to examine more closely how the narrative arranges the contentions between Son and Jadine and what effects are produced by the text's favouring of Son. In the course of the narrative, Jadine suffers from a number of discomforting dreams and visions. Indeed, dreams are important as indications of unease and unresolved problems as well as of aspirations and hopes. Jadine's first unnerving dream, which she experiences shortly after arriving on the island, is a figurative formulation of her identity confusion, suggesting that she does not know what kind of woman she is; that is, she does not know what hat she is wearing. 'After an hour she woke rigid and frightened from a dream of large hats. Large, beautiful women's hats like Norma Shearer's and Mae West's amd Jeanette MacDonald's although the dreamer is too young to have seen their movies or remembered them if she had. Feathers. Veils. Flowers. ... Hat after lovely hat surrounding her until she is finger-snapped awake' (41). The hats are associated with a parade of Hollywood screen idols, who, as we saw in *The Bluest Eye*, are often used in Morrison's work to signify the production of ideals of beauty and desire.[13] If Jadine's dreams are troubled and signify her uneasy sense of inauthenticity, Son's are far more complacent – he dreams of the warm and nurturing South, where women mind the pie tables in the basement or welcome him into their homes and their beds.

Before Jadine ever meets Son, he spends nights in her bedroom attempting to colonise her dreams, trying to insinuate himself into them and manipulate them. He wants her to share his romanticisation of the South and to want the kind of life about which he feels nostalgic, so he seeks to keep her dreaming so that 'she could long as she had longed for nothing in her life for the sound of a nickel nickelodeon' (119). Son sees his relationship with Jadine as a competition in dreams: 'at any moment she might talk back, or worse, press her dreams of gold and cloisonné and honey-coloured silk into him and then who would mind the pie table in the basement of the church?' (120). Though Son ridicules the fears of the women in Valerian's house that he is there to rape them, he certainly does violate Jadine's privacy and sleep: 'He used to slip into her room ... in order to manipulate her dreams, insert his own dreams into her so that she would ... dream steadily the dreams he wanted her to have about yellow houses with white doors ... ' (119).

No wonder, in the final scenes of the novel that concern Jadine, she has done with dreaming. Morrison likens her to the queen of the soldier ants who is programmed to carry out the duties that ensure the survival of her species – she has no need of males apart from the one moment of impregnation which lasts her a lifetime. 'Soldier ants have no time for dreaming. Almost all of them are women and there is so much to do' (293). After describing in detail the functions of the queen, the narrator comments: 'That is all. Bearing, hunting, eating, fighting, burying. No time for dreaming, although sometimes, late in life … she might get wind of a summer storm one day' and recall her moment of mating (294). Similarly, it is suggested, Jadine will pursue her goals relentlessly, but it will be hard, 'so very hard to forget the man who fucked like a star' (294). The final image of Jadine's association with the queen of the soldier ants is the relentless independence she insists on. Jadine's independence is associated with a fear of losing control (the reins she must always keep hold of) as well as a fear of her sexuality (the image of the male dog mounting and pinning down the female). And because it seems funded by Valerian and inflected by 'white culture', female independence has a problematic status in this novel.

Jadine's vision of the night women is perhaps her most significant dream. 'This was not the dream of hats for in that she was asleep, her eyes closed. Here she was wide-awake, but in total darkness … ' (261). Although the cast of black women who crowd into her airless room in Eloe is usually taken to represent fertility and maternity, as well as the true and ancient properties that Jadine is neglecting, the women are not all representative of nurturing black womanhood. Son's first wife, Cheyenne, known amongst men for 'the best pussy in Florida' is there, as is Francine, attacked by dogs while running and now confined to an institution. The range of women she dreams seems to her to represent an admonishment of her choices and, although each bares a breast, they offer not to nurture her but to invalidate her way of being a woman and to compete with her for 'femaleness'. In fighting Son after his return from Eloe she realises that she is fighting the night women: 'the mamas who had seduced him and were trying to lay claim to her. It would be the fight of their lives to get away from that coven that had nothing to show but breasts' (265). She experiences them as persecutory, concerted (despite their differences) in victimising and chastising her. 'And the breasts they thrust at her like weapons were soft, loose bags, closed at the tip with a brunette eye' (264). In Jadine's mind, if she is not who she is now, she is onion-heeled, potbellied, her hair in braids and her breasts sagging. The narrative emphasises that these are Jadine's slightly paranoid views, but what then really are the qualities that the night women represent? Thérèse, for example, is indeed consistently hostile toward Jadine and does define herself in relation to her breasts; she prides herself on her powers of lactation, although it is a long time since Enfamil has deprived her of her livelihood as a wet-nurse. Thérèse, who delights in and mothers Son, gives him the choice of joining the blind chevaliers rather than continuing his search for Jadine. As she sets him on his course, she counsels him against Jadine – 'Forget her. There is nothing in her parts for you. She has forgotten her ancient properties' (308). But how much do Ondine and Thérèse, who despise each other, and who both appear in the line-up, have in common? What signals of inauthenticity make the yellow-clad, egg-holding woman in the Paris supermarket spit at Jadine?

The problematic question of authenticity, which swirls round Jadine, is an important one in relation to African American culture and memory. In her essay, 'Memory and Mass Culture', Susan Willis asks whether it is 'possible for social minorities to enact memory and recovery of history in culture without simply bowing to the dominant culture's requirement that all marginal groups be authentic'.[14] Willis cites Morrison's exposure of power relations in this regard in *Song of Solomon*, where she has Pilate behave as a mammy in a head rag in order to effect Milkman's release from jail. 'Morrison's treatment shows that authenticity has no real attachment to people's histories and experiences but resides in the dominant culture's ideological stereotypes.'[15] The example of Pilate is an appropriate one, but the question is more difficult in relation to the representation of black women in *Tar Baby*. Although it could be argued that Morrison is simply raising the question of authenticity rather than prescribing its content, it is difficult to ignore the text's censure of Jadine, the very one who is protesting prevailing stereotypes of black women. Whom must Jadine emulate in the novel's terms in order to be deemed authentic, or (in the novel's terms) in touch with her ancient properties?

The scene at the swamp of Sein de Vieilles is at first sight evidence of Jadine's reluctance to join with the women who know their 'sacred properties' and is often cited to show Jadine's symbolic reluctance to blacken herself. But surely she can not be blamed for not wanting to sink in the muck that the text has already described as foul and noxious (8). The narrative seems first to applaud Jadine's canny survival strategies, as witnessed in her ability to dance dextrously with the tree and save herself, only then to fault her for not wanting to be tarred.[16]

> The women hanging from the trees were quiet now, but arrogant – mindful as they were of their value, their exceptional femaleness; knowing as they did that the first world of the world had been built with their sacred properties … they wondered at the girl's struggle down below to be free, to be something other than they were. (184)

It is true that Jadine's aspirations and values detach her from the old ways, but the images of the women who represent those old ways are ambivalent and the nature and specificity of the old ways themselves largely unexamined.[17]

Jadine is often criticised for refusing to take care of her aunt and uncle and 'be a daughter', but early in the novel, when she arrives on the island, she talks about buying a store they could all run and 'live together like a family at last' (46). The response of her aunt and uncle is to 'smile generously, but their eyes made her know they were happy to play store with her, but nothing would pull them away from the jobs they had had for thirty years or more' (46). Yet, at the end of the novel, when Jadine is on her way back to Paris, her leaving is figured as an abdication of responsibility towards the old folks who reared her and made sacrifices for her. Ondine chastises her sadly: 'A daughter is a woman who takes care of them that took care of her … I don't want you to care about me for my sake, I want you to care about me for yours' (282). Has Son been a better son because he mailed money orders home to his father from wherever he was in the world?

As a novel that airs contentions, *Tar Baby* attempts to

preserve the complexities of different views, but in the case of Jadine in particular, it ends up reducing complexity and courting predictability. Jadine resists notions of essential blackness – just because you are black does not mean you automatically love Mingus and have to straighten your hair. Morrison represents her nevertheless as a predictable type – the sophisticated model, the art student who prefers Picasso to the Ithumba masks, who is almost obscenely turned on by a coat made of clubbed baby seals, who fears her sexuality and vulnerability and needs to be in control. Motivated but uptight, she wants things done on time, while Son is prepared to trust that they will be done in time. Jadine is presented as prescriptive; Son is allowed to be open. She conforms time and again to dominant, white American values; he resists them.

Son's resistance to the white world, symbolised by Valerian, demands closer scrutiny, since it receives far less critical qualification in the novel than Jadine's tainted and defensive feminism. Jadine's complaint, that Son is a Mama-spoiled black man, holds in relation to the narrative's treatment of Son, as the text itself avoids confronting his violence and invests itself increasingly in his resistance to white colonialist domination. Indeed, despite his faults – a tendency to smash, kill or hang out of a window those who anger him – he is the favoured Son, a position that comfortably tolerates if not licenses his sexist attitudes. When he tells Jadine that he has killed someone, he enjoys her fear: 'Suddenly he liked it. Liked her fear. Basked in it as a cat in a steam-pipe and it made him feel protective and violent at the same time' (177–8). We see him laughing as he shares with Valerian a joke about the three coloured whores who went to heaven; he gives Valerian's cyclamens a sharp tweak to 'jack' them up and make them behave nicely, just like women, and when he takes Jadine back to Eloe, his male friends regard her as a 'prize woman', 'a Cadillac he had won, or stolen, or even bought for all they knew' (256). His friend explains more truly than he knows when he remarks, 'Son knows people. He gets confused when it comes to women' (258). Lest Son seem too complicit with the chauvinism he finds on the Isle des

Chevaliers and in Eloe, Morrison allows him to defend himself against charges that he regards women as inferior. He responds to Jadine's 'barking' about sexual equality – it is no accident that the verb consigns her to the realm of the dogs against whom she seeks to define herself – by offering a paean to the prowess of the women of Eloe: Rosa, capable of building her own house; his mother, able to rope horses; Cheyenne, skilled enough to 'drop a pheasant like an Indian' (271).

Having been 'mixed up' for much of the novel by his love for Jadine, which amounts to a seduction and corruption by cloisonné and raw silk, he is suddenly brought to his senses in his last frantic search for Jadine by the image of Alma Estee in her synthetic wig, the colour of dried blood. The island girl, perverted by American consumer culture, looks like a 'bougainvillea in a girdle, like a baby jaguar with lipstick on, like an avocado with earrings' (302). When previously he visited Gideon and Thérèse, Alma Estée begged him to buy and send her the wig she wanted. Now, when she appears in the red wig, 'which she had to buy herself because he had not sent her one as he promised to do', he approaches her, bent on rescuing another 'tar baby' from inauthenticity: '"Oh, baby baby baby baby" he said, and went to her to take off the wig, to lift it, tear it, throw it far from her midnight skin and antelope eyes' (302). Like Hagar, whose desperate attempts to look good sends her on a final orgy of purchasing, and who returns home drenched and smudged, eventually to die, Alma Estée is a familiar figure in Morrison's persistent cautions against consumer values and American standards of beauty. Son's crusade to rescue Alma Estée from American-style consumerism and restore her female authenticity seems a little hollow, since he has quite forgotten her and the promise he glibly made her until he sees her in the cheap wig. In the last pages of the novel, Alma Estée is used as a grotesque parody of the look, the consumables, and the produced desires that define Jadine. Yet she contrasts with Jadine who is linked imagistically to the perpetrators while Alma Estée is aligned with the victims. Her doe-like 'antelope' eyes are different from the predatory, rodent-like 'mink eyes' of Jadine (214); and Alma

Estée's wig, the colour of 'dried blood', makes her symbolically the bleeding victim, whereas Jadine's coat of clubbed baby seals puts her in the camp of the predators. Furthermore, Jadine serves Valerian as a kind of handmaiden of white privilege and power, and is seen by Son to bask in 'the cold light that came from one of the killers of this world' (205). The coat she enjoys, that comes from other killers of this world, is just another sign of the way she has sold out.

The closing chapters show Jadine on her way back to Paris and probable marriage to Ryk; Margaret, Sydney and Ondine remain on the island living in a slightly altered relation to Valerian. Although these three seem to wield more power than they did, the relationship of Valerian to his wife and his servants still demonstrates his superior and patriarchal power. The traumatised son, Michael, is still absent, and the escaping Son is on the road to liberation from his obsession with Jadine, running into the hills to join the mythic blind horsemen, who symbolise a refusal to co-operate with the forces of imperial and colonial power. Jadine, certainly, seems not to have solved anything through her various flights to and from the island; the more highly-favoured Son may be solving something, it is suggested, as he follows the advice of Therese, the islander who will not even look at Americans, let alone work in their houses. If Morrison finds herself in the early 1980s at a juncture where African Americans are in need of a wider repository of mythology, it is possible that Son's quest may turn out to be the antithesis of Milkman's.[18] Whereas Milkman needed to take possession of his family history to understand his place in America at the beginning of the civil rights movement, Son seems to have to dispossess himself of American history, or rather, to go further back to an originary moment of trauma for the slaves and the land to which they were brought in order to find a sustaining cultural memory of resistance.

Beloved: the possessions of history

A situation has not been satisfactorily liquidated, has not been fully assimilated, until we have achieved, not merely an outward reaction through our movements, but also an inward reaction through the words we address to ourselves, through the organization of the recital of the event to others and to ourselves, and through the putting of this recital in its place as one of the chapters in our personal history.[1]

BELOVED (1987) is the novel that demonstrates most obviously Morrison's concern to bear witness to the forgotten or erased past of African Americans. However, as I have been arguing, it is not a new direction or departure within her work, which manifests throughout a strong interest in histories that haunt, in what is difficult or painful to remember. The process of writing *Beloved*, Morrison owns, was one of confronting not only her own reluctance to write about slavery, but the 'national amnesia' on the subject.

Then I realized I didn't know anything about it, really. And I was overwhelmed by how long it was. Suddenly the time – 300 years – began to drown me.... I thought this has got to be the least read of all the books I'd written because it is about something that the characters don't want to remember, I don't want to remember, black people don't want to remember. I mean, it's national amnesia.[2]

By dedicating *Beloved* to the 'Sixty Million and more' Morrison draws overt attention to the history of slavery as a holocaust:

I'm trying to explore how a people – in this case one individual or a small group of individuals – absorbs and rejects
information on a very personal level about something
[slavery] that is undigestible and unabsorbable, completely. Something that has no precedent in the history of the
world, in terms of length of time and the nature and
specificity of its devastation. If Hitler had won the war and
established his thousand-year-Reich, at some point he
would have stopped killing people, the ones he didn't want
around, because he would have needed some to do the labor for nothing. And the first 200 years of that Reich
would have been exactly what that period was in this
country for Black people. It would have been just like that.
Not for five years, not for ten years, but for 200 years or
more.[3]

Morrison's interviews from 1987–89, when *Beloved* was
being written and published, attest to her own passionate reclamation of an unspeakable history. *Beloved* is born from her
recognition that traditional slave narratives always 'drew a veil'
over the shocking and painful incidents of their past, pleading
that such things were too terrible to relate. Morrison regards the
genre of the slave narrative, shaped and constrained as it was by
the Abolitionist cause, as unable to bear the fullest possible witness to the interior lives of the slave-narrators. There are many
stories told in this novel, each a testimony to a slightly different
aspect of slave experience, none balking from revealing the psychic and physical horrors of slavery. In addition to exploring the
trauma that slavery wreaked on those who survived into the
post-Civil War period, Morrison ambitiously attempts an
imaginative testimony, through the figure of Beloved, of those
who did no*t* survive, those sixty million and more to whom the
novel is dedicated. The novel challenges its readers to recognise
the unbearable poignancy of the claims of the past – the loss suffered not just by those who survived, but by those who did not.

The trauma of Sethe, a mother who could not suffer her
children to be taken back into slavery, is not represented
through her inability to remember the past; indeed, Sethe
appears to suffer from insatiable memory. The narrator empha-

sises that there is no limit to what her brain can absorb about the past and Sethe herself bemoans the fact that she does not shut down, go mad, or refuse to accept further information and images. When Paul D tells her about Halle watching the boys steal her milk and then smearing his face with Clabber, she takes it all in:

> She shook her head from side to side, resigned to her rebellious brain. Why was there nothing it refused? No misery, no regret, no hateful picture too rotten to accept? Like a greedy child it snatched up everything. Just once could it say, No thank you? I just ate and can't hold another bite? I am full God damn it of two boys with mossy teeth, one sucking on my breast, the other holding me down, their book-reading teacher watching and writing it up. I am still full of that. God damn it, I can't go back and add more.... But my greedy brain says, Oh thanks, I'd love more – so I add more. (70)

Although she works hard at trying not to remember, her brain is devious, the narrator explains, overwhelming her with memories, not even requiring the occasion of strong associational stimulus. 'The plash of water, the sight of her shoes and stockings awry on the path ... or Here Boy lapping in the puddle near her feet, and suddenly there was Sweet Home rolling, rolling, rolling out before her eyes' (6). In this instance, Sethe does not bemoan the extent to which she can take in 'a hateful picture, too rotten to accept'; she laments the way her mind returns to the shameless beauty of Sweet Home, whose landscapes are so vivid and strong that she can hear the wind soughing in the beautiful sycamores. The loveliness of the Kentucky farm is described as 'shameless', and in judging the landscape ethically, Sethe is judging herself: the scenes of horror accommodated in that beauty ought to obliterate all memories of the hills' loveliness. Sethe sees in memory the bodies of lynched 'boys' hanging in those soughing trees and is shamed because she remembers the wonderful trees more vividly than the atrocities of lynching. Why do the trees appear beautiful still? 'Try as she might to make it otherwise, the sycamores beat out the children every time and she could not forgive her memory for that' (6). Could it be argued on the strength of this passage that Sethe does indeed block the memories that are traumatic, her mind refusing to reproduce the horrors she has witnessed during slavery? It is not repression of memory that presents the problem here, but Sethe's consciousness of the amorality of her memories, which refuse to obey her judgement of events at Sweet Home.[4] She struggles with her aesthetic responses to the hills of Sweet Home and later feels 'punished' for her 'terrible memory'. Far from fixated on particular horrific scenes, or dysfunctional in not being able to recall the past, Sethe lives in a constant state of being overwhelmed by vivid memories. These sometimes glory in the beauty of the Kentucky landscape, eclipsing the horrors that took place within it, and sometimes dwell hungrily on details of degradation and scenes of exquisite pain from her past life. These examples serve to show Sethe in constant relation to and struggle with her memory, berating either its capaciousness for pain or preference for pleasure.

Despite Sethe's energetic and unregenerate memory, there is one incident that she does not dwell on, at least in the first half of the novel – the actual killing of the 'crawling already? baby' in the woodshed. All other memories crowd in on her and well up unbidden, but the reader does not hear the details of the baby's death from Sethe. When she explains to Paul D that Schoolteacher did track her down after her escape from Sweet Home, she offers a very selective narrative:

> 'And he didn't take you back?'
> 'Oh, no. I wasn't going back there. I don't care who found who. Any life but not that one. I went to jail instead. Denver was just a baby so she went right along with me.' (42)

As Denver puts it: 'Her mother had secrets – things she wouldn't tell; things she halfway told' (38). Almost exactly half-way through the novel, the reader encounters a graphic scene disclosing Sethe's attempts to kill her children. The scene unfolds largely through the eyes of the white men who, under the Fugitives Bill, have come to claim Schoolteacher's human property. After a description of Sethe in the woodshed, the narration moves to Schoolteacher's understanding of what has just happened, expressed in indirect discourse:

> Right off it was clear, to Schoolteacher especially, that there was nothing there to claim.... Two were lying open-eyed in sawdust; a third pumped blood down the dress of the main one – the woman Schoolteacher bragged about, the one he said made fine ink, damn good soup, pressed his collars the way he liked besides having at least ten breeding years left. But now she'd gone wild, due to the mishandling of the nephew who'd overbeat her and made her cut and run. Schoolteacher had chastised that nephew, telling him to think – just think – what would his own horse do if you beat it beyond the point of education. (149)

The narrative choice to handle the novel's central incident this way has the effect of making the reader understand more compellingly Sethe's horrific actions. Schoolteacher's perspective reveals why Sethe cannot permit her children to be captured and taken back into slavery, for they will be returning to the world effectively signalled in his dehumanising, bestialising view of slaves.

In the first half of the novel, Sethe's secret, the narrative's secret, is the way Beloved dies; it is the point towards which the narrative continually moves and draws back – the unspeakable heart of the story, the central incident that gradually impresses its shape on the reader through the accumulation of surrounding details and incidents long before the narration of Schoolteacher's attempt to recapture Sethe and her children. In the first few pages of the novel, the narrator has already developed a tissue of details surrounding the death of Sethe's 'crawling already?' daughter. The house is haunted by a baby, who throws a spell 'as powerful' as the way her mother loved her (4); there was a headstone for her grave whose inscription Sethe had to purchase with sexual favours (5); the baby's throat was cut (5). References to preachers, abolitionists and a town filled with disgust, hint very indirectly at Sethe's opprobrium – her part in her daughter's death (5). Denver tells Paul D that her sister died in their house and Paul D remembers a story of haunting from

Sweet Home concerning a 'headless bride' (13). This detail also seems to anticipate the arrival of Beloved, whose head was almost severed when her throat was cut. Through hints and insinuations the narrative circles around its central unspeakable incident, enacting the symptoms of trauma in its own fragmentation and blockages.

Sethe may choose not to tell or to 'tell things halfway' only, but that does not mean she does not remember them. Where Morrison signals Sethe's trauma is in the body. The skin on her back, for example, around the tree of scars, feels no sensation, has 'been dead for years' (18).[5] The absence of physical sensation in various bodily ways signals the emotional dissociation Sethe experiences, for she knows very well that her days are committed to warding off feeling. When Paul D arrives at 124 Bluestone, she finds herself wondering if this man is trustworthy enough to hold her and allow her to 'feel the hurt her back ought to. Trust things and remember things because the last of the Sweet Home men was there to catch her if she sank' (18). Through Paul D's descriptions of the chain-gang, Sethe's memory of her mother's mouth, misshapen from the bit, and Beloved's choric accounts of the destruction of slave bodies on a slave ship, the novel underscores the body's traumatic responses to pain and torture. It is significant that Baby Suggs, preaching in the clearing, emphasises love of one's own flesh as the cornerstone of antidotal healing and self-possession:

> Here ... in this place, we flesh; flesh that weeps, laughs; flesh that dances on bare feet in grass. Love it. Love it hard. Yonder they do not love your flesh. They despise it. They don't love your eyes; they'd just as soon pick em out. No more do they love the skin on your back. Yonder they flay it. (88)

There are other sensory and sensual deprivations through which Morrison indicates Sethe's response to the trauma of motherhood under slavery and, in particular, Beloved's death. Sethe does not apprehend colour. It is as if the death of her child has drained all the colour out of the world, but unlike Baby Suggs who dies 'starved for color' (39), Sethe does not see or miss its absence.

> Sethe looked at her hands, her bottle-green sleeves, and
> thought how little color there was in the house and how
> strange that she had not missed it ... Deliberate, she
> thought, it must be deliberate, because the last color she
> remembered was the pink chip in the headstone of her
> baby girl.... Every dawn she saw the dawn, but never
> acknowledged or remarked its color. There was something
> wrong with that. It was as though one day she saw red
> baby blood, another day the pink gravestone chips, and
> that was the last of it. (39)

Her refusal to see colour is a traumatic commemoration – as the
blood drained from her daughter's body, so the colour drains
from Sethe's subsequent world. Perceptions of the world are
therefore powerfully marked by the central traumatic incident.
By allowing Sethe overwhelming and abundant recall of the past
– which serves the narrative purposes of making the past vivid to
the reader – yet revealing that she lives in a world of profound
sensory deprivation, Morrison signals the trauma in other ways
than simply through the characteristic dysfunctions of memory.
The body memorialises trauma in particular somatic symptoms,
which function in Sethe's case to emphasise her dissociation
from feeling and affect.[6] A related response on Denver's part to
the traumatic consequences of her sister's death is her tempo-
rary deafness.

Beloved's arrival and presence gradually unleash in Sethe a
chain of repressed memories, not about the trauma of Beloved's
death, since, as I have argued, those memories are painfully
available to Sethe, but about maternal loss. Sethe's confrontation with her own feelings of abandonment and 'mother-lack'
develops Morrison's indictment of slavery as an institution devoted to distorting and truncating maternal subjectivity. About
four weeks after her arrival at 124 Bluestone, Beloved asks Sethe
if her woman 'never fixed her hair' (61). Sethe explains how she
rarely saw her mother, but on one occasion, her mother showed
her the brand under her rib and informed her that she could
know her by her mark. Later when they 'cut her down nobody
could tell whether she had a circle and a cross or not, least of all

me and I did look' (61). At this point, Sethe begins frantically to fold laundry: 'She had to do something with her hands because she was remembering something she had forgotten she knew. Something privately shameful that had seeped into a slit in her mind right behind the slap on her face and the circled cross' (61). It is not quite clear at this point what is so shameful about the memory that Sethe recovers. It is a memory of an account of her origins. Nan, the one-armed woman who cares for her and nurses her, tells her that she was the only child of her mother that was not the product of rape by sailors – the only child her mother conceived in love. The narrator explains that, as a small girl, Sethe was not impressed by this account; as a grown woman 'she was angry, but not certain at what' (62). First the recall of Nan's words is experienced as something shameful; then it is described as provoking inexplicable anger. At this point, the reader cannot understand the valency of these memories any better than Sethe. It is only much later, in Sethe's 'monologue' (Section Three) that the shame and anger are clarified. Sethe is explaining that her plan was to take herself and her children to the other side where her mother is. 'You came right on back like a good girl, like a daughter which is what I wanted to be and would have been if my ma'am had been able to get out of the rice long enough before they hanged her and let me be one' (203). She continues: 'I wonder what they was doing when they was caught. Running, you think? No. Not that. Because she was my ma'am and nobody's ma'am would run off and leave her daughter, would she? Would she, now?' (203). The answer to Denver's earlier question 'Why did they hang your ma'am?' is probably that she was running away, possibly an act of abandonment that Sethe wants to avoid recognising, but that makes her feel shamed and angry. When Nan was telling Sethe that her mother kept her when she threw her other children away off the ship, it was in some way to comfort her, saying in effect that even though her mother had been running away, Sethe did mean more to her mother than any other child she had borne:

> The one from the crew she threw away on the island. The others from more whites she also threw away. Without

names, she threw them. You she gave the name of the black man. She put her arms around him. The others she did not put her arms around. Never. Never. Telling you. I am telling you, small girl Sethe. (62).

Nan's words are not comfort, for although Sethe was conceived willingly and named, she was also deprived of her mother and left behind when she attempted to escape. Sethe's desire for her mother, her identification with her – 'mark the mark on me too' (61) – suggests that in regarding her children as extensions of herself and in seeing their protection as the preservation of the best part of herself, she replays her longing for a mother who would similarly protect and stay with her. Taken from her mother after a few weeks of nursing, and suckled by the one-armed Nan, who never has quite enough milk for her, Sethe is determined that she will bring her milk to her hungry babies. Through Sethe's emerging memories of her mother, Morrison suggests a genealogy of mothering under slavery that would logically produce the excesses and extreme forms of Sethe's maternal subjectivity.

As I have suggested, the narrative itself, at least in the first half of the novel, conveys the nature of the traumatic past through its discontinuity and fragmentation. The narrative texture is built up of memories that disrupt linear time and blur the boundaries between past and present experience. If trauma is a 'disease of time', the narrative represents it through chronological disruption and the visitation of the past as a concrete, material reality. Sethe finds the past welling up in her daily experience as if it were happening again; she lives the past as if it were the present. What the trauma of slavery has done is to disturb linearity and chronology. Time itself is haunted, and narrative denies history, which is an ordering of time. First-time readers often report that a second reading is necessary to assimilate the details of the text in the light of the revealed incident in the woodshed. The narrative must be replayed. This essential second reading provides a greater sense of narrative continuity and coherence as it allows the reader to share more fully the testimony to the trauma that the narrative offers. In this way, the story is revisited or 'passed on', a phrase that reverberates with different meanings in the novel. Questions of repetition and transmission also govern the narrative enterprise in other ways. As the materialised ghost, Beloved occasions a repetition of the past so that Sethe can confront her guilt and pain, but *Beloved* is itself a repetition of Margaret Garner's story.[7]

Many narratives guard a mystery and hint at a revelation or explanation that will clarify that mystery for the readers. Withholding information and creating suspense is a basic feature of narrative, but is the way *Beloved* hints at, and gestures towards the unspeakable event at its centre of a different order than ordinary narrative suspense? The narrative enacts a circling or repetition around the traumatic event. In this way it accords significantly with psychoanalytic accounts of traumatic repetitions – 'unavailable to the consciousness but intruding repeatedly on sight'.[8] In addition, the reader's initial experiences of the novel are apprehended in the two aspects of trauma that are at 'the heart of this repetitive seeing': 'belatedness and incomprehensibility'.[9] Morrison herself suggests that she wanted her readers to be pitched into the narrative without warning, much in the way that the slaves found themselves confused and aboard ships.

As I noted earlier, fiction engaged with representing trauma has a wide range of ways to represent or even reimpose traumatic experience. Although it is true enough to say that Sethe has been traumatised by the past, the novel's grasp of historical trauma is too deep to be satisfactorily represented in one character. Morrison ingeniously allows Sethe to remember too much and too well, but at the same time, a fragmented and discontinuous narrative performs a repression of memory. Sethe's memory is represented as bodily so that the arrest of affect is figured as sensory deprivation, which underlines that while traumatised subjects may remember, they are numb to the affect of the experience. And in *Beloved*, the reader is urged to inhabit the subject position both of the victim, who reverberates with the effects of the unresolved past, and that of the healing listener.

Until Paul D arrives, Sethe has been living enslaved, as it were, by her memories. 'Her brain was not interested in the future. Loaded with the past and hungry for more, it left her no room to imagine, let alone plan for the next day' (70). Her day consists of beating back the past, keeping it at bay, yet still dwelling within it. When Paul D offers her a life with him, the following exchange takes place:

> 'Maybe I should leave things the way they are,' she said.
> 'How are they?'
> 'We get along.'
> 'What about inside?'
> 'I don't go inside' (45)

It is Paul D, rather than Beloved, who functions as the catalyst that begins Sethe's exploration and confrontation of what is 'inside'. When he, Denver and Sethe return from the carnival, the narrator signals the possibility of a joined future by describing their shadows linked and holding hands, even though the three of them walk separately. All the while, Sethe is musing over his invitation that they make a life together. It is only when Sethe begins to imagine, to desire, a future that the ghost who has been haunting 124 Bluestone materialises. While victims of trauma are possessed by their history, rather than possessing it, Sethe's possession is made literal and real in the form of Beloved.

The specific moment of Beloved's materialisation is significant, suggesting not only the possessiveness of the past, but also Sethe's need to work through that past if she is to move forward, and her need to confront her own guilt at having survived. As Dominick LaCapra observes, 'victims of trauma may experience not only "guilt" about surviving but intense anxiety about rebuilding a life and beginning again. One basis of anxiety is the feeling that building a new life is a betrayal of loved ones who died or were overwhelmed in a past that will not pass away.'[10]

Critics have explored the many ways in which Morrison's novel depends on the tradition of the ghost story. It includes most of the 'manifestations traditional to stories of haunted houses: noises, displaced objects, smells, lights, a brooding atmosphere, and the sensitivity of an animal to the presence of the ghost.'[11] Likewise, as Carole Schmudde explains, Beloved possesses many of the characteristics typically attributed to ghosts, including new skin marked only by the scars of her violent death, 'supernatural strength', and the ability to change shape and form at will. She can cast a spell on Paul D, lift heavy weights with a finger and must ultimately be exorcised from the community 'by a ritual act of prayers and chanting'. Haunting has traditionally involved 'an old house or other locale and rest-lessness of a spirit'; the first 'an unbroken link with the past', the second provoked by 'the shock of a violent death'.[12] The history of the ghost tale in African American literature also bears on Morrison's deployment of the genre. It was originally used by white slave owners, as Geraldine Smith-Wright has shown, but became a site where Blacks could reconcile 'African beliefs about the supernatural with their experience as slaves'.[13] Morrison links her interest in memory and its operations to the tradition of the ghost story through the concept of rememory, which asserts the reality of past ideas and experiences:

> Some things go. Pass on. Some things just stay. I used to think it was my rememory. You know. Some things you forget. Other things you never do. But it's not. Places, places are still there. If a house burns down, it's gone, but the place – the picture of it – stays, and not just in my re-memory but out there, in the world. (35–6)

Denver asks if other people can see the picture and Sethe assures her they can, confirming therefore that memories are not just private and invisible, but independent entities existing in the outside world. Beloved, in this sense, is a coalition of rememories.

What is so poignant about Beloved is Morrison's represen-tation through her of the countless silenced subjects whose claims against history, the past, the living can never be made good.[14] Beloved's testimony, offered tantalisingly and con-fusingly in her 'monologue' (210–13), strains notions of the individual, discrete subject; of chronology; and of the difference between the living and the dead. Despite critical attempts to fix Beloved's identity as Sethe's daughter or as an imposter, it seems clear enough that the ghost is a layering of unstable and suggestive identities, whose fundamental unknowability is the very point. In the last paragraphs the narrator says that the community 'never knew where or why she crouched, or whose was the underwater face she needed like that' (275). What Morrison does is to create a ghost who suggests a number of possible identities but resists particularisation. Beloved is Sethe's dead daughter and more; as a choric and composite character she recalls the capture of slaves in Africa, the horrors of the Middle Passage; the sexual enslavement of young black women by white men. Sethe believes for a time that Beloved has been locked up by some white man and never allowed out. Sethe says 'that she must have escaped to a bridge or someplace and rinsed the rest out of her mind' (119). Whatever Beloved's multiple identity, she intrudes, an ungovernable past, with her own impossible agenda.

Beloved is not only a site on to which each member of the household can project her particular, unresolved emotional problems; she is also paradoxically a non-self, whose yearning to be a self is represented in terms of a fierce and insatiable desire as well as a profound sadness. One moment Beloved is choking Sethe in an act of appropriation, rage and vengeance, the next she is soothing Sethe's bruised neck with exquisite tenderness. Beloved's exclusion from another realm of desire – sexual – is emphasised when Denver finds her gazing with rapt attention at two turtles, struggling to couple as they emerge from the water:

> A turtle inched along the edge, turned and climbed to dry ground. Not far behind it was another one, headed in the same direction. Four placed plates under a hovering motionless bowl. Behind her in the grass the other one moving quickly, quickly to mount her. The impregnable strength of him – earthing his feet near her shoulders. The embracing necks – hers stretching up toward his bending down, the pat pat pat of their touching heads. No height was beyond her yearning neck, stretched like a finger towards his, risking everything outside the bowl, just to touch his face. The gravity of their shields, clashing, countered and mocked the floating heads touching. Beloved dropped the folds of her skirt. It spread around her. The hem darkened in the water. (105)

The significance of the turtles and the wet hem is not revealed until later in the novel when Morrison expresses Beloved's sexuality through these images. At one point Denver asks
Beloved why she does not cry when she feels the pain of an
extracted tooth; Beloved does begin to cry, remembering
different episodes of sadness and pain: 'And she did. Sitting here
holding a small white tooth in the palm of her smooth smooth
hand. Cried the way she wanted to when turtles came out of the
water, one behind the other ... The way she wanted to when
Sethe went to him standing in the tub under the stairs' (134).
The sight of the turtles focuses the desire that Paul D has noticed
'shining' in Beloved; like the turtles she seems to be an amphibious creature, and when she comes to Paul D, her skirts as
unwieldy as a carapace, she hoists them and turns 'her head over
her shoulder the way the turtles had' (116). Beloved's yearning
to be 'touched on the inside part' and called by her name (116),
is in some ways the reverse of Paul D's. He has been working
assiduously for years to keep his 'inside part' – his heart – un-
touched and invulnerable. The rusty tin in which he has buried
the 'red heart' suggests the defences against loving and vulnerability that slave experiences have produced. By pushing him
out of the house where he is ensconced with Sethe, Beloved
propels him from Sethe's bed, forcing him to sleep in the rocking chair downstairs, to move to the storeroom, the keeping
room, and eventually to sleep unsheltered under the night sky.
Literally, 'she moved him' (114). Just when Paul D, who has
always yearned for a family and kin, finds Sethe and wants to
'take root', Beloved keeps him on the move, propelling him to
replay the past and make better peace with it. In seducing him,
demanding to be called her name and touched on the inside, she
causes his rusty tin to flake away and exposes the feeling heart
that he has been bent on protecting. When Paul D returns to the
storeroom after Beloved has been banished, we are told that
looking at it in daylight, he cannot imagine

> the desire that drowned him in there and forced him to
> struggle up into that girl like she was the clear air at the
> top of the sea. Coupling with her wasn't even fun. It was

more like a brainless urge to stay alive. Each time she came, pulled up her skirts, a life hunger overwhelmed him and he had no more control over it than over his lungs. And afterward, beached and gobbling air, in the midst of repulsion and personal shame, he was thankful too for having been escorted to some ocean-deep place he once belonged to. (264)

The passage is an instance of the way Morrison associates the subterranean and oceanic with Beloved and how she uses Beloved to propel others to confront the primal underwater urges in themselves. On the one hand, Paul's hunger for Beloved is like an urge for the 'clear air at the top of the sea'; on the other, she is an escort to an 'ocean-deep' place recalling his individual beginning – the womb – as well as the oceanic beginning of life forms. Beloved enables Paul to plumb the depths of desire that drowns and engulfs, and to find salvation from it. Furthermore, Beloved's amphibious nature indexes her ambiguous identity. Her association with the sea and submergence allows Morrison to overdetermine her composite identity as the drowned from slave ships, the child who loses its mother, the aquatic, foetal, pre-self, and the transgressor of human boundaries between air and water.[15]

Once the tobacco tin is open, Paul D is at the mercy of his feelings and, it is important to note, his hurting memories. In a subsequent chapter, the reader encounters Paul D sitting on the steps of the porch, holding his wrist between his knees, not to keep his hands still but because he had nothing else to hold on to. 'His tobacco tin, blown open, spilled contents that floated freely and made him their prey and play' (218). His mind playing over the past, Paul D wonders, 'plagued by the contents of his tobacco tin', what difference there really was between Garner's rule at Sweet Home and Schoolteacher's (220). The point is that Paul's open tin does not so much put him in touch with what he cannot remember, as it allows him to re-experience memories and process them anew. Beloved herself, whose agenda is to find what she has been denied, clamours for life, love, identity and sexual experience. Her possible pregnancy at the end of the novel is, like all her impossible desires to 'be' in this world, a simulacrum – truly a phantom pregnancy.

Just as Beloved's presence is responsible for opening and renewing Paul D's heart, she also propels the hermit-like Denver to separate from 124 Bluestone and to venture into the outside world. Denver, who has grown up under the sign of loss and leaving, is desperately dependent on Beloved for a sense of self. Convinced that she loves her lost sister more than anyone else, the baby ghost having been her secret company all her life, she believes she will risk anything to keep and please Beloved. Denver's bodily ailment, her resistance to hearing, is her defence against the trauma of her sister's death and her mother's status as a murderess. After she attends Lady Jones's school and a fellow pupil, Nelson Lord, tells her that her mother went to prison, she simply stops hearing. Since it is not worth going to Lady Jones if you cannot hear, Denver stays at home, never venturing outside the yard and keeping watch for the 'thing' that can provoke her mother to kill her own children. In the 'quiet' she plays with the ghost. She learns to read people's faces and figure out what they are thinking so that she does not need to rely on her auditory sense. In the quiet too, she can better fantasise about the return of her father. Just as Sethe began to stutter after her mother's death, Denver registers the horror of her mother's story by ceasing to hear. The sound of the ghostly 'crawling already? baby', crawling on the stairs, is the first thing she hears after she has been deaf for some time. Deafness enables her to turn off the world's judgements of her mother, to stay alert for her own safety, and to be attuned to, and in readiness for, the return of her ghost sibling.

As Beloved's hold on Sethe and demand for her undivided attention increases, Denver finds herself marginalised. The lifelong worry that something would provoke her mother again to kill now becomes the worry that Sethe will not stand up to Beloved, whose insatiability is effectively killing her. Denver's gradual reconnection to the community (she finds work and brings home gifts of food) prepares for her rescue of Sethe with the community at the point when Sethe has relinquished all power to Beloved.

Beloved performs, impossibly, the subjectivity of one who dies too early to know herself as a subject, one who must speak though she has never had language.[16] She enacts the physically separated but psychologically unseparated child's longing for fusion and desire for the mother's face as a mirror of itself, the reflection where it will learn to distinguish itself as a self. She is all those for whom satisfaction is impossible and whose claims for life and self must forever go unsettled. Sethe regains 'the property of her own person' through the presence of the child,[17] but what does Beloved gain, let alone regain? Bloated by her cravings for sweetness and her desire for attention and affection, the final vision of Beloved is grotesque – pregnant, inflated, swelling, insatiable. She is in the process of feeding off and consuming Sethe's life at the point of her exorcism from 124 Bluestone. Morrison makes Beloved gothically monstrous by the time the community comes to replay, and this time deliver, Sethe from the past, so that the reader feels relief at the ghost's banishment. We must choose for the living; despite all mourning and guilt, the ghosts of the past must not usurp life. One of the reasons why Sethe's estranged friend Ella consents to aid Sethe is that she would not want any child ghosts of the past to invade her present. Having been abused by white men, and having refused to nurse the 'hairy white thing' which is the product of her rape by the 'lowest of the low', Ella believes she understands Sethe's position.

Nevertheless, the epilogue with its refrain, 'it was not a story to pass on', captures the poignancy of Beloved's condition. She is a roaming loneliness that cannot be rocked; as those who knew her forget her, her claims remain unanswered. She is normalised into being part of the everyday atmosphere: her 'clamor for a kiss' becomes just 'weather. Not the breath of the disremembered and unaccounted for, but wind in the eaves, or spring ice thawing too quickly' (275).

Morrison's epigraph from Romans 9:25 reads 'I will call them my people, which were not my people; and her beloved, which was not beloved.'[18] Although sometimes taken to support the view that Beloved is an imposter, or is at least mistaken in her recognition of Sethe as her mother, these lines can be read in other ways.[19] They are resonant particularly in relation to the final paragraphs of the novel, which, through evoking Beloved's loneliness and absence, create a sense of the irony of her name – the fact that disremembered and unaccounted for, she cannot really be beloved. Does the novel do better than Sethe's community in being able to call beloved that which was not beloved? In the light of Morrison's interest in historical reclamation, the epigraph can be interpreted as dwelling on the inclusion of the excluded – on a reversal of naming and status. It promises reparation, acknowledgement. It is a performative utterance, which suggests that by the declaration of words, community and connection are created where outsiders and unlovingness prevailed. The narrative project hovers between the epigraph and the final paragraphs: even as it insists on inscribing Beloved as unaccounted for and disremembered – one whose story is inadvisable or impossible to transmit – it also transmits that story, enrolling the unbeloved as beloved, enlarging the sense of 'my people'.

The last paragraphs of the novel capture the paradox of Beloved and of the narrative enterprise, offering as they do a simultaneous contradiction in the phrase, 'not a story to pass on'. There is a significant difference between 'this was not a story to pass on' and 'this is not a story to pass on'.[20] In the first case, the past tense keeps us in the context of the community about which Morrison has just been writing; they have forgotten and disremembered Beloved. 'Pass on' here has the sense of 'transmit.' But if we allow the meaning of 'pass on' to emerge from the context of the novel, we must remember the sense in which it has already been used. When Sethe is explaining the concept of rememory to Denver, she uses 'pass on' in the sense of 'die': 'Some things go. Pass on. Some things just stay' (35). 'Pass on' as 'disappear' means something quite opposed to 'transmit'. In the last paragraph of the novel, the present tense in 'this is not a story to pass on' suggests that this story must not disappear or die, that this is not a story that will die or fade away.

'A sweettooth for pain': history, trauma and replay in *Jazz*

> The past, until you confront it, until you live through it, keeps coming back in other forms. The shapes redesign themselves in other constellations, until you get a chance to play it over again.[1]

Towards the end of *Jazz* (1992), the narrator confesses a craving or sweet tooth for pain:

> Pain. I seem to have an affection, a kind of sweettooth for it ... I break lives to prove I can mend them back again. And although the pain is theirs, I share it, don't I? Of course. Of course. I wouldn't have it any other way. But it is another way. I am uneasy now. Feeling a bit false. What, I wonder, what would I be without a few brilliant spots of blood to ponder? Without aching words that set, then miss, the mark? (219)

As the narrator (or, as Morrison prefers to say, the voice) self-consciously interrogates its power in the universe of its fiction, it reflects, as any narrative consciousness with a metafictional impulse may do, that lives are fractured and chaos imposed so that the narrator can mend them and restore order.[2] This is the narrator's storm, and it is the eye (I) in it. But further, the narrative voice is admitting here a dependence on painful stories and a sudden uneasy sense of its vampiric relation to their creation and telling. Does it share their pain or feed off it, satisfying the craving for story, for someone else's tragedy? The moment of uneasiness draws attention to the ethics of a fiction that represents traumatic history – the problematic implications of writing a history of pain.

Jazz, like *Beloved*, is a novel that deals with the re-enactment of hurtful and unassimilated experiences, but instead of being literally haunted by the past, the characters in this novel repeat the traumatic aspects of their past lives in relation to a current and tragic situation. Joe's murder of his young girlfriend and Violet's stabbing of the corpse as it awaits burial indicate a powerful eruption of their unresolved pasts into the present.

In *Jazz*, the reader experiences the narrator's enactment of the processes of creating and remembering, of improvising on the painful past, in order to understand and assimilate not only the tortured individual histories of Joe and Violet, but their larger historical context – the period of the Great Migration and the Harlem Renaissance. Like *Beloved*, *Jazz* is a novel historicising racial trauma, but in this novel it is primarily through the mediations and intrusions of a highly self-conscious narrator or voice that the reader is propelled into thinking about the act of reimagining, producing and consuming a history marked by trauma. The voice in *Jazz* is intimate, personal, gossipy, and is concerned with its own musings, its misreadings, its false predictions. At the very outset of the novel, having preconceived its characters, the voice misleads the reader into thinking that a second tragedy will occur:

> It promised to be a mighty bleak household, what with the birds gone and the two of them wiping their cheeks all day, but when spring came to the City, Violet saw, coming into the building with an Okeh record under her arm and carrying some stewmeat wrapped in butcher paper, another girl with four marcelled waves on each side of her head. Violet invited her in to examine the record and that's how that scandalizing threesome on Lenox Avenue began. What turned out to be different was who shot whom. (6)

What turns out to be different, not only from the Dorcas-Joe-Violet threesome, but from the narrator's implications, is that no one shoots anybody. The reference to a 'scandalizing threesome' provokes an anticipation of something far less innocent than

Felice's dinner at the Traces, and the dancing that ensues. On that occasion, the extent of the pain is only 'too much hot pepper' on Mrs Trace's catfish, which Felice eases with a drink of water. It is after this episode that the narrator muses on its sweet tooth for pain and reminds the reader that imagining past lives can never be a predictable or perfunctory exercise. 'I thought I knew them and wasn't worried that they didn't really know about me... They knew how little I could be counted on; how poorly, how shabbily my know-it-all self covered helplessness. That when I invented stories about them – and doing it seemed to me so fine – I was completely in their hands, managed without mercy' (220). What Morrison undercuts here is exactly the sense of omnipotence that her narrator inscribes in the earlier musing about making and breaking lives. The narrator also claims here a spontaneity in creativity and a responsiveness to the process and patterning that may emerge in contradiction of the original conception. If the threesome of Felice, Joe and Violet was originally seen as a traumatic re-enactment of the Dorcas, Joe, Violet triangle, then the joke (peppery catfish as the extent of the pain) is on the narrator, who concedes fallibility and replaces hubris with humility. The narrator discovers through the process of repetition that the story does not always have to end scandalously or tragically. The improvisation in this novel means that the narrative voice is itself surprised by its own creation, which asserts itself against preconceived pattern. In a recent interview, Morrison says:

> So when I was thinking who was going to tell this story, the idea of 'who owns jazz' or who knows about it, came up. ... I decided that the voice would be one of assumed knowledge, the voice that says 'I know everything'. ... Because the voice has to actually imagine the story it's telling ... the story ... turns out to be entirely different from what is predicted because the characters are evolving.... It reminded me of a jazz performance ... Somebody takes off from a basic pattern, then the others have to accommodate themselves.[3]

Morrison shows that narrative improvisation means taking risks, responding spontaneously to what emerges in the process of creation. This is one of the ways in which Morrison's novel approximates jazz music. Jazz, Morrison has observed, symbolises an 'incredible kind of improvisation, a freedom in which a great deal of risk is involved'.[4] As Leo Ostransky describes jazz improvisation, it is always an act that depends on but resists repetition:

> Early moments in improvising sessions usually consist of each performer's blowing himself out, so to speak – ridding himself of those musical ideas close to the surface of his memory, those that come to mind too easily and too readily. As the session progresses, however, ... the performer ... feels compelled to reach out, or perhaps inward. In such moments, great jazz may be born.[5]

If the voice talks at times about its relation to the narrative it is creating and to the characters who seem to know themselves (and the voice) better than it knows them, it also inscribes its relation to the readers of the novel. On a number of occasions, the narrator's telling is figured as its product. That is, the book itself is conceived as a narrative performance, the narrator becoming indistinguishable from the story it makes. If in Yeatsian terms one cannot tell the dancer from the dance, then it makes sense for the narrative voice to present itself as the book it writes.[6] Dramatising the connection that takes place between performer and listener, it shows that writing and interpretation are truly acts of 'concert'. Since the book is powerless unless picked up and read, its pages turned, the reader's response is the very condition of its existence. Morrison's last words evoke the erotics, not so much of reading, but of being read: 'I like your fingers on and on, lifting, turning.... Talking to you and hearing you answer – that's the kick.... Look where your hands are. Now' (229). Reading, it wants to say, is a 'hands on' participatory experience. As the book conjures the reader, 'make me, remake me', it articulates both the plenitude of experience that this imaginative performance promises, but also its precarious reliance on the reader for its power to communicate. The narrator's words echo the advice that Alice Manfred, the dead girl's aunt, has given Violet earlier in the novel: 'You got anything left to you to love, anything at all, do it.... Mind what is left to you … I'm saying make it, make it' (112–13). In its emphasis on the possibility of making and remaking, Morrison's *Jazz* puts its faith in the agency and creativity that can arise even out of extremely painful experiences.

I began my account of the narrator's relation to the painful story being told by focusing on the admission that it would be nothing without a few brilliant spots of blood to ponder. I want now to turn to the documentary evidence those spots of blood recall in order to explore more fully the history of Harlem that the novel reimagines. The evidence on which Morrison's fictive history of Harlem is based is a photograph in *The Harlem Book of the Dead*. Morrison's novel improvises on the history of the jazz age through the story that Van Der Zee's photograph inspires. As author of the Foreword to *The Harlem Book of the Dead*, Morrison surely saw the manuscript of this book and read the photographer James Van Der Zee's description:

> She was the one I think was shot by her sweetheart at a party with a noiseless gun. She complained of being sick at the party and friends said, 'Well, why don't you lay down?' and they taken her in the room and laid her down. After they undressed her and loosened her clothes, they saw the blood on her dress. They asked her about it and she said, 'I'll tell you tomorrow, yes, I'll tell you tomorrow.' She was just trying to give him a chance to get away. For the picture I placed the flowers on her chest.[7]

The poetic text supplied by Owen Dodson reads:

> They lean over me, and say:
> 'Who deathed you who,
> who, who, who, who….
> I whisper: 'Tell you presently….
> Shortly…. this evening….
> Tomorrow….'
> Tomorrow is here
> And you out there safe.
> I'm safe in here, Tootsie.[8]

As the poem suggests, and as Felice points out in Morrison's novel, the wounded young woman – Dorcas – is giving herself a chance to get away, as much as she is protecting her lover. Not badly wounded, yet determined to bleed to death, she conceals her shoulder injury from others and escapes both treatment and life.

Around the arresting image of the young woman slain by her lover, Morrison builds an intricate narrative, more complicated in its overlapping of human motivations, desires and emotions than Van Der Zee's depiction of her death as an instance of the ultimate protectiveness of love – 'she was just trying to give him a chance to get away'. As Henry Louis Gates has noted, 'just as Morrison's *Beloved* was sparked by an actual historical event, so too is *Jazz*'.[9] *Beloved* begins in the newspaper account of Margaret Garner and child-murder, but takes us far beyond the action, providing in effect an imaginative history of motherhood under slavery; *Jazz* takes us from Dorcas's corpse to an exploration of the forces that have produced black Harlem. Through the local tragedy of Dorcas, Joe and Violet, Morrison summons the political and social history of African Americans at the time that Harlem is being hailed as a new beginning. Morrison's focus is on the first two decades of this century, the migration from the South to the industrial cities of the North, and the erosion of civil rights through Supreme Court decisions such as *Plessy* v *Ferguson* (1896), which effectively established apartheid by legitimising separate but equal public facilities. Morrison draws on the history of race riots in the deadly post-Reconstruction years to show the coalescence of long-preparing forces that made the City a place of promise and doubled the population of Harlem between 1910 and 1920.

It has been suggested that *Beloved* was the beginning of a planned trilogy of novels which would record the history of African Americans from slavery to the present. *Beloved* is set in 1873 and reaches back eighteen years and more in its account of Sethe and the Sweet Home slaves; *Jazz* begins in 1926, but reaches back to the 1870s when Violet and Joe were young. In addition to creating a chronological continuity with its predecessor, this second novel specifies a very important moment in African American history. By setting her novel in the mid-1920s, Morrison locates it squarely in the time of the Harlem

Renaissance, a time when young black intellectuals such as
Alain Locke, W. E. B. Du Bois, and E. Franklin Frazier saw themselves as engaged in 'history-making and race-building'.[10] It was
a time when poets and writers including Langston Hughes,
Countee Cullen and Zora Neale Hurston won prizes in the literary competition sponsored by *Opportunity Magazine* and
ushered in what the *New York Herald Tribune* called a 'Negro
renaissance'.[11] And increasingly at this time, Harlem itself
became the focus of literary attention and representation: Carl
van Vechten's notorious novel *Nigger Heaven* was published in
1926 to be followed in 1928 by Claude McKay's *Home to
Harlem*. This was also the time in which jazz music was not only
being played but recorded. In 1926 Louis Armstrong's release of
'Heebie Jeebies' introduced the style of scat singing – an instru-
mental solo performed by the voice to vocables or nonsense
syllables,[12] and Duke Ellington recorded 'Rainy Nights' and
'East St. Louis Toodle-Oo', as well as 'Trombone Blues', the
record responsible for some trouble in *Jazz* as it prompts a teenage girl to leave her baby sister unattended while she dashes into
her house to fetch it. Violet wanders off with the baby and a
neighbour remarks of the jazz-struck sister, 'She'll know more
about blues than any trombone when her mama gets home' (21).

Although Morrison is writing about the time of the Harlem
Renaissance, she avoids recreating the exotic cultural world, the
jungle of dance and music in familiar and formulaic representations of this jazz age, the world of the 'niggerati', as Zora Neale
Hurston called it. The Harlem Renaissance of the 1920s is often
cited as symbolic of black liberation. According to Nathan
Huggins it was a time of sophistication, 'the final shaking off of
slavery from the minds, spirits, and characters of African Americans. It was a period when the African American came of age –
when the 'New Negro' was born – with the clearest expression
of this transformation visible in its remarkable outpouring of
literature, art, and music.'[13] But Morrison is sceptical of accounts
of the period that focus solely on its literary and artistic productions and in *Jazz* she avoids mention of the 'renaissance'
altogether. She has expressed the view that this awakening was

not really an African American enterprise because 'in some ways it was somebody else's interest that made it exist'; she chooses to write about the ordinary folk rather than the Harlem intellectuals and poets.[14] What was 'ours' about Harlem at that time, she implies in *Jazz*, was something altogether less glamorous. Langston Hughes himself noted that 'non-theatrical, non-intellectual Harlem was an unwilling victim of its own vogue', and that 'ordinary Negroes hadn't heard of the Negro Renaissance. And if they had, it hadn't raised their wages any.'[15] As in-house editor of *The Black Book* in 1974, Morrison says she

> had gotten tired of histories of black life that focused only on leaders, leaving the everyday heroes to the lumps of statistics. She wanted to bring the lives of those who always got lost in the statistics to the forefront – to create a genuine black history book 'that simply recollected life as lived'.[16]

Following the spirit of *The Black Book*, Morrison chooses to write about the 'ordinary Negro' rather than the Harlem intellectuals and poets and social hostesses. Her characters are a small-time, unlicensed hairdresser and a sample-case man – Violet and Joe – rather than the amazing cosmetics and hair-straightening heiress, A'lelia Walker, whom Langston Hughes described as 'the joy-goddess of Harlem's 1920s' at whose parties 'Negro poets mingled with downtown poets. ... And a good time was had by all'.[17] Joe and Violet's work reminds us of the wealthy Walker, whose mother made a fortune with a hair-straightening technique, but it also underlines Morrison's decision to focus on the ordinary. *Jazz* is therefore a history of Harlem that is interested in the improvisation of lives out of a painful past rather than concerned to represent a glorious moment of cultural awakening. In accordance with Morrison's emphasis on daily life and ordinary people, public events are muted and backgrounded; they form a texture rather than dominate the plot. Characters in *Jazz* do not join Marcus Garvey's group, or participate in the NAACP, but many of them do indeed witness the parades and silent marches that took place in the streets of Harlem. In a variety of quiet ways, *Jazz* reveals how subjectivities and identities are produced through the conditions of racism and oppression specific to the first three decades of the twentieth century. To read accounts of life in Harlem at this time is to realise not only how densely and deftly Morrison has grounded *Jazz* in the city's rich and complex history, but how her novel dialogues with other accounts of Harlem's history – that of Alain Locke, James Weldon Johnson, Langston Hughes and, later, Nathan Huggins – fleshing them out at times, and at others endorsing or sceptically ironising them.

Part of the great migration from the South, Joe and Violet travel North by rail in 1906; they are moved 'five times in four different cars to abide by the Jim Crow law' (127), until 'out of Delaware and a long way from Maryland', there is 'no green-as-poison curtain separating the colored people eating from the rest of the diners' (31). As they feel the rhythm of the train on the tracks and dance on their way into the city, the narrator fills out a picture of 'the specter' that they and millions of others like them have left behind. 'The wave of black people running from want and violence crested in the 1870s; the '80s; the '90s but was a steady stream in 1906 when Joe and Violet joined it' (33). Metonymically evoking the race riots of the early twentieth century, Morrison lists a number of places: Springfield Ohio, Springfield Indiana,[18] Greensburg Indiana, Wilmington Delaware, New Orleans Louisiana, and 'the raving whites' who 'foamed all over the lanes and yards of home' (33). Lynchings may have been decreasing slightly, but as John Hope Franklin points out, it was the epidemic of race riots that swept the country early in the century that aroused greatest anxiety and discomfort.[19] While Violet and Joe, like millions of others, head to Harlem to escape the wave of violence and persecution, Morrison emphasises that the city is not merely a place of refuge, but a new beginning: 'I'm crazy about this City', confesses the narrator, drawing us into the past of 1926 where her characters believe that 'all the wars are over and there will never be another one…. History is over, you all, and everything's ahead at last' (7). Knowing Morrison's abiding concern with the presentness of the past, we may suspect that despite the buoyancy of optimism in 'everything's ahead at last', this novel too will show that history is never over. As much as Joe recounts in his narrative the many times in which he has changed – 'You could say I've been a new Negro all my life' (129) – what happens between Joe and Violet and Dorcas is a convergence of old, unresolved hurts and unsatisfied hungers that well up from the past. Joe called himself Trace because according to his foster mother his parents disappeared without a trace, but we soon know that there are indeed traces of his mother and that while the past may leave one traumatised, no past is radically untraceable. The more Joe tries to constitute himself as 'new', to kick over the traces, the more assertive the past becomes in his present.

Enthusiastic accounts of Harlem as a new beginning contextualise Joe's claims to personal transformation. Joe's phrase 'a new Negro' resonates with the well-known text which coined that phrase: in 1925 Alain Locke, the first black Rhodes scholar and a professor of philosophy at Howard, wrote about 'the New Negro' in Harlem, signalling through the appellation a new psychology of self-respect and an optimism about the possibilities of black community and culture in Harlem:

> The tide of Negro migration, northward and city-ward, is not to be fully explained as a blind flood started by the demands of war industry ... or the pressure of poor crops with increased social terrorism in certain sections of the South and Southwest. Neither labor demand, the boll weevil nor the Ku Klux Klan is a basic factor, however contributory any or all of them may have been. The wash and rush of this human tide on the beach line of the northern city centers is to be explained primarily in terms of a new vision of opportunity, of social and economic freedom, of a spirit to seize, even in the face of an extortionate and heavy toll, a chance for the improvement of conditions.[20]

Locke hails Harlem, which has 'the largest Negro community in the world', as prophetic of a 'transformed and transforming psychology' which is permeating the masses, and looks forward to the flowering of self-expression in the 'new Negro' and a 'spiritual Coming of Age'.[21] Nathan Huggins points out that 'black men's dreams would find in Harlem a capital for the race, a platform from which the new black voice would be heard around the world, and an intellectual center for the New Negro'.[22]

Even more buoyant about the prospects of cultural and community life in Harlem, James Weldon Johnson wrote in *Black Manhattan* (1930) of the metropolis as the great hope of the future: 'It strikes the uninformed observer as a phenomenon, a miracle straight out of the skies.' He described the city as neither a slum, nor a 'quarter' but a section of 'handsome dwellings, with streets as well paved, as well lighted and as well kept as any other part of the city'.[23] In *Jazz*, the narrator's rhapsody expressing the newcomers' delight in the City dwells on the 'thrilling, wasteful street lamps' that burn continuously and make the stars irrelevant (35). But while Morrison captures some of the excitement of the new beginning that the city represented, she is also firmly focused on its limitations and the disabling aspects of the past from which it arises. And while Johnson extolled this clean, well-lighted place, others were already noticing its decline into slum.

First Joe and Violet live in the Tenderloin, a district on the Lower East Side, but just before the war they move uptown where 'whole blocks was let to colored. Nice … These had five, six rooms; some had ten and if you could manage fifty, sixty dollars a month, you could have one' (127). In the early 1920s, however, the average Harlemite worked, as in the 1890s, in menial or unskilled positions and earned less than other New Yorkers (about $1300 a year as opposed to $1570) and paid far more for housing.[24] As E. Franklin Frazier noted, there were two types of business in New York in terms of hiring policy: 'those that employ Negroes in menial positions and those that employ no Negroes at all'.[25] Violet starts out 'going into service' and Joe tells us he works shoe leather, rolls tobacco, cleans fish at night and toilets by day until he gets a job waiting tables. Then he does hotel work and eventually, when rents are 'raised and raised again', and the price of uptown meat doubles while that of Whites' meat stays the same, Joe begins selling beauty products. Langston Hughes's observation about ordinary people not

having heard of or profited from the Renaissance gains resonance in the context of Joe's efforts to make a living.[26] In Joe's
account of his and Violet's painful struggle to improve their
lives in the city, Morrison undercuts any notion of Harlem as an
idealised, monolithic community. 'When we moved from 140th
Street to a bigger place on Lenox, it was the light-skinned renters
who tried to keep us out. Me and Violet fought them just like
they was whites. We won' (127). Before the end of the nine-
teenth century, Harlem had been a much sought neighbourhood
boasting many fine homes and apartment buildings. As Cary
Wintz explains, confidence in the future of this area of the city
encouraged speculation and when the speculative boom col-
lapsed in the early years of the twentieth century, many inves-
tors found their buildings standing empty. Pressure for housing
from the swelling black population in other areas of the city
(Tenderloin and San Juan Hill) meant that Harlem property
began to be subdivided and leased to black tenants. Despite the
attempts of white residents to resist this tide, by 1910 Harlem
was a largely black neighbourhood.[27] Through Joe's reference to
the 'light-skinned renters', Morrison signals awareness that although Harlem may be hailed as the capital of the race, the Mecca for Blacks throughout the world, it is a complex, multi-lay-
ered community, by no means impervious to, but rather
constituted by, the stratifications of colour that govern the rest
of the United States.

The power of gradations of colour to determine social status
and class is also clear in the way Violet and Joe earn a living. By
focusing on the small-time hairdressers and sample-case men,
Morrison subtly reminds the informed reader of the cosmetics
and hair-straightening heiress, A'lelia Walker, whose prece-
dence in Harlem at this time is evidence that beauty processes
and products were, for some, a fabulously lucrative business. As
E. Franklin Frazier wrote of Madame Walker: 'It was in the
manufacture of cosmetics that Negroes – women – first achieved
a spectacular success.... The numerous beauty shops, which
constitute a large proportion of Negro business undertakings,
have provided outlets for these products.'[28] The community's

great beauticians had both wealth and social influence in Harlem and 'no beautician in New York was qualified or authorized to practice the Walker System unless she had received a diploma from the college, creating along with other schools and systems such as Nu-Life, Poro, and Apex, a highly controlled and organized beauty industry'.[29] Violet is a private operator rather than a licensed beautician, which means she lacks the necessary diploma from one of the beauty schools and systems and cannot work in a salon but instead travels to the homes of her customers. We learn that two hairdressers see Joe with Dorcas at the Mexico club, and enjoy gossiping about them; they have a grudge against Joe's wife because she steals their business, but admit that 'crazy as she was she did do hair well and if she wasn't so crazy she could have got a license proper instead of taking away their trade' (201). The products Joe sells recall those advertised in the pages of black newspapers of the time. Around 1907 papers began to sport advertisements for beauty products such as 'Black-No-More', 'Fair-Plex Ointment', 'Cocotone', and 'Golden Brown'. One of the 'Cleopatra' products Joe sells is 'Nut Brown' (68), and the name 'Cleopatra' itself suggests a sultry exoticism that is burnished rather than black. Advertisements for 'Golden Brown' urged users not to be 'fooled by so-called "skin-whiteners". But you can easily enhance your beauty, lighten and brighten your dark or sallow skin by applying Golden Brown ... It won't whiten your skin – as that can't be done.'[30] By making both Joe and Violet small-time operators in one of the most powerful areas of Harlem business, Morrison again draws attention, as she did in *The Bluest Eye*, to the business of beauty and the commodity culture that disseminates standards of beauty and self-worth dependent on a hierarchy of skin and hair types. Furthermore, associations drawn from the occupations of Joe and Violet lead the reader on a mysterious trail into the peculiarly linked past histories of Joe and Violet. Golden Gray brings these histories together: accidentally present at Joe's birth, he supplants Joe by becoming an object of fascination for the wild woman – Joe's mother – who will not mother her son. In Violet's family, he is the wonderboy with the 'carefully loved hair' and, although never seen by Violet, becomes her desired blond brother, friend, lover, self.

The episodes in the novel concerning Golden Gray constitute an imaginative fable, a digressive improvisation on the Southern past from which Joe and Violet have emerged but which they play out rather than escape in the City. Golden Gray is the son of a young white woman, Vera Louise Gray, and the black hunter, Henry LesTroy or Lestory, also known as Hunters Hunter. Morrison deliberately associates Golden Gray with Violet's work as a hairdresser: his legendary golden curls, 'the kind her grandmother soaped and played with and remembered for forty years' are not, the narrator tells us, the kind that Violet washes and treats (17). That kind, it is implied, needs straightening tongs and marcelling irons. The hair that Violet straightens and sets is not only different from the kind idolised by her grandmother, but Violet herself has internalised Golden Gray as the object of her desire. His image 'tore up' Violet's girlhood as if they had been the best of lovers, and moreover, she admits that when she was seeking Joe in the cane fields she was 'holding onto him but wishing that he was the golden boy I never saw either' (97).

When Violet's mother threw herself down a well, Violet was left in the care of her grandmother, True Belle, a mammy figure of the old South, whose charge – Golden Gray, her mistress's illegitimate son – captured her strongest affections. The narrator muses:

> Maybe that is why Violet is a hairdresser – all those years of listening to her rescuing grandmother, True Belle, tell Baltimore stories. The years with Miss Vera Louise in the fine stone house on Edison Street, where the linen was embroidered with blue thread and there was nothing to do but raise and adore the blond boy who ran away from them depriving everybody of his carefully loved hair. (17)

The link between Golden Gray and the skin and hair products that Violet and Joe now deal with is further underlined in the memory that Hunters Hunter has of the wild woman who is Joe's mother:

[I]t saddened him to learn that instead of resting she was hungry still. Though for what, exactly, he couldn't say, unless it was for hair the color of a young man's name. To see the two of them together was a regular jolt: the young man's head of yellow hair long as a dog's tail next to her skein of black wool. (167)

Although the exact nature of Wild's hunger is unclear – Hunters Hunter implies that it is desire for Golden Gray – Wild's refusal to mother her son bequeaths him a desperate hunger and desire for her, which he will take with him to the City to displace on to Dorcas. Joe's searches for Wild before he leaves the South lead him eventually to the cave his berry-black mother inhabits. In here he finds the green dress that once belonged to Vera Louise Gray. (The dress is in the hut and used to cover the injured, pregnant Wild; Hunters Hunter remembers that when Vera Louise wore it you could hardly distinguish between her and the grass.) The narrator emphasises the presence of Golden Gray's clothes: 'Also. Also, a pair of man's trousers with buttons of bone. Carefully folded, a silk shirt, faded pale and creamy – except at the seams' (184). Unhousebroken, Wild leaves traces of her sloven self all over the country, but in her secret cave, a domestic space, among filched items of civilised life, the clothes of the white woman and the golden man are carefully folded. Henry Lestory reports the community view that Wild set great store by the 'queer boy' – Golden Gray (168). What becomes of Wild we never know. Perhaps she perished in the cane field burnings that drove hundreds of workers from the area. 'The cane field where Wild hid … burned for months…. Would she know? he wondered. Would she understand that fire was not light or flowers moving toward her, or flying golden hair? That if you tried to touch or kiss it, it would swallow your breath away?' (174). In turn, Wild is the 'girl' who changes Golden Gray's mind after he resolves to blow off his own father's head. The narrator does not divulge how the girl dissuaded him; nor do we know how she came to have his trousers and shirt in her cave. But instead of the savage and bestial creature others think her, Morrison's narrator comes to see her ultimately as 'a playful woman who lived in a rock':

I'd love to close myself in the peace left by the woman who lived there and scared everybody. Unseen because she knows better than to be seen. After all, who would see her, a playful woman who lived in a rock? Who could, without fright? Or her looking eyes looking back? I wouldn't mind. Why should I? She has seen me and is not afraid of me. She hugs me. Understands me. Has given me her hand. I am touched by her. Released in secret. Now I know. (221)

While Wild does not – will not – reach out and touch her desperate son's hand, she does touch and hug the narrator. Similarly, the narrator discovers that Golden Gray merits more sympathy than she initially accorded him: 'Not hating him is not enough; liking, loving him is not useful. I have to alter things. I have to be a shadow who wishes him well' (161). Travelling back to the past of Joe and Violet, the narrator works with the stuff of Southern legend and mythology – scenes of confrontation over paternity and miscegenation; the mammy who adores the white child; the savage wild woman who can mother no one. This foray into a tradition that extends from post-Confederation to Faulkner and beyond allows Morrison to refigure that past with a hint of parody, and yet to rescue figures such as the half-breed and the wild woman from stereotype by allowing her narrator to challenge preconceived opinions and be touched by the wild woman, to become a shadow that wishes Golden Gray well.

Despite the relief of leaving the South with its lynchings and smoking cane fields, Joe and Violet experience significant loss in moving North. In a mellow scene that takes place just before Joe and Violet leave for the City, Violet is described as settling herself down for a deep sleep after a long, hard day's work. Her ritual of face cleaning, slipping on a freshly laundered white shirt and unwinding her hair is pleasantly sensual: 'Finally she sat on the bed to unwind her hair. Most of the knots fixed that morning had loosened under her headcloth and were now cupfuls of soft wool her fingers thrilled to. Sitting there, her hands deep in the forbidden pleasure of her hair, she noticed she had not removed her heavy work shoes' (225). As Violet tells Felice: 'Before I came North I made sense and so did the world. We didn't have nothing but we didn't miss it' (207). In the City, however, Violet says that she forgot it was her life and

> just ran up and down the streets wishing I was somebody else.... Now I want to be the woman my mother didn't stay around long enough to see. That one. The one she would have liked and the one I used to like before.... My grandmother fed me stories about a little blond child. He was a boy, but I thought of him as a girl sometimes, as a brother, sometimes as a boyfriend. He lived inside my mind. Quiet as a mole. But I didn't know it till I got here. The two of us. Had to get rid of it. (208)

Felice then recounts Violet's narrative to herself, now able to perceive the story's relevance to the ring she has to recover: 'Reminds me of the tricky blond kid living inside Mrs. Trace's head. A present taken from whitefolks, given to me when I was too young to say No thank you' (211). As the object of both Wild's and Violet's desire, Golden Gray is the one who doubly displaces Joe, claiming the daydreams and the attention of his abandoning mother and his wife. The Golden Gray fable works economically, therefore, to suggest the psychic freight that Joe and Violet bring to the City – that great expectorate of what is dormant inside its 'new' inhabitants. Relating particularly to skin and hair, Morrison's representation of the Southern past draws on the pervasive metonymies of racial identity that continue to shape and disrupt lives in the City.

A number of critics have already shown that jazz as a musical form is relevant to the novel's structure, patterning and voice,[31] but what I want to emphasise is the cultural significance of jazz in the 1920s as an integral part of the novel's concern with the painful aspects of African American history. The music is in the history and the history is in the music. Two incidents in the novel register the communal and public importance of jazz. In the first, Joe tells of 'feeling proud of the colored troops' – the 'three six nine' infantry – and dancing in the street along with everyone else. The return of the 'three six nine' was a momentous occasion that acknowledged the success of these black soldiers and celebrated their part in securing freedoms and rights to all. After marching in the regular way up Fifth Avenue to cheering crowds, the black soldiers entered Harlem and marked their 'homecoming' by parading up Lenox Avenue to a jazz step. Both their success in combat and the hope and promise signalled by the end of the war prompted this joyous musical expression. The image of the black troops breaking into jazz step carries a poignant irony if we remember Morrison's character Shadrack in *Sula*, who returned from the war having seen its atrocities and was unable to ponder much more than a community's suicidal urges. He reminds us of the cost to black soldiers whose patriotism was enlisted abroad, but whose oppression continued to be sanctioned at home.

In the second incident, Alice Manfred takes her orphaned niece to the Silent Protest Parade on Fifth Avenue in July 1917. By way of protesting against the East St. Louis riots and other violence, the NAACP organised a silent parade. Banners read 'Thou Shalt not Kill'; 'Mother, do Lynchers go to Heaven?'; 'Mr. President, Why not make America Safe for Democracy?' and 'Pray for the Lady Macbeths of East St. Louis.'[32] Leaflets were distributed by the parade committee saying: 'We march because we want to make impossible a repetition of Waco, Memphis and East St. Louis, by rousing the conscience of the country and to bring the murderers of our brothers, sisters and innocent children to justice.' Morrison refers to such 'explanatory leaflets' being passed out by Colored Boy Scouts (58), and tells us that Alice Manfred cannot connect the explanations to her orphaned niece Dorcas. Although some insisted that the rioters were disgruntled war veterans who had fought in all-coloured units and came home to white violence, and others said Whites were terrified by the wave of Southern refugees coming North, Alice blames the violence on 'the music'. Her brother-in-law was not a veteran; nor did he need a white man's job. He owned a pool-hall. Further, he was pulled off a streetcar and 'stomped to death'. His home was torched and his wife, who had just returned from identifying him was 'burned crispy' in the flames. Rejecting the violence against Blacks as a cause of the riots, Alice attributes the tragedy to the 'lowdown' music. Like many others she censoriously perceives jazz music as the cause of 'Imminent Demise' and is wary of the 'nasty dancing' and the songs that 'used to start in the head and fill the heart' but 'had dropped on down.... [l]ower and lower until the music was so lowdown that you shut the window' (56). Since jazz music was associated with Storyville (the prostitution district) in New Orleans, 'jazz became a symbol of crime, feeble-mindedness, insanity and sex, and was under constant attack by the press from the early 1920's on. It was seen as a symptom of general cultural decay.'[33] Blaming the incendiary music and the morals and ways of life that it encourages – 'It made you do unwise disorderly things. Just hearing it was like violating the law' (58) – is a puritanical gesture of self-blame and a denial of the power-ful tensions in black–white political relations.

However, there is one way in which Alice is close to the truth about the power of the music. When she stands with her niece Dorcas at the parade and fails to connect the silent marchers to the explanation offered in the leaflet, it is only through sound, the music of the drums, that she begins to understand a connection and the solemn sound of the drums becomes a life-line: 'Then suddenly like a rope cast for rescue, the drums spanned the distance, gathering them all up and connected them: Alice, Dorcas, her sister and brother-in-law, the Boy Scouts and the frozen black faces, the watchers on the pavement and those in the windows above' (58). Thereafter, Alice finds that rope, the music, relatively secure except when it expresses desire or long-ing. And although she knows from its bad press, sermons and editorials that jazz is not 'serious music' but just 'colored folks' stuff – harmful, certainly; embarrassing, of course; but not real, not serious' (59) – she recognises, and is afraid of, the complicat-ed anger, appetite and hunger that the music both expresses and inspires. Alice's blame of the 'lowdown' music becomes a recog-nition that the longing and appetite it sings of cannot simply be dismissed as brazen and immoral. If the drums at the Fifth Avenue parade become a rope of 'fellowship, discipline and tran-scendence' (60), they also connect Alice to the rage and want in other music: 'It was impossible to keep the Fifth Avenue drums separate from the belt-buckle tunes vibrating from pianos and spinning on every Victrola' (59). The music is not just sassy and sexy, and the desires it evokes are not just sexual; it is also, in its capacity to destabilise, politically powerful. Unbidden, the lines of a song play in Alice's head: '"When I was young and in my prime I could get my barbecue any old time." They are greedy, reckless words, loose and infuriating, but hard to dismiss because underneath, holding up the looseness like a palm are the drums that put Fifth Avenue into focus' (60).

Holding her aunt's hand at the parade, Dorcas also hears the drums. Whereas her aunt begins to see that the music expresses meanings beyond the 'life below the sash', Dorcas takes that life as her principal reality. 'While her aunt worried about how to keep the heart ignorant of the hips and the head in charge of both, Dorcas lay on a chenille bedspread, tickled and happy knowing that there was no place to be where … someone was not licking his licorice stick, tickling the ivories, beating his skins, blowing off his horn while a knowing woman sang … ' (60). The ways of describing clarinet and piano, drums and horn here conjure Dorcas's sensual hungers, especially for sweet things. When Joe first meets her she is in a candy store, but she not only has a sweet tooth for candy. She shares with the narrator a sweet tooth for pain. The other side of her hunger for music and candy is a powerful urge for the dangerous and even self-destructive. Dorcas remembers the protest parade her aunt took her to as a kind of funeral march for her parents. Given her experiences in East St. Louis at the scene of her mother's burning, she responds very differently to the sound of the drums. 'Back in East St. Louis, as the little porch fell, wood chips – ignited and smoking – exploded in the air. One of them must have entered her stretched dumb mouth and traveled down her throat because it smoked and glowed there still. Dorcas never let it out and never put it out' (62). In this way, Dorcas is also linked with Joe's mother, Wild, who may have perished in the cane fields by swallowing fire which could, if you tried to kiss or touch it, 'swallow your breath away' (174). The spark that Dorcas swallows does not take her breath away, but leaves her volatile and inflammable, reckless and possibly dangerous. Ready to catch fire, blaze and burn, an adolescent Dorcas advertises a hunger for loving that, despite her aunt's efforts to 'privatize' her niece, is 'like a public secret' (67). The City, seeping music, calls 'come and do wrong' and Dorcas responds by beginning an affair with Joe Trace, which ignites his hunger for fulfillment and for doing something wild himself. Dorcas is, one might say, another walk for Joe on the wild side.

When the jilted Joe goes looking for Dorcas, it is as if he once again seeks his wild woman mother. He sets out to find Dorcas, he thinks, as a conciliatory lover, but he is also the sum of Joes that successive transformations have not banished. Especially, he is a disappointed son and a consummate hunter: 'When I find her, I know – I bet my life – she won't be holed up with one of them. His clothes won't be mixed up with hers. Not her. Not Dorcas. She'll be alone. Hardheaded. Wild, even. But alone' (182). And Dorcas, having dismissed Joe more cruelly than she intended, knows that he will try to find her: 'He is coming for me. Maybe tonight. Maybe here' (190). Not only does Dorcas know that if you play you pay, but, as Henry Louis Gates points out in a recent essay on O. J. Simpson and the Million Man March, Morrison is 'less interested in the grand passions of love and requital than she is in the curious texture of communal amnesty'; her novel deals with the 'culturally-vexed status of the so-called crime of passion'.[34] It is noticeable that Joe, forgiven by the community and eventually his wife, goes officially unpunished for Dorcas's death. Are we to say then, that not only did Dorcas have it coming to her, but she was looking for it? Dorcas herself accedes to the view that she brought it on herself, but her status as sacrificial victim ought to provoke some disquieting reflection. Joe and Violet work through the aftermath of the murder – the 'sad stuff' and the 'bad stuff' (7) – with each other and their community. Everyone releases a pent-up tension or learns something new about themselves from Dorcas's death. Alice Manfred recognises her emotional stranglehold on herself, and Felice comes to understand the meaning of the ring she loaned Dorcas. It is also the occasion that generates the reader-writer community, for without the improvisation on Van Der Zee's photograph there would be no narrative. Well might the narrator register a slight qualm about its vampiric tendencies, for the few brilliant spots of blood on which it depends are Dorcas's. As in *Beloved*, a dead girl provides the occasion for the narrative. It is interesting that in 1985, when she was writing *Beloved*, Morrison spoke in an interview of her plans to incorporate in one novel the story of Margaret Garner and the story behind the photograph by Van Der Zee:

> And I call her Beloved so that I can filter all these confrontations and questions that she has in that situation, which is 1851, and then to extend her life, you know, her search, her quest all the way through as long as I care to go, into the twenties where it switches to this other girl. Therefore, I have a New York uptown-Harlem milieu in which to put this love story, but Beloved will be there also.[35]

Yet what originally aroused Morrison's interest in these two incidents was that each featured a woman who sabotaged herself. In each case 'a woman loved something other than herself so much. She had placed all of the value of her life in something outside herself.'[36] In *Beloved*, Sethe certainly remains true to that conception; her painful journey is to locate the best part of herself inside rather than outside herself. In *Jazz*, Dorcas betrays Joe because he credits her with having a self rather than trying to mould her and produce her himself. 'Joe didn't care what kind of woman I was. He should have. I cared. I wanted to have a personality and with Acton, I'm getting one' (190). Having snared the prize that Acton represents – his savvy self is enough – she wins the envy of other girls and defines herself in the process. 'I'm Acton's and it's Acton I want to please. He expects it. With Joe I pleased myself because he encouraged me to. With Joe I worked the stick of the world, the power in my hand' (191). So when Joe comes looking for Dorcas and shoots her, she knows that she is being called on to name her assassin. 'They need me to say his name so they can go after him … I know his name but Mama won't tell. The world rocked from a stick beneath my hand, Felice. There in that room with the ice sign in the window' (193). But in the next sentence Morrison writes: 'Felice puts her ear on my lips and I scream it to her. I think I am screaming it. I think I am' (193). The ambiguity of the referent of 'it' means that Dorcas could be screaming what we have just heard, that she will not tell his name, or she could be contradicting what she has just avowed, and indeed screaming 'it' – his name. Even if Dorcas does sabotage herself, the tendency to blame her for her death does not deal with the complexities of her marginalisation in this narrative. If Beloved remains at the close of *Beloved* as the loneliness that cannot be stilled, Dorcas remains at the close of *Jazz* as the cost of the blues.

The emphasis in the last chapters moves from pain and expiation to tentative reconciliation and repair. Music and dancing point the way to the gradual coming together of Violet and Joe at the end of the novel: 'Somebody in the house across the alley put a record on and the music floated in to us through the open window. Mr. Trace moved his head to the rhythm and his wife snapped her fingers in time. She did a little step in front of him and he smiled. By and by they were dancing' (214). The bringer of music, Felice informs them that they need a Victrola in the apartment. And as a kind of double of Dorcas, she provides Joe and Violet metaphorically with an opportunity for replay. Morrison continues the analogy with music as she points out in her most optimistic ending, that the past is not an abused record, with 'no choice but to repeat itself at the crack and no power on earth [to] lift the arm that held the needle' (220). It is possible to make it and remake it, to go round once more and get out of the groove in which we have been stuck – Sethe replays the approach of the slave catcher in *Beloved*, and Violet and Joe rehearse their past in relation to Felice, probably a happy substitute for Dorcas. Morrison first provokes the notion of repetition compulsion but then tempers it with a saving variation – the repressed returns but there is also another day. All Morrison's novels are at some level about the return of the unaccounted for or the forgotten in history and public and private life. In her last two novels, however, components of a historical trilogy, Morrison produces hopeful endings, neither of which forecloses on, or writes off, pain as it tentatively suggests the possibility of a renovated future. Violet asks: 'What's the world for if you can't make it up the way you want it?' (208). Morrison's history of the jazz age is an attempt to express and assimilate the pain of the past but also to acknowledge the agency and power of its inheritors to make and remake it. A sweet tooth for pain – this could also be formulated as the 'blues temperament' or the urge to 'finger the jagged edge' – also surely accommodates a taste for hope and pleasure.

Critical overview

WHEN the Swedish Academy awarded Morrison the Nobel Prize for Literature in 1993, she was described as one 'who, in novels characterized by visionary force and poetic import, gives life to an essential aspect of American reality'.[1] The assessment captures two important trajectories of the now vast body of criticism on Morrison's work. One broad strand of Morrison criticism has focused on the 'visionary force and poetic import' of the novels. Her texts are examined for their unusually poetic language, figuration and use of a diverse range of mythologies. The 'universal' and 'transcendent' qualities of her work are emphasised over the cultural and social specificities. The next part of the quotation from the Nobel Prize dedication character-ises another general strand in criticism, which focuses on Morri-son's attention to the specificities of race and the socio-historical context of African American experience. Although the phrase 'gives life to an essential aspect of American reality' does not clearly specify the African American community – some would argue that it deliberately avoids mention of race – it does gesture towards the context of American social and political life which shapes, and is shaped by, African American culture and identity. It draws attention to Morrison's status as an African American writer and her expressed desire to give voice to black experience in America. In their preface to a recent volume of criticism on Morrison, Gates and Appiah draw together these two strands: 'Morrison's greatest capacities as a writer are her ability to create a densely lyrical narrative texture that is instantly recognizable as her own and to make the particularity of the African-American "experience" the basis for a representation of humanity *tout court*.'[2]

Morrison's first novel, *The Bluest Eye*, was published in 1970 and out of print by 1974. Her second, *Sula* (1973), was greeted with mixed reviews, but was nominated in 1975 for the National Book Award in Fiction. Since the publication of *Song of Solomon* (1977), she has been a much-lauded writer[3] and immensely popular, although her works are acknowledged to be 'difficult'. Her writing is also provocative and her work has been the site of critical engagement over a wide variety of often controversial issues: the nature of black feminism, the attraction of black women's texts for white Anglo-American critics, and the assumption that ethnic minority literature (in this case, black women's texts) provides documentary/realistic evidence of ethnic life.[4] The last few years have seen an increasing number of book-length studies devoted to Morrison, as well as a welter of articles, essays and book chapters. There is a range of collections of essays on Morrison, as well as journal numbers devoted entirely to her work. Criticism on her work is now a corpus so large that it contains the widest diversity of theoretical approaches and methodological affiliations. It is testimony not only to the industry of academia but to Morrison's capacity as a contemporary novelist that her work invites such a broad spectrum of critical approaches. I propose to illustrate that diversity in this overview by discussing briefly some of the full-length critical studies on Morrison and then reviewing by theme and critical affiliation a range of articles and essays.[5]

Among the book-length studies of Morrison, Trudier Harris's *Fiction and Folklore: The Novels of Toni Morrison* (1991) locates Morrison's work in relation to a specifically African American literary tradition – the folktale. Harris argues that Morrison manages to steep her novels in folkways and simulate the 'ethos of folk communities', achieving art that is genuinely representative of the folk.[6] Drawing on a philosophic and political (rather than literary) tradition in African American culture, Denise Heinze's approach in *The Dilemma of 'Double-Consciousness'*

(1993) draws on Du Bois's notion of 'double-consciousness', which enables her to see Morrison as attempting the accommodation of 'two often competing literary selves'.[7] Heinze's study is, however, less an interrogation of Du Boisian double-consciousness and the interesting and complex rethinking of that concept by Ellison, Gates and Appiah, than it is an analysis of major themes in Morrison's work. Dorothea Drummond Mbalia, *Toni Morrison's Developing Class Consciousness* (1991), draws on the ideology of Nkrumaism which 'uses dialectical and historical materialism first to explain the uniqueness of the African's oppression ... grounded in race and class, and second to propose a viable solution to that oppression'.[8] Morrison's 'grand theme' is self-discovery, according to Karen Carmean, *Toni Morrison's World of Fiction* (1993). Carmean also takes issue with critics who insist that Morrison's writing has become more politicised, arguing that 'politics is not a new aspect of her novels. ... [It] just plays a more obvious role in *Beloved* and *Jazz* because of their subject matter and the nature of their stories.'[9] Post-structural concepts of division and dissolution provide the framework for Philip Page's analysis of American and African American culture in *Dangerous Freedom: Fusion and Fragmentation in Toni Morrison's Novels* (1995). In *Toni Morrison's Fiction* (1996), Jan Furman emphasises the centrality of black women's lives in Morrison's novels and explores the depiction of social and family cultures of violence, while Barbara Hill Rigney, *The Voices of Toni Morrison* (1991), turns to French feminist theorists (Irigaray, Cixous, Duras, Wittig) to help her investigate 'Morrison's marginality and her difference' and argues that Morrison's work represents an 'exemption from "phallocratic law"' in its pursuit of a black feminist aesthetic.[10]

Since the early 1980s, critical texts dealing with the 'Afro-American novel' have included a chapter on Morrison; she has also been an important focus in studies on black women novelists.[11] Beginning with Barbara Christian's *Black Women Novelists: The Development of a Tradition* (1980), there have been a number of publications devoted to a specifically black women's literary tradition. Among these are Marjorie Pryse and Hortense Spillers (eds), *Conjuring: Black Women, Fiction and Literary Tradition* (1985); Susan Willis, *Specifying: Black Women Writing the American Experience* (1987); Michael Awkward, *Inspiriting Influences: Tradition, Revision and Afro-American Women's Novels* (1989); Mae Gwendolyn Henderson, 'Speaking in Tongues: Dialogics, Dialectics, and the Black Woman Writer's Literary Tradition' (1989). Henry Louis Gates has noted that 'Black women novelists … are more widely read by a broader cross section of the American reading public than any other Black writers have ever been in this century'.[12] As editor at Random House, Morrison herself has encouraged and done much to foster the growing prominence of black women writers such as Gayl Jones, Toni Cade Bambara and Angela Davis.

Perhaps as a result of the burgeoning field of African American women writers, comparative studies of Morrison and other African American women writers have increased over the last few years. In *Race, Gender, and Desire: Narrative Strategies in the Fiction of Toni Cade Bambara, Toni Morrison, and Alice Walker* (1989), Elliot Butler-Evans compares Morrison with two other African American women writers, exploring in each the conflicting discourses of race and gender. Adam McKible's recent essay on Morrison also deals with Gayl Jones, Octavia Butler and Sherley Anne Williams. Both Gina Wisker and Madelyn Jablon compare *Beloved* and Walker's *Temple of My Familiar*.[13] *Beloved* has also been frequently discussed in relation to Sherley Anne Williams's *Dessa Rose*[14] and other slave narratives.[15] A number of critics have addressed Morrison's work alongside that of her male counterparts, especially James Baldwin, Richard Wright and Ralph Ellison. Kimberley Drake discusses Wright's *Native Son* and Morrison's *The Bluest Eye*, and Pamela Glenn Menke explores constructions of gender in Ellison, Baldwin, Morrison and Walker. *Invisible Man* is frequently invoked in discussions of Morrison: Michael Awkward sees Morrison as rewriting Ellison in *The Bluest Eye*'s rape scene; and both Kimberley Benston and Utelinde Wedertz-Furtado offer readings of *Song of Solomon* with close reference to Ellison's text.[16]

Morrison's work is often read alongside and compared to a

wide range of canonical British and American writers from
Christina Rossetti and Virginia Woolf to James Joyce and Philip
Roth. Rather than studies of influence, comparisons of Morrison
and Faulkner that generate new readings of each have begun to
engage critical attention in a sustained way.[17] David Cowart has
written on Morrison in relation to Faulkner and Joyce; Harold
Bloom on Morrison's 'descent' from Woolf and Faulkner; Eileen
Barrett on Woolf and Morrison; and Naomi Rand on Morrison,
Leslie Silko Marmon and Philip Roth.[18] There are relatively few
studies like that of Marilyn Mobley Sanders, *Folk Roots and Mythic
Wings in Sarah Orne Jewett and Toni Morrison: The Cultural
Function of Narrative* (1991) discussing Morrison in relation to other
American women writers. In genre studies, Morrison's work has
provoked a wide variety of responses and has been discussed as
magic realism, African American gothic, postmodern narrative,
Utopian fiction and literature of the fantastic.[19] Her novels have
also been discussed in terms of their generic affiliations to the
slave narrative (*Beloved*), fairytale, folktale and fable. Classical
and African mythology and biblical allusion have been fruitful
and perennial topics in Morrison criticism.[20] Film studies have
also influenced approaches to Morrison's work.[21]

   Morrison's critique of consumer capitalism and her repeated engagement with questions of commodity culture have been
the subject of vigorous critical scrutiny. In particular, Susan
Willis explores African American cultural heritage in relation to
popular, commodity and consumer culture.[22] Willis identifies
the problem at the centre of Morrison's work as the main-
tenance of cultural heritage once 'the relationship to the black
rural South has been stretched thin over distance and generations'.[23] Her analysis of lack, deformity and self-mutilation as
figures for liberation is provocative, as is her definition of 'funk'
as 'the intrusion of the past into the present', a North American
'variant of the magic realism' associated with Gabriel García
Márquez.[24] In 'I Shop Therefore I Am: Is There a Place for Afro-
American Culture in Commodity Culture?' Willis draws on
advertising and mass media culture to explore contemporary
commodity fetishism. And in a recent essay, 'Memory and Mass

Culture', she probes the influence of mass culture on the relation of history to memory.[25]

An important segment of criticism on Morrison is materialist, feminist and psychoanalytic scholarship. Margaret Backus combines these approaches in a provocative article exploring the dysfunctionality of the family system as a consequence of 'the formation and gendering of the subject within capitalism'.[26] Other readings informed by psychoanalytic approaches include Alisha Coleman's 'One and One Makes One: A Metacritical and Psychoanalytic Reading of Friendship in Toni Morrison's *Sula*', Jennifer Fitzgerald's 'Selfhood and Community: Psychoanalysis and Discourse in *Beloved*', and Iyunolu Osagie's 'Is Morrison Also Among the Prophets?: "Psychoanalytic" Strategies in *Beloved*'. Morrison's work – *Beloved* in particular – has attracted a wide variety of feminist approaches to questions about family violence, sisterhood, mother-daughter relationships, maternal subjectivity, language, sexuality and race.[27] The construction of masculinity and the figure of the father receive far less attention, though Marianne Hirsch has focused on paternal issues in *Song of Solomon* and Vanessa Dickerson's 'The Naked Father in Toni Morrison's *The Bluest Eye*' addresses questions of male sexuality and fatherhood.[28]

Articles and essays that have explored Morrison's work in relation to Africanist thought and aesthetics include Vashti Lewis, 'African Tradition in *Sula*', and William Handley, 'The House a Ghost Built: *Nommo*, Allegory, and the Ethics of Reading in Toni Morrison's *Beloved*'. Handley reads *Beloved* in the light of the West African concept, *nommo*, the 'magic power of the word to call things into being'.[29] With the publication of *Tar Baby* in 1981, Morrison opened up opportunities for discussing the construction of African American identity in relation to Afro-Caribbean and Pan-American communities. Stelamaris Coser, *Bridging the Americas: The Literature of Toni Morrison, Paule Marshall, and Gayl Jones* (1995) sets Morrison's work in relation to Pan-American writing, focusing particularly on the intertextual relationships between García Márquez's magic realism and Morrison's *Tar Baby* and *Song of Solomon*. Coser's analysis of 'the Americas' is, however, restricted to Latin America and the United States, with a few references to Mexican American writing. The notion of an African diaspora is explored in Evelyn Hawthorne's essay on *Tar Baby*, which reads Morrison's novel in the light of African American diasporic thought dating back to the founders of Sierra Leone and Liberia in 1787 and 1802.[30]

The area of criticism from which my own study arises is literature as a form of cultural and historical memory. How Morrison invokes and responds to historical events and contexts such as the civil rights movement and the Black Aesthetic movement is the focus of chapters in Melissa Walker, *Down from the Mountaintop: Black Women's Novels in the Wake of the Civil Right's Movement* (1991) and Madhu Dubey, *Black Women Novelists and the National Aesthetic* (1994). Critics are increasingly interested in addressing questions of history and memory in Morrison's fiction, especially *Song of Solomon* and *Beloved*. Recent studies include Rebecca Ferguson, 'History, Memory, and Language in Toni Morrison's *Beloved*'; Deborah Guth, 'A Blessing and a Burden: The Relation to the Past in *Sula, Song of Solomon*, and *Beloved*'; and Caroline Rody, 'Toni Morrison's *Beloved*: History, "Rememory", and a "Clamor for a Kiss"'. Focusing particularly on history, memory and loss are essays by Robert Grant, 'Absence into Presence: The Thematics of Memory and "Missing" Subjects in Toni Morrison's *Sula*'; Emily Miller Budick, 'Absence, Loss, and the Space of History in Toni Morrison's *Beloved*'; and Susan Comfort, 'Counter-Memory, Mourning and History in Toni Morrison's *Beloved*'.[31] Morrison's management of traumatic history and pain are raised in Kristin Boudreau, 'Pain and the Unmaking of Self in Toni Morrison's *Beloved*', and Laurie Vickroy, 'The Traumatized Child in Toni Morrison and Marguerite Duras', which explores the relationship of 'trauma to social oppression' and demonstrates how that relationship is manifest in the way Duras and Morrison critique colonialism.[32]

Since *Beloved* is so obviously a novel about history as a haunting, its relations to the ghost story have been widely explored: Carol Schmudde, 'The Haunting of 124' and Geraldine

Smith-Wright, 'In Spite of the Klan: Ghosts in the Fiction of Black Women Writers'.[33] Also in relation to *Beloved*, the question of apocalypse engages critics such as Mark Ledbetter,'An Apocalypse of Race and Gender: Body Violence and Forming Identity in Toni Morrison's *Beloved*', and Josef Pesch, '*Beloved*: Toni Morrison's Post-Apocalyptic Novel'. Susan Bowers, '*Beloved* and the New Apocalypse' places Morrison's work within a tradition of African American apocalyptic writing. She argues that Morrison is working from a West African philosophical perspective (involving communion with one's ancestors): 'Morrison presents an apocalyptic demolition of the boundaries between earthly and spiritual realms, an invasion of the world of the living by the world beyond the veil'.[34] James Berger, 'Ghosts of Liberalism: Morrison's *Beloved* and the Moynihan report', also explores the representation of trauma as apocalypse in *Beloved*.

The publication of *Jazz* has provoked renewed attention to the relations between Morrison's novels and music. Craig Werner's *Playing the Changes: From Afro-Modernism to the Jazz Impulse*, concentrates in its epilogue on *Jazz*, arguing that it reflects where Afro-American musical and artistic energies lie today. Alan Rice, 'Jazzing It Up a Storm: The Execution and Meaning of Toni Morrison's Jazzy Prose Style', argues that Morrison's entire corpus is influenced by the rhythms of black musical tradition. Rice differentiates his approach to Morrison's novels from those typical of the 'Anglocentric world of academia' that concentrate on Morrison's debt to Faulkner, but ignore the influence of African American expressive forms. Rice argues that one ought 'to examine Faulkner's borrowings from African American culture in the South'; both Faulkner and Morrison are responding to similar influences and it is no surprise that their writing should bear resemblances.[35] Other responses to jazz in Morrison's work are Anthony Berret, 'Toni Morrison's Literary Jazz', Paula Gallant Eckard, 'The Interplay of Music, Language, and Narrative in Toni Morrison's *Jazz*' and Barbara Williams Lewis, 'The Function of Jazz in Toni Morrison's *Jazz*'. In relation to *The Bluest Eye* and especially *Song of Solomon*, critics have explored the blues in Morrison's work: Joyce Wegs, 'Toni

Morrison's *Song of Solomon*: A Blues Song'; and Joseph Skerrett Jr, 'Recitation to the *Griot*: Storytelling and Learning in *Song of Solomon*,' which sees Milkman as a Bluesman.

The oral tradition, call and response, and reader participation are enduringly the focus of Morrison's critics. Joyce Middleton has argued that 'the art of an oral tradition in the novel invests itself in the reader as a participant'.[36] While there has been debate about the extent to which readerly participation is an essential aspect of 'black' art, reader response criticism has found Morrison a rewarding site. Critics have followed Morrison's own remarks on the subject: 'In the same way that a musician's music is enhanced when there is a response from the audience, ... to have the reader work *with* the author in the construction of the book – is what's important ... To construct the dialogue so that it is heard.'[37] The intimate relationship between book and reader that all her work invites is most complexly thematised in *Jazz*, as its final lines indicate: 'I like your fingers on and on, lifting, turning.... Talking to you and hearing you answer – that's the kick.... Look where your hands are. Now' (229).

An overview of Morrison's work and the criticism it has inspired reveals a daring and explorative artist whose work now represents a rich testimony to the past and to the special ways in which imaginative literature can speak of that past.

Postscript on *Paradise*

WHEREAS Morrison's previous work has articulated the importance of bearing witness to the past and of coming to terms with traumatic history through memory and narrative, her most recent novel (published while this book was in press) explores the excesses of commemoration as a symptom of enduring trauma. *Paradise* (1998) is about a town 'deafened by the roar of its own history'.[1] Like its predecessors it is concerned with remembering black history, but it also explores how too zealous a remembrance of the past can hold a community in its grip. The community of the all-black town, once called Haven, later Ruby, has memorialised its history in a   way that threatens its capacity to adapt and respond to the present.

Paradise focuses on a more isolated and self-sufficient black community than the neighbourhood in *Sula*; like *Song of Solomon* it is intimately concerned with genealogies and histories from slavery through to the twentieth century. It resonates with *Tar Baby* in its exploration of tensions between gender and race issues and its interest in the African diaspora; it shares with *Beloved* a concern with the aftermath of violent and scarring historical moments, the nature of mothering under pressure, and the haunting power of the past. Like *Jazz*, it is interested in the gradations of colour that produce and stratify black communities. In *Jazz* Morrison explores one response to the 'huge backlash' that took place during Reconstruction when the renewed persecution of black people 'prompted many of them to move to places like New York, Chicago, and Detroit – the big industrial centers where there was safety in numbers.'[2] Morrison notes another response to that backlash:

> During Reconstruction, which occurred after 1865 ... there was a lot of migration of black people. They built towns, and in some places – particularly the West – they were very well organized and prosperous. There were over 100 black towns in Oklahoma, with their own banks, schools, and churches – beautiful buildings.[3]

In *Paradise* Morrison envisions the survival of one of those Oklahoma black towns where paradise is ownership and freedom from fear, harassment and rejection – where to be separate is very heaven.

While *Beloved* dealt with slavery and its immediate aftermath, and *Jazz* with the 1920s in Harlem, *Paradise* captures the spirit of the 1970s in different parts of America, but reaches back to the 1890s in its account of the history of the town. Even as *Paradise* recognises the importance of memory and history, however, it explores their limitations. As the narrator says of the town's mind-reading midwife, Lone DuPres: 'Yet she knew something more profound than Morgan memory or Pat Best's history book. She knew what neither memory nor history can say or record: the "trick" of life and its "reason"'(272). Magic, miracle and faith have a part alongside history and memory in this novel. Through the 'practising' clairvoyant midwife, and through the gift of Consolata Sosa (she is miraculously able to 'step in' between the dying and death), the reader is exposed to a world beyond the ordinary realm of history.

If *Beloved*, *Jazz* and *Paradise* form a trilogy, as Morrison once envisioned, it is a very loose one. There is no obvious overlap of character or setting; nor can the strong historical focus of these novels be said to distinguish them markedly from Morrison's other work. As I have argued throughout this book, all her writing is powerfully engaged with African American history. Morrison did once say of *Beloved* that 'this story is about ... the tension between being yourself, one's own Beloved, and being a mother. The next story has to do with the tension between being one's own Beloved and the lover.'[4] If 'love, or its deprivation, and its impact on self-image is played across time' in her trilogy,[5] then *Paradise* is about being one's own Beloved and a believer, the seeker and receiver of spiritual love.[6] In this novel Morrison is interested in what the dreams of paradise tell about the dreamer. She shows how much is revealed about a people, its history and culture, by what kind of paradise it envisions, whom that paradise includes and excludes, and where it is to be found.

The novel bears a familiar Morrison signature: an intimate, powerful voice that holds its narrative cards close to the chest and releases details out of their chronological order so that the reader is confused, intrigued and hungry for more pieces of the puzzle. The novel begins in 1976 with its climactic event well under way in the first chapter, and then weaves back into the past; only near its close does it resume the narration of that event. Just as *Jazz* tells of Dorcas's death in its opening pages, *Paradise* begins with the men of Ruby leading a deadly raid on the Convent. Whereas *Jazz* experimented with the metafiction of the narrator as book and attempted to capture the voice of jazz itself in the often misled and misleading narrator, *Paradise* returns to a less conceptually postmodern narrator. Apart from a sermon by Reverend Misner and the history book entry by Patricia Best, the narration belongs to this steady, sympathetic, story-telling voice, whose ability to inhabit many points of view and to pull the past into relation with the present reminds the reader of Morrison's Faulknerian heritage. This is a narrator whose rich and startling lyricism is still the hallmark of Morrison's prose.

Morrison's novels have always focused on ordinary people in history but in *Paradise* the range of characters is wider than in any previous novel and the focus on any particular character diffused. Its protagonists are the inhabitants of two adjacent communities: the town of Ruby (referred to as 'this hard-won heaven') and the neighbouring Convent, initially an embezzler's obscenely opulent mansion, then a mission for inculcating Catholicism into Indian girls, and more recently a haven for all kinds of women seeking refuge from the ravages of love, motherhood, men and themselves. Some women of the town themselves find succour and respite there – a desperate, pregnant teenager, a troubled daughter, a mother almost mad from tending her sick children. Soane Morgan and Consolata are firm friends, and she and Lone DuPres, also a foundling, find they speak similar languages of faith and miracle.

These two havens advance the discourse of paradise invoked by the title and provide the focus for Morrison's investigation of what paradise can mean beyond the definitions of Dante and Milton.[7] Morrison has observed that traditional notions of paradise always describe 'male enclaves, while the interloper is a woman, defenseless and threatening. When we get ourselves together and get powerful is when we are assaulted.'[8] In contrast to the black 'dreamtown', Morrison therefore poses a female community, not consciously aiming to be a haven, but approaching that state by offering its inhabitants what they need most.[9] Although the women fight among themselves, and although there is sin, sex and death at the Convent, there is also complete freedom to come and go, the plenty of the miraculous gardens, and as a result of Consolata's mediations, consolation, relief from pain, and saving.

Structurally, Morrison's novel is itself a collectivity of women, each chapter bearing the name of a woman from the town or the Convent. Through the use of chapter titles, Morrison rebuilds and commemorates a community of women that flexes and crosses spatial, racial and ideological boundaries to create a literary *Paradise*. The first chapter, 'Ruby', is the name of the town and the sister of the twin brothers who now lead the raid on the Convent. The young Ruby became sick on the journey to relocate Haven in the 1940s but when her family sought medical care, they found that no 'colored people' were allowed in the wards: 'She died on the waiting room bench while the nurse tried to find a doctor to examine her. When the brothers learned that the nurse had been trying to reach a veterinarian, and they gathered their dead sister in their arms, their shoulders shook all the way home' (113). The name of the town commemorates the woman; more strongly, though, it recalls through her the rejection and racism that necessitates this now fiercely separate community. But 'Ruby' also alludes to the Biblical comparison: 'Who can find a virtuous woman? for her price is far above rubies' (*Proverbs*, xxxxi.10). The town's name reverberates ironically in relation to the allusion, drawing attention to the patriarchal attitudes of its leaders and their difficulties in evaluating virtue and appreciating the value of women.

Subsequent chapters are named for Mavis, Grace (Gigi), Seneca and Divine (Pallas), women living at the Convent, each on the run from their tangled and painful histories. 'Consolata' fleshes out the history of Connie, the last of the nuns' era, who is now virtually blind and often drunk, and whose strange gifts arise from the blend of her Catholic upbringing and Afro-Brazilian past. Not herself a nun, Consolata was 'kidnapped' in 1925 at the age of nine by Sister Mary Magna, who was working at that time with an order of nuns in South America. Sister Mary rescues two other children from the 'shit-strewn paths' of the city and takes them back to the ship with her: 'They were six American nuns on their way back to the States after twelve years of being upstaged by older, sterner Portuguese Orders. Nobody questioned Sisters Devoted to Indian and Colored People paying cut-rate passage for three certainly not white urchins in their charge' (223). Two of the three children rescued are placed in an orphanage in Puerto Limón, Costa Rica, but Consolata comes to the Convent – 'an asylum/boarding school for Indian girls in some desolate part of the North American West' (223–4). The South American Consolata shares with African Americans a heritage from the era of slavery – a heritage that one day makes itself conscious when she sees some of the men of Ruby and experiences 'a memory of just such skin and just such men … And although they were living here in a hamlet, not in a loud city full of glittering black people, Consolata knew she knew them' (226). As if to shatter the narrow and exclusive notion of blackness to which the citizens of Ruby subscribe, as well as expose their rigid but transgressed morality, Morrison has Consolata embark on a searingly intense relationship with one of the town's leaders.

Three chapters are named for inhabitants of the town: 'Patricia' focuses on the town's school teacher and historian,

'Lone' is for the midwife whose prescience about the Convent assault sends her on the road out of Ruby to try and prevent the slaughter, and 'Save-Marie', the final chapter, ends with the funeral of a girl who has played only a very small part in the novel, but whose death is symbolic of the town's new willingness to admit mortality.

From the first scene, Morrison is concerned to show the desperate fidelity the townsmen of Ruby have to their own history, and indeed, immortality:

> From Haven, a dreamtown in Oklahoma Territory, to Haven, a ghosttown in Oklahoma State. Freedmen who stood tall in 1889 dropped to their knees in 1934 and were stomach-crawling by 1948. That is why they are here in this Convent. To make sure it never happens again. That nothing inside or out rots the one all-black town worth the pain (5).

The Old Fathers made a virtue of their colour and forever shunned any lighter-skinned Blacks, attempting to prevent marriages that drew partners from the outside who were not dark enough. 'The rejection, which they called the Disallowing, was a burn whose scar tissue was numb by 1949, wasn't it? Oh no' (194). Intent on self-protection in response to 'the Disallowing', the townsfolk have developed a blood fetish. Patricia Best summarises: 'Unadulterated and unadulteried 8-rock blood held its magic as long as it resided in Ruby. That was their recipe. That was their deal. For Immortality' (217). Only the blackest Blacks ('8-rock' because that is the deepest stratum in mining) are regarded as its true inhabitants. Even the town's nativity performance attests to its blood rule – it features seven Marys and seven Josephs, representing the remaining seven families whose blood lines have not been contaminated (211). Patricia Best's father was the first of the New Fathers to violate the unspoken blood rule, and, as the product of a disapproved alliance, she is never wholly accepted.

The novel probes the problem of exclusivity: how does one keep an all-black town viable and thriving? How to negotiate the relations of inside to outside when borders are inevitably permeable? As the young Reverend Misner, a voice for the future, observes: 'In their view Booker T. solutions trumped Du Bois problems every time' (212), which is to say that some of the town's citizens regard separation, even apartheid, as preferable to the complex negotiations of 'double consciousness'. In a vain attempt to banish sin and death, and thus to imitate the conditions of the traditional Paradise, there is no cemetery in the town and no death admitted. The Convent and its unconventional women come to be associated with sin; hence the raid on the unarmed women whose experiences at the Convent give rise to a version of paradise very different from that of the town.

The Convent women become scapegoats not only for every aberration in Ruby's family life, but also for the unsettling militancy and disobedience of the young people who hang out at the town's sacred monument – the Oven:

> It was a secret meeting, but the rumors had been whispered for more than a year. Outrages that had been accumulating all along took shape as evidence. A mother was knocked down the stairs by her cold-eyed daughter. Four damaged infants were born in one family…. Trips to Demby for VD shots common. And what went on at the Oven these days was not to be believed. (11)

The Oven is a *lieu de memoire* and a central symbol of the town's commitment to a god-fearing, communal life, but it also draws attention through its enigmatic motto to the impossibility of denying change and the importance of reinterpreting tradition. Initially it was a common kitchen, a place where everyone's bread could be baked. The Old Fathers who founded the town put 'most of their strength into constructing the huge, flawlessly designed Oven that both nourished them and monumentalized what they had done' (6–7). Morgan, the ironmonger, set the motto into an iron plate and no one quite knew where the words came from. They could have been invented, stolen or forged: 'words that seemed at first to bless them; later to confound them; finally to announce that they had lost' (7). When Haven was relocated and revived as Ruby in the late 1940s, the Oven was dismantled and carefully reassembled. Its motto, whose significance is contested, could mean 'Beware the Furrow of his Brow', an injunction to live within God's ways, or a warning to those who originally spurned the blue-black-skinned families and forced them to found their own town. In the novel's present, the days of black power, there are those in the younger generation, including the new minister, who want the motto to assert a timely agency and righteous aggressiveness: 'Be the Furrow of his Brow'.

Song of Solomon dealt with the need for prideful memory and the importance of bearing witness to the past and one's genealogy. In that novel, Milkman Dead experienced a wake-up call to history. The inhabitants of Ruby, however, have to wake up *from* history. As I have discussed in previous chapters, trauma often expresses itself in the dysfunction of memory. The inability to remember an event, to narrate or to place it in time is itself a symptom of the unspeakability of the occurrence. The historical trauma of Ruby's ancestors has produced a fixation on memorialisation and a need to repeat the conditions of their rejection and the town's founding. *Paradise* pushes towards the realisation that collective memory and tradition must continually adapt and respond to the present if they are to avail change and help to make a desired future. It is not a question of revising or rewriting history, but of seeing new significance in traditional accounts and artefacts. Those, like Misner, who are new to the town are struck by the inability of many of its citizens to engage with the present or future:

> Over and over and with the least provocation, they pulled from their stock of stories tales about the old folks, their grands and greatgrands; their fathers and mothers. Dangerous confrontations, clever maneuvers. Testimonies to endurance, wit, skill and strength. Talk of luck and outrage. But why were there no stories to tell of themselves? About their own lives they shut up. Had nothing to say, pass on. As though past heroism was enough of a future to live by. As though, rather than children, they wanted duplicates. (161)

Morrison's critical emphasis on duplication here is also expressed in the novel's unusually large cast of twins: Deacon

and Steward; Coffee and Tea; Brood and Apollo; Merle and
Pearl. Deek and Steward are the self-styled leaders of the town
and keepers of its faith: 'The twins have powerful memories.
Between them they can remember the details of everything that
ever happened – things they witnessed and things they did not'
(13). The raid on the Convent is a watershed, however, after
which a cavernous difference opens up between the twins.
Whereas Deek would have gone forward to know the realm that
Consolata's gift of 'stepping in' revealed, Steward pulled a
trigger on the revelation. And as Consolata's killer, Steward
recalls Deek's own abjection of her when he ended their passionate affair twenty-two years ago. His twin now becomes the
mirror of his own shame: 'It was as though he had looked in his
brother's face and did not like himself anymore' (300). One
morning he finds himself unable to cover his feet and walking
barefoot to speak to Reverend Misner. Deek tells a story of his
grandfather, whose name was Coffee before he changed it to
Zechariah. His twin was known as Tea. Harassed by whitemen
and forced at gunpoint to dance, Tea performs, but Coffee takes
a bullet in the foot and walks many miles barefoot, defining his
difference from his brother forever. Coffee became one of the
Old Fathers of Haven; Tea was not asked to join them on their
journey to Oklahoma (302). The story is about being able to see
but not accommodate the other's difference. Whereas Tea and
Coffee remain sundered, Deek and Steward do not, because, in
their case, difference is eventually accommodated. Deek does not
have to step into his grandfather's shoes, so to speak, and he and
his brother do not have to be replicas of each other or of the past.
The allowance of differentiation indicates a self that augurs well
for the future in that it can reproduce rather than clone itself.
Double-consciousness replaces duplication.

A summary of the town's failure is given to Reverend
Misner, who sees the travesty that the 'dreamtown' has produced, but nevertheless decides to stay among these flawed,
proud and outrageously beautiful people:

> Whether they be the first or the last, representing the old-
> est black families or the newest, the best of the tradition or

the most pathetic, they had ended up betraying it all. They think they have outfoxed the whiteman when in fact they imitate him. They think they are protecting their wives and children, when in fact they are maiming them. And when the maimed children ask for help, they look else-where for the cause…. Unbridled by Scripture, deafened by the roar of its own history, Ruby, it seemed to him, was an unnecessary failure. How exquisitely human was the wish for permanent happiness, and how thin human imagination became trying to achieve it…. How can they hold it together, he wondered, this hard-won heaven defined only by the absence of the unsaved, the unworthy and the strange? (305–6)

If the town excludes the unsaved, the unworthy and the strange, the Convent takes in members of all those categories and helps them to confront their problems. Inhabiting the memories of her Afro-Brazilian past, Consolata leads the Convent women in a ritualistic exorcism of their pain. As a 'new and revised Reverend mother' she calls them together, makes them lie on the marble floor, and paints around the shape of each, thereby creating a template of every woman. At first reluctant, they then join the rituals, shaving their heads and eating blood-less food. Whereas the invading men see proof of the Convent's unnatural practices, depravity and filth in the women's paint-ings on their body shapes, others later recognise these as the 'turbulence of females trying to bridle, without being trampled, the monsters that slavered them' (303).

Consolata endorses a marriage rather than division of spirit and flesh, for, after all, 'Eve is Mary's mother. Mary is the daughter of Eve' (263). And in a vision of paradisal home-coming, she offers consolation for present pain: 'She spoke of fruit that tasted the way sapphires look and boys using rubies for dice. Of scented cathedrals made of gold where gods and god-desses sat in the pews with the congregation…. Then she told them of a woman named Piedade [the word means 'mercy', 'pity', 'compassion' in Portuguese] who sang but never said a word' (263–4).[10] Later she tells further stories about Piedade, whose 'breath smelled of pineapple and cashews', and 'whose voice made proud women weep in the streets' (285). The women begin to dream collectively, each entering and experiencing the traumatic re-enactments of the other. All visit the overheated Cadillac in which Mavis's newborn twins suffocated: 'They enter the heat in the Cadillac.... They inhale the perfume of sleeping infants and feel parent-cozy although they notice one's head is turned awkwardly. They adjust the sleeping baby head then refuse, outright refuse, what they know and drive away home' (264). The women begin to externalise what is internally unassimilable, painting on to their templates their pain and wounds. Seneca, abandoned as a five-year-old by her teenage mother, who always maintained that they were sisters, is given to cutting herself in frequent bouts of exquisite, ritualised, self-torture; she 'duplicated in robin's egg blue one of her more elegant scars, one drop of red at its tip' (265). Later, however, when she has the urge to slice open her own thigh, she chooses rather to mark the image of her body, which has become 'the open body' on the floor. Indeed, the Convent women become so focused on the templates that 'they had to be reminded of the moving bodies they wore, so seductive were the alive ones below' (265). That the adjective 'alive' is applied to the templates is a form of transference and it prepares the reader for the novel's finale, which depends on the miracle of life transferred to a new realm or mode.

Women from the town who visit the Convent begin to detect the changes taking place there; its inhabitants are no longer haunted. As the narrator points out, however, they may not be haunted, but they are hunted. In both *Jazz* and *Paradise*, Morrison explores the way women are pursued as the objects of projected male rage and insecurity. Joe re-enacts the trauma of his mother's abandonment of him; the townsmen collectively re-enact the traumatic effects of 'the Disallowing', seeing the women as a threat to Ruby's psychic intactness. In neither case is Morrison concerned with official, legal punishment, but rather with community management of the disaster. And in both cases she allows the perpetrators a second chance. Joe and Violet work through the death of Dorcas together, while in *Paradise* the miraculous disappearance of the bodies ensures that the towns-men of Ruby escape prosecution for the murder of the Convent women.

The arresting opening line of the novel, 'they shot the white girl first' makes the reader realise that colour was never an issue among the women in the Convent and underlines, therefore, the way gender and race are rigid and defining categories from the posse's point of view. Unarmed, the women defend themselves as best they can with kitchen skillets and knives; they crash portraits of Saint Catherine of Siena around the ears of their attackers, and hurl alabaster ashtrays at their temples (286). In the novel's climactic scene, Consolata cradles the body of the woman shot first and 'begins to step in, deep, deeper to find the pinpoint of light' (289). Hearing shots from another room, she enters it, bellowing to the men to stop their attack. Her words, 'Your're back', seem at first an address to her erstwhile lover, Deek Morgan, but they are directed to the woman whose dying she has just intercepted. In the moment that Deek and Steward witness the miracle of her interception, Steward shoots Con-solata through the forehead. The three remaining women have disappeared, although some of the men shooting at them say they 'went down in the grass' (292). When Roger Best, who owns a hearse, arrives to deal with the bodies, he finds none. Mavis's Cadillac is also gone. While a strictly rational explana-tion is possible, there are signs for those prepared to read them that a miracle has taken place.

The aged and prescient midwife, Lone, interprets the miraculous disappearance of the dead bodies as an act of divine grace: 'God had given Ruby a second chance. Had made Himself so visible and unarguable a presence that even the outrageously prideful ... ought to be able to see it. He had actually swept up and received His servants in broad daylight, for goodness sake! right before their very eyes, for Christ's sake! (297–8).

When visiting the Convent shortly after the assault, the Reverend Misner and his new affianced, Anna Flood, see some-thing that they afterwards describe as a door or maybe a window. While they argue about what each thought they saw, they avoid knowing that what they have seen is the escape hatch to somewhere beyond: 'Whether through a door needing to be opened or a beckoning window already raised, what would happen if you entered? What would be on the other side? What on earth would it be? What on earth?' (305). And when the minister is later conducting the funeral service for Save-Marie, he sees 'the window in the garden, felt it beckon toward another place – neither life nor death – but there, just yonder, shaping thoughts he did not know he had' (307). The fact that the minister is presiding over a funeral means that 'the reaper was no longer barred entry from Ruby ...' (296) and that there is now 'a real and formal cemetery in a town full of immortals. Something seismic had happened since July' (296).

For others, the Convent victims are already being mytholo-gised as warrior women, honing their amazonian power in prep-aration of splendid vengeance. Billie Delia, who has found occa-sional solace and understanding at the Convent, is not puzzled by the disappearance of the dead and dying women. She awaits their return:

> When will they reappear, with blazing eyes, war paint and huge hands to rip up and stomp down this prison calling itself a town.... A backward noplace ruled by men whose power to control was out of control and who had the nerve to say who could live and who not and where; who had seen in lively, free, unarmed females the mutiny of the mares and so got rid of them. She hoped with all her heart that the women were out there, darkly burnished, biding their time, brass metaling their nails, filing their incisors – but out there. Which is to say that she hoped for a miracle. (308)

In the final scenes of the novel, the reader is invited to walk through the beckoning window or door to a realm 'just yonder' as each of the Convent women revisits a significant aspect of her past on her way to her future. In these visitations, the women are often with companions and in some cases depart into the blue – 'violet so ultra' it breaks your heart (312), viridian lake water (310), the framing cerulean blue sky (318). Gigi spends a moment with her father, who has been granted a reprieve from death row. Pallas returns to the house of her mother Dee Dee, now under a compulsion to paint her neglected daughter and trying for the fifteenth time to catch her likeness. Mavis has a satisfying lunch with her daughter Sally, but Seneca's runaway mother Jean misremembers the street name of their apartment and so loses the opportunity to make herself known to her daughter. Consolata returns home to Piedade to be sung to and caressed as she rests her head in a welcoming lap.

As the novel's epigraph from the Nag Hammadi tractate, 'The Thunder, Perfect Mind', promises, 'they will live and they will not die again'. The novel closes with a vision of Consolata's paradise, a beatific seashore realm, but not one divorced from this world and its detritus – discarded bottle tops, an old dead radio in the surf, a sandal. Here Piedade's song sings the weary home:

> When the ocean heaves sending rhythms of water ashore, Piedade looks to see what has come. Another ship, perhaps, but different, heading to port, crew and passengers, lost and saved, atremble, for they have been disconsolate for some time. (318)

'Disconsolate' is a nice pun, for in this paradise, mercy and compassion (Piedade) attend consolation (Consolata) and await the needy. The narrator concludes: 'Now they will rest before shouldering the endless work they were created to do down here in Paradise' (318). In an interview that appeared just after the novel's publication, Morrison expressed regret about that final capitalisation:

> The last word in the book, 'paradise,' should have a small 'p', not a capital P. The whole point is to get paradise off its pedestal, as a place for anyone, to open it up for passengers and crew. I want all the readers to put a lowercase mark on that 'p.'[11]

Morrison's concern here underscores her notion of paradise as democratic and open. 'Down here' as opposed to up there, it is recognisably earthly, imperfect, accessible, and welcomes both lost and saved. Deliberately not exclusive, it is no doubt able to accommodate even other versions of paradise.

Notes

Chapter 1

1 This introductory chapter emphasises Morrison's engagement with history and argues that the discourse of memory and trauma in relation to African American history is an illuminating intertext for her work. That is not to underestimate, of course, the influence of other intertexts, but these have, for the most part, already been the subject of some critical scrutiny. As subsequent chapters will show, Morrison engages with a wide range of existing literary and cultural forms: the ghost tale, the slave narrative, the tar baby and flying African myths, the formal qualities of jazz and the texts representing the Harlem Renaissance.

2 See David W. Blight, 'W. E. B. Du Bois and the Struggle for American Historical Memory', in Geneviève Fabre and Robert O'Meally (eds), *History and Memory in African-American Culture* (Oxford, Oxford University Press, 1994), p. 49.

3 Blight, 'W. E. B. Du Bois', p. 46, p. 50.

4 Christina Davis, 'An Interview with Toni Morrison' [1988], in Danille Taylor-Guthrie (ed.), *Conversations with Toni Morrison* (Jackson, University of Mississippi Press, 1994), pp. 224–5 (hereafter referred to as *Conversations*). I draw extensively on interviews with Morrison, not to suggest that her stated 'intentions' about her work should govern interpretation of it, but to emphasise her concern with black history and the relation of artistic production to historical and social forces.

5 See Karen Carmean, *Toni Morrison's World of Fiction* (Troy, NY, Whitson, 1993). Carmean insists on the political nature of all Morrison's work and also emphasises Morrison's interest in using her novels to 'bear witness' (p. 17) in the process of retrieving and recovering the lost history of black Americans. My approach is

similar, but focuses on Morrison's inscription and management of racial trauma in American culture and history.

6   See Maurice Bloch, 'Internal and External Memory: Different Ways of Being in History', in Paul Antze and Michael Lambek (eds), *Tense Past: Cultural Essays in Trauma and Memory* (London, Routledge, 1996), p. 229. On social and cultural memory, see James Fentress and Christopher Wickham, *Social Memory* (Oxford, Blackwell, 1992).

7   Ernest Renan, 'What is a Nation?', in Homi Bhabha (ed.), *Nation and Narration* (London, Routledge, 1990), p. 11. See the discussion of Renan in William Boelhower, 'Ethnographic Politics: The Uses of Memory in Ethnic Fiction', in Amritjit Singh, Joseph Skerrett, Jr, Robert Hogan (eds), *Memory and Cultural Politics: New Approaches to American Ethnic Literatures* (Boston, Northeastern University Press, 1996), p. 21.

8   Singh *et al.*, *Memory and Cultural Politics*, p. 5.

9   See Linda Anderson, 'The Re-Imagining of History in Contemporary Women's Fiction', in Linda Anderson (ed.), *Plotting Change: Contemporary Women's Fiction*, (London, Edward Arnold, 1990), p. 141.

10 Charles Ruas, 'Toni Morrison' [1981], *Conversations*, p. 114.

11 Colette Dowling, 'The Song of Toni Morrison' [1979], *Conversations*, p. 54.

12 Jean Strouse, 'Toni Morrison's Black Magic', *Newsweek* (March 1981), p. 53.

13 Nellie McKay, 'An Interview with Toni Morrison', *Conversations*, p. 138.

14 Claudia Tate, 'Toni Morrison', [1983], *Conversations*, p. 158.

15 Tate, 'Toni Morrison', p. 158.

16 Betty Fussell, 'All that Jazz' [1992], *Conversations*, p. 283.

17 Strouse, 'Toni Morrison's Black Magic', p. 54.

18 Mel Watkins, 'Talk with Toni Morrison' [1977], *Conversations*, p. 45.

19 Ruas, 'Toni Morrison', p. 99.

20 Ruas, 'Toni Morrison', p. 100.

21 Sandi Russell, 'Conversations from Abroad', in Nellie McKay (ed.), *Critical Essays on Toni Morrison* (Boston, G. K. Hall, 1988), p. 45.

22 Nellie McKay, 'Introduction', in McKay, *Critical Essays on Toni Morrison*, p. 3. McKay is citing Susan Blake, 'Toni Morrison',

Dictionary of Literary Biography – Afro-American Writers After 1955 (Detroit, Gale Research Co., 1984), p. 188.

23   Ruas, 'Toni Morrison', p. 98.

24   McKay, 'An Interview with Toni Morrison', p. 138.

25   Clayborne Carson *et al.* (eds), *Eyes On The Prize: Civil Rights Reader* (New York, Penguin, 1991), p. 28.

26   Carson *et al.*, *Eyes on the Prize*, p. 29.

27   See Dowling, 'The Song of Toni Morrison', p. 50.

28   Bessie W. Jones and Audrey Vinson, 'An Interview with Toni Morrison' [1985], *Conversations*, p. 174.

29   The ruling in *Plessy* v *Ferguson* enshrined the apartheid philosophy (which would only later become law in South Africa) that facilities for Blacks could be separate so long as they were equal.

30   The play has been performed only once; Morrison has not published the script and refuses to allow scholars to scrutinise it.

31   See the interview with Rosa Parks by Howell Raines, reprinted in Carson *et al.*, *Eyes on the Prize*, p. 45–7.

32   A fuller account of these events can be found in Carson *et al.*, *Eyes on the Prize*, pp. 45–7.

33   Rosemary Lester, 'An Interview with Toni Morrison' [1983], in McKay, *Critical Essays on Toni Morrison*, p. 51.

34   Lester, 'An Interview with Toni Morrison', p. 51.

35   See Carson *et al.*, *Eyes on the Prize*, p. 163.

36   See the discussion by David J. Garrow in Carson *et al.*, *Eyes on the Prize*, p. 204.

37   Strouse, *Newsweek*, p. 56.

38   Carson *et al.*, *Eyes on the Prize*, p. 234.

39   Stokely Carmichael, 'What we Want', excerpted in Carson *et al.*, *Eyes on the Prize*, p. 282.

40   See Clayborne Carson's account of black power in Carson *et al.*, *Eyes on the Prize*, p. 247.

41   William L. Vandeburg, *New Day in Babylon: The Black Power Movement and American Culture, 1965–1975* (Chicago, University of Chicago Press, 1992), p. 58.

42   Vandeburg, *New Day in Babylon*, p. 51.

43   See Vandeburg, *New Day in Babylon*, p. 58.

44   Homi Bhabha, *The Location of Culture* (London, Routledge, 1994),

p. 9. Bhabha's reading of Fanon in the light of contemporary postcolonialist concerns provides an interesting frame for Morrison's *Beloved*, to which he makes frequent reference in the introduction.

45   Bhabha, *The Location of Culture*, p. 3, p. 2.

46   See Singh *et al.*, *Memory and Cultural Politics*, p. 11. See also the editors' discussion of Werner Sollors, *The Invention of Ethnicity* (New York, Oxford University Press, 1989) and the concept of internal colonisation.

47   Vandeburg, *New Day in Babylon*, p. 59.

48   Vandeburg, *New Day in Babylon*, p. 9.

49   Madhu Dubey, *Black Women Novelists and the Nationalist Aesthetic* (Bloomington, Indiana University Press, 1994) p. 163, n. 1.

50   See Dubey, *Black Women Novelists and the Nationalist Aesthetic*, for a sustained discussion of the relation of women novelists to the Black Aesthetic.

51   Lester, 'An Interview with Toni Morrison', p. 53.

52   See the discussion of this article by Elaine Jordan, 'Not My People', in Gina Wisker (ed.), *Black Women's Writing* (London, Macmillan, 1993), p. 115.

53   *Black Creation Annual*, 'Conversation with Alice Childress and Toni Morrison', *Conversations*, p. 4.

54   Jones and Vinson, 'An Interview with Toni Morrison', p. 183.

55   Ntozake Shange, 'Interview with Toni Morrison', *American Rag* (November 1978), 52.

56   Gloria Naylor, 'A Conversation: Gloria Naylor and Toni Morrison' [1985], *Conversations*, p. 209.

57   Gail Caldwell, 'Author Toni Morrison Discusses Her Latest Novel *Beloved*' [1987], *Conversations*, p. 244–5.

58   Toni Morrison, *The Nobel Lecture in Literature, 1993* (New York, Knopf, 1994), p. 15.

59   Morrison, *The Nobel Lecture in Literature*, p. 14.

60   Morrison, *The Nobel Lecture in Literature*, p. 17, p. 18.

61   See Judith Butler's analysis of the speech in terms of the violence that language can do, not merely represent, in Judith Butler, *Excitable Speech: Politics of Performance* (New York, Routledge, 1997), pp. 6–13,

62   Davis, 'An Interview with Toni Morrison', pp. 224–5.

63   Davis, 'An Interview with Toni Morrison', p. 225.

64   Jones and Vinson, 'An Interview with Toni Morrison', p. 176.

65   Camille Billops, James Van Der Zee, Owen Dodson, *The Harlem Book of the Dead* (New York, Morgan and Morgan, 1978), Foreword.

66   William Zinsser (ed.), *Inventing the Truth: The Art and Craft of the Memoir* (Boston, Houghton Mifflin, 1987), pp. 103–24.

67   Morrison, 'The Site of Memory' in Zinsser, *Inventing the Truth,* p. 111.

68   Morrison, 'The Site of Memory', p. 111.

69   Robert Stepto, 'Intimate Things in Place: A Conversation with Toni Morrison' [1976], *Conversations*, p. 20.

70   Benedict Anderson, *Imagined Communities* 2nd edition (London, Verso, 1991), p. 6.

71   Toni Morrison, 'Memory, Creation, and Writing', *Thought: A Review of Culture and Idea* 59 (1984), 389.

72   Morrison, 'Memory, Creation, and Writing', p. 389.

73   See Shoshana Felman and Dori Laub, *Testimony: Crises of Witnessing in Literature, Psychoanalysis, and History* (London, Routledge, 1992), p. xiv, who refer to the present effects of the trauma of the Second World War.

74   Toni Morrison (ed.), *Race-ing Justice and En-Gendering Power: Essays on Anita Hill, Clarence Thomas, and the Construction of Social Reality* (New York, Pantheon Books, 1992), p. x.

75   Morrison, *Race-ing Justice*, p. xi.

76   Morrison, *Race-ing Justice*, p. xxvii.

77   Morrison, *Race-ing Justice*, pp. xxviii–xxix.

78   Morrison, *Race-ing Justice*, pp. xix–xx.

79   Morrison, *Race-ing Justice*, pp. xiv–xv.

80   Morrison, *Race-ing Justice*, p. x.

81   Toni Morrison, *Playing in the Dark: Whiteness and the Literary Imagination* (New York, Vintage Books, 1992), pp. 9–10.

82   Morrison, *Playing in the Dark*, p. 12.

83   Morrison, *Playing in the Dark*, p. 25.

84   Morrison, *Playing in the Dark*, p. 5.

85   Morrison, *Playing in the Dark*, p. 6.

86   Ralph Ellison, *Shadow and Act* (New York, Vintage Books, [1953] 1974), p. 276.

87   Bonnie Angelo, 'The Pain of Being Black: An Interview with Toni Morrison' [1989], *Conversations*, p. 258.

88   Felman and Laub, *Testimony*, p. 15.

89   Felman and Laub, *Testimony*, p. 15.

90   Cathy Caruth, 'Introduction', to Part II, 'Recapturing the Past' in Cathy Caruth (ed.), *Trauma: Explorations in Memory* (Baltimore, Johns Hopkins University Press, 1995), p. 151.

91   See Allan Young, *The Harmony of Illusions: Inventing Post-Traumatic Stress Disorder* (Princeton, New Jersey, Princeton University Press, 1995), p. 7.

92   Caruth, *Trauma: Explorations in Memory*, p. 5.

93   See Ruth Leys's excellent critical discussion of this assumption in 'Traumatic Cures: Shell-shock, Janet and the Question of Memory', in Antze and Lambek, *Tense Past: Cultural Essays in Trauma and Memory*, pp. 123–4.

94   Judith Lewis Herman, *Trauma and Recovery* (New York, Basic Books, 1992), p. 1.

95   See Leys, 'Traumatic Cures', pp. 120–1; Herman, *Trauma and Recovery*, pp. 175–7.

96   Pierre Janet, *Psychological Healing: A Historical and Clinical Study* (New York, 1919) vol. 1, pp. 661–2; cited in Leys, 'Traumatic Cures', p. 124.

97   See Catherine Belsey, *Critical Practice* (London, Routledge, 1980), p. 75. See also the recent discussion of postmodern fragmentation in Lynne Layton, 'Trauma, Gender Identity and Sexuality: Discourses of Fragmentation', *American Imago* 52:1 (1995), 107–25.

98   The phrase is from Stephen Heath, 'Narrative Space', *Screen* 17:3 (1976), 85.

99   Hayden White, 'The Burden of History', in Hayden White, *Tropics of Discourse: Essays in Cultural Criticism* (Baltimore, Johns Hopkins University Press, 1978), p. 50.

100 See Danille Taylor-Guthrie, 'Introduction', *Conversations*, p. viii.

101 In *Sula*, as John Leonard notes in Gates and Appiah, *Toni Morrison: Critical Perspectives Past and Present* (New York, Amistad, 1993), p. 38, Sula's startling speech about black men gives a deliberate twist to the notion of victim and counters Jude's self-pitying pose: 'I don't know what the fuss is about. I mean everything in the world loves you. White men love you. They spend so much time worrying about your penis they forget their own' (*Sula*, p. 103).

102 bell hooks, *Yearning: Race, Gender and Cultural Politics* (Boston, South End, 1990), pp. 216–17.

103 See Erwin Randolph Parson, 'Ethnicity and Traumatic Stress: The Intersecting Point in Psychotherapy', in Charles Figley (ed.), *Trauma and its Wake: The Study and Treatment of Post-Traumatic Stress Disorder* (New York, Brunner/Mazel, 1985), pp. 314–37.

104 Irving M. Allen, 'PTSD Among African Americans', in Anthony J. Marsella, Matthew J. Friedman, Ellen T. Gernety and Raymond M. Scurfield (eds), *Ethnocultural Aspects of Posttraumatic Stress Disorder: Issues, Research, and Clinical Applications* (Washington, APA, 1996), p. 233.

105 Kai Erikson, 'Notes on Trauma and Community', in Caruth, *Trauma: Explorations in Memory*, p. 185.

106 Laura Brown, 'Not Outside the Range: One Feminist Perspective on Psychic Trauma', in Caruth, *Trauma: Explorations in Memory*, p. 107. See also Maria Root, 'Reconstructing the Impact of Trauma on Personality', in L. S. Brown and M. Ballou (eds), *Personality and Psychopathology* (New York, Guildford, 1992), pp. 229–65.

107 Brown, 'Not Outside the Range', p. 102.

108 Today in post-apartheid South Africa, the Truth and Reconciliation Commission, working through a variety of centres and committees, (the Human Rights Violation Committee, the Reparation and Rehabilitation Committee, and the Centre of the Study of Violence and Reconciliation, for example) attempts to deal with a population traumatised by an apartheid government over the past fifty years.

109 Maria Root, 'Women of Color and Traumatic Stress in "Domestic Captivity": Gender and Race as Disempowering Statuses', in Marsella, *et al.*, *Ethnocultural Aspects of Posttraumatic Stress Disorder*, p. 374.

110 David Aberbach, *Surviving Trauma: Loss, Literature and Psychoanalysis* (New Haven, Yale University Press, 1989), p. 2.

111 Aberbach, *Surviving Trauma*, p. 9.

112 Felman and Laub, *Testimony*, p. xviii.

113 Toni Morrison, 'A Bench By the Road', *The World* 3:1 (1989), 4.

114 Felman and Laub, *Testimony*, p. 57.

115 See Kali Tal, *Worlds of Hurt: Reading the Literatures of Trauma* (Cambridge, Cambridge University Press, 1996) pp. 53–4. Tal is outspokenly critical of Felman and Laub's emphasis on the listener's contact with survivor testimony, which she formulates as an 'appropriative gambit of stunning proportions'.

116 Dominick LaCapra, *Representing the Holocaust: History, Theory, Trauma* (Ithaca, Cornell University Press, 1994) p. 198.

117 Caruth, *Trauma: Explorations in Memory*, p. 11.

118 See Denise Heinze, *The Dilemma of 'Double-Consciousness': Toni Morrison's Novels* (Athens, University of Georgia Press, 1993), p. 11.

119 Angelo, 'The Pain of Being Black', pp. 247–8

120 See Laurie Vickroy, 'The Politics of Abuse: The Traumatized Child in Toni Morrison and Marguerite Duras', *Mosaic* 29:2 (1996), 91–109. Vickroy argues that Morrison is a 'textual' therapist. Although she is not alone in casting the writer as therapist, her attribution raises questions about the implications of the comparison. Is the text the traumatised patient? And what about the role of the reader?

121 Sigmund Freud, *Beyond the Pleasure Principle*, trans. and ed. James Strachey (New York, Norton, 1961), p. 11.

122 Freud, *Beyond the Pleasure Principle*, p. 37.

123 Freud, *Beyond the Pleasure Principle*, pp. 36–7.

124 Freud, *Beyond the Pleasure Principle*, p. 37.

125 Morrison often represents death or mutilation horrifically in instances of burning: not only in *Sula* does Eva set Plum alight and Hannah burn, but in *Tar Baby*, Margaret burns her son's flesh with a cigarette; in *Beloved*, Sixo is set alight, the burned bodies of boys hang in the trees, and in *Jazz*, Dorcas' mother burns 'crispy' while Dorcas swallows a smouldering chip from the torched house.

126 Barbara Johnson, '"Aesthetic" and "Rapport" in Toni Morrison's *Sula*', *Textual Practice* 7:2 (1993), 172.

127 Johnson, '"Aesthetic" and "Rapport"', p. 171.

128 LaCapra, *Representing the Holocaust*, p. 66.

129 LaCapra, *Representing the Holocaust*, p. 199.

130 Craig Werner, *Playing the Changes: From Afro-Modernism to the Jazz Impulse* (Urbana, University of Illinois Press, 1994), p. 289.

131 Morrison, *The Nobel Lecture in Literature*, pp. 20–1.

132 Morrison, *The Nobel Lecture in Literature*, p. 21.

Chapter 2

1   Toni Morrison, 'Unspeakable Things Unspoken: The Afro-American Presence in American literature', in Harold Bloom (ed.), *Toni Morrison: Modern Critical Views* (New York, Chelsea House Publishers 1990), p. 214.

2   Sandi Russell, 'Conversations From Abroad', in Nellie McKay (ed.), *Critical Essays on Toni Morrison* (Boston, G. K. Hall, 1988), p. 45.

3   Gloria Naylor, 'A Conversation: Toni Morrison and Gloria Naylor' [1985], *Conversations*, p. 199.

4   Toni Morrison, *The Bluest Eye* (Harmondsworth, Penguin, [1974], 1994), p. 209.

5   Gershen Kaufman, *Shame: The Power of Caring* 3rd edition, (Rochester, Shenckman Books, 1992), p. xxi; see also Eve Kosofsky Sedgwick and Adam Frank (eds), *Shame and its Sisters: A Silvan Tompkins Reader* (Durham, Duke University Press, 1995).

6   Kaufman, *Shame*, p. xiii.

7   Kaufman, *Shame*, p. 9

8   Toni Morrison, *The Bluest Eye* (London, Picador, [1970], 1990), pp. 6–7. Further references are to this edition and will be made parenthetically in the text.

9   In this regard, see bell hooks's powerful characterisation of anger against racism as 'killing rage' in *Killing Rage: Ending Racism* (London, Penguin, 1996), pp. 9–20.

10   Susan Willis, 'I Shop Therefore I Am: Is There a Place for Afro-American Culture in Commodity Culture?', in Cheryl Wall (ed.), *Changing Our Own Words: Essays on Criticism, Theory and Writing* (New Brunswick, Rutgers University Press, 1989), p. 174.

11   Willis, 'I Shop Therefore I Am', p. 174.

12   See Morrison, 'Afterword', *The Bluest Eye*, p. 210.

13   Laura Brown, 'Not Outside the Range: One Feminist Perspective on Psychic Trauma', in Cathy Caruth (ed.) *Trauma: Explorations in Memory* (Baltimore, Johns Hopkins University Press, 1995), p. 100.

14   Brown, 'Not Outside the Range', p. 101.

15   Brown, 'Not Outside the Range', p. 103.

16   Brown, 'Not Outside the Range', p. 108.

17 Shoshona Felman and Dori Laub, *Testimony: Crises of Witnessing in Literature, Psychoanalysis, and History* (London, Routledge, 1992), p. 57.

18 See the discussion of Claudia as a moral agent in Lynne Tirrell, 'Storytelling and Moral Agency', *The Journal of Aesthetics and Art Criticism* 48:2 (1990), 115–26.

19 Michael Awkward, 'Roadblocks and Relatives: Critical Revision in Toni Morrison's *The Bluest Eye*', in McKay, *Critical Essays on Toni Morrison*, p. 63.

20 Awkward, 'Roadblocks and Relatives', p. 66.

21 Awkward, 'Roadblocks and Relatives', p. 64.

22 Ralph Ellison, *Invisible Man* (New York, Vintage, [1947], 1995), p. 60.

23 I am grateful to my student, Jennifer Rosenitch, for making this point.

24 Felman and Laub, *Testimony*, p. 75.

25 The quotation is from Edward O. Wilson, *On Human Nature* (Cambridge, Harvard University Press, 1978); cited in Bessel A. van der Kolk and Onno van der Hart, 'The Intrusive Past: The Flexibility of Memory and the Engraving of Trauma', in Caruth, *Trauma: Explorations in Memory*, pp. 158–82.

Chapter 3

1 Sigmund Freud, *Beyond the Pleasure Principle*, trans. and ed. James Strachey (New York, Norton, 1961), p. 11.

2 Cathy Caruth (ed.), *Trauma: Explorations in Memory* (Baltimore, Johns Hopkins University Press, 1995), p. 5.

3 See Pierre Nora, 'Between History and Memory: Les Lieux de Mémoire', in Geneviève Fabre and Robert O'Meally (eds), *History and Memory in African-American Culture* (New York, Oxford University Press, 1994), pp. 284–300.

4 See Melissa Walker, *Down from the Mountaintop: Black Women's Novels in the Wake of the Civil Rights Movement, 1966–1989* (New Haven, Yale University Press, 1991), who historicises Morrison's writing of *Sula* in relation to the events of 1973. Walker notes that 'in 1973 it would have been virtually impossible for readers of a novel like *Sula* to be oblivious to the public history of years that saw the passing of the Voting Rights Act, the escalation

of the Vietnam War, with its disproportionate number of African-American casualties: Lyndon Johnson's announcement that he would not seek re-election; the assassination of Martin Luther King, Jr; increasing outbreaks of urban riots; the election and re-election of Richard Nixon; and the systematic attack on the advocates of black power'(p. 128).

5   Walker sees the novel as pointing to the reasons why African Americans have been campaigning for civil rights. It offers a history of the 1920s until the civil rights movement and, despite its affirmation of village values, incorporates many of the reasons for that movement.

6   On Sula's defiance of morality, see Hortense Spillers, 'A Hateful Passion, a Lost Love', in Henry Louis Gates Jr and K. Anthony Appiah (eds), *Toni Morrison: Critical Perspectives Past and Present* (New York, Amistad, 1993), p. 214.

7   Recently, Craig Werner has attempted to show how *Jazz* reactivates some of Morrison's concerns in her MA thesis on Faulkner and Woolf. The thesis contrasts Faulkner's rejection of characters who choose alienation (seeing it as a flaw) with Woolf's understanding that objective detachment is necessary for a meaningful life. Werner argues that *Jazz* critiques Woolf's insistence on detachment, showing it to be merely 'a self-protective delusion' (Craig Hansen Werner, *Playing the Changes: From Afro-Modernism to the Jazz Impulse* (Urbana, University of Illinois Press, 1994), p. 295). At the same time, Morrison's novel reflects concerns that are quite similar to those of Woolf. *Jazz* brings together divergent perspectives, incorporating some of Woolf's views, especially 'that recreating the self requires a deep awareness of interior processes' (p. 296). While Morrison's MA thesis may be relevant to *Jazz* in the ways Werner suggests, it is also, I suggest, immediately illuminating in relation to *Sula*.

8   Morrison, MA thesis (Chloe Ardellia Wofford, 'Virginia Woolf's and William Faulkner's Treatment of the Alienated', Cornell University, 1955), p. 39.

9   Barbara Johnson's brilliant reading of the novel in '"Aesthetic" and "Rapport" in Toni Morrison's *Sula*', *Textual Practice* 7:2 (1993), 165–72, draws attention to Sula's unusual, and at times puzzling, disinterestedness. Johnson focuses on the moment when Nel discovers Jude and Sula together and in disbelief at the adulterous scene before her waits for one of them to say something by way of explanation. 'I waited for Sula to look up at me any minute and say one of those lovely college words like *aesthetic* or *rapport*, which I

never understood but which I loved because they sounded so comfortable and firm' (*Sula*, p. 105). In Johnson's reading, such words provide a key to the novel, since the first represents the domain of the artistic, of forms, and implies a detachment and difference. The second signals the 'dynamics of interconnectedness.' Johnson argues that the novel functions for the reader as a test of readerly aesthetics or rapport, interest or disinterest in the succession of horrible images, painful truths and losses that it articulates. Johnson interrogates the readerly response to the horrible images we see: 'Do we just sit back and watch? What is the nature of our pleasure in contemplating trauma?'(p. 171).

10   Focusing on an imagined danger, Chicken Little alerts everyone in the barnyard of the impending sky fall and they all – Ducky Lucky, Turkey Lurkey, Goosey Loosey – follow him to tell the king. Less alert to the clear and present danger of predators such as Foxy Loxy, Chicken Little's sky falls in in a different way when the fox eats him.

11   Robert Grant, 'Absence into Presence: The Thematics of Memory and "Missing" Subjects in Toni Morrison's *Sula*', in Nellie McKay (ed.), *Critical Essays on Toni Morrison* (Boston, G. K. Hall, 1988), p. 98.

12   The dream may encode more than unresolved responses to the death of the mother, for the label on the tin of the baking powder to which Morrison alludes featured in the 1940s a supposedly welcoming kitchen scene: a kindly, smiling white woman sits plucking a goose, while in the foreground a young blue-eyed, blonde girl sweeps the hearth clean. Assumptions about ideal femininity and the domestic space may also be of relevance as Sula defines herself against Nel's aspirations.

13   See Johnson, '"Aesthetic" and "Rapport"' on this point, p. 168 ff.

14   Johnson, '"Aesthetic" and "Rapport"', p. 169.

15   Grant, 'Absence into Presence', p. 95.

16   Walker, *Down from the Mountaintop*, p. 128.

17   See Houston Baker's comparison of Morrison's 'Bottom' with the Dixie Pike village in Jean Toomer's *Cane* in 'When Lindbergh Sleeps with Bessie Smith: The Writing of Place in *Sula*,' in Gates and Appiah, *Toni Morrison: Critical Perspectives Past and Present*, p. 243.

18   See Baker, 'When Lindbergh sleeps', pp. 248–9, for a different interpretation of the significance of the butterflies as 'graceful flight and sexual delight'.

Chapter 4

1   See Marianne Hirsch, 'Knowing Their Names: Toni Morrison's *Song of Solomon*', in Valerie Smith (ed.), *New Essays on Song of Solomon* (Cambridge, Cambridge University Press, 1995) whose Lacanian reading also emphasises the paternal and contends that Morrison's novel theorises paternity through an exploration of 'the myths and realities of paternal "absence"' (p. 75).

2   Toni Morrison, *Song of Solomon* (London, Picador, [1977], 1989), p. 89. References are to this edition and will hereafter be made parenthetically in the text.

3   See, for example, Kimberley W. Benston, 'Re-weaving the "Ulysses Scene": Enchantment, Post-Oedipal Identity, and the Buried Text of Blackness in Toni Morrison's *Song of Solomon*', in Hortense J. Spillers (ed.), *Comparative American Identities: Race, Sex, and Nationality in the Modern Text* (New York, Routledge, 1991), pp. 87–109, who notes that Macon's journey allows him to find 'an ensemble performance of black historicity enacted by the collective African-American body' (p. 102).

4   See in particular Robert Holton, 'Bearing Witness: Toni Morrison's *Song of Solomon* and *Beloved*', *English Studies in Canada* 20:1 (1994), 79–90; and Melissa Walker, *Down from the Mountaintop: Black Women's Novels in the Wake of the Civil Rights Movement, 1966–1989* (New Haven, Yale University Press, 1991), pp. 131–47.

5   Cathy Caruth, 'Unclaimed Experience: Trauma and the Possibility of History', *Yale French Studies* 79 (1991), 192; reprinted in Cathy Caruth, *Unclaimed Experience: Trauma, Narrative, and History* (Baltimore, Johns Hopkins University Press, 1996), p. 24.

6   For criticism on the black family in relation to the Moynihan report, see Hirsch, 'Knowing Their Names', p. 71; and James Berger, 'Ghosts of Liberalism: Morrison's *Beloved* and the Moynihan Report, *PMLA* 111:3 (May 1996), 408–20.

7   Virginia Hamilton, *The People Could Fly: American Black Folktales* (New York, Knopf, 1985), p. 169.

8   Patrick Bjork, *The Novels of Toni Morrison* (New York, Peter Lang, 1992) emphasises that the recovery of names in *Song of Solomon* allows Milkman to challenge the invisibility imposed by history on his family and African Americans in general.

9   See Walker, *Down from the Mountaintop*, and Utlelinde Wedertz-Furtado, 'Historical Dimensions in Toni Morrison's *Song of Solomon*', in Gunter H. Lenz (ed.), *History and Tradition in*

Afro-American Culture (Frankfurt, Campus Verlag, 1984), pp. 222–41.

10   See Jane Bakerman's treatment of this relationship in 'Failures of Love: Female Initiation in the Novels of Toni Morrison', *American Literature* 52:4 (1981), 541–63.

11   For a more positive reading of the way Pilate allows Morrison to rewrite the traditional male quest motif, see Benston, 'Re-Weaving the "Ulysses Scene"', who reads Pilate as the healer of divisions between 'self-finders and culture-bearers'(p. 101). See also Denise Heinze, *The Dilemma of 'Double Consciousness': Toni Morrison's Novels* (Athens, University of Georgia Press, 1993), pp. 137–9 for discussion of critical views of Pilate.

Chapter 5

1   See the excellent analysis of Margaret's trauma by Margot Gayle Backus, '"Looking for That Dead Girl": Incest, Pornography, and the Capitalist Family Romance in *Nightwood, The Years* and *Tar Baby'*, *American Imago* 51:4 (1994), 421–45.

2   What Morrison articulates here is what has recently been termed 'betrayal trauma'; see Jennifer Freyd, *Betrayal Trauma: The Logic of Forgetting Childhood Abuse* (Cambridge, Harvard University Press, 1996). Freyd has written of abuse by parents, asserting that it is of a different order than other traumas because the violation of dependency, trust and love in the child–parent relationship constitutes a profound betrayal.

3   See Peter B. Erickson, 'Images of Nurturance in *Tar Baby'*, in Henry Louis Gates and Anthony Appiah (eds), *Toni Morrison: Critical Perspectives Past and Present* (New York, Amistad Press, 1993), p. 295, who discusses the implications of Margaret's failure in nurturing.

4   See Backus, '"Looking for That Dead Girl"', p. 438.

5   When Valerian decides to move to the island, he is described as 'measuring French colonial taxes against American residential ones' (p. 51).

6   See Evelyn Hawthorne, 'On Gaining the Double-Vision: *Tar Baby* as Diasporean novel', *Black American Literature Forum* 22:1 (1988), 97–107.

7   See Craig Werner, 'The Briar Patch as Modernist Myth: Morrison,

Barthes, and *Tar Baby* As-Is', in Nellie McKay (ed.), *Critical Essays on Toni Morrison* (Boston, G. K. Hall, 1988), p. 155 for a genealogy of the tar baby myth and its metamorphoses through African trickster tale, Afro-American folktale, retold in Harris's *Uncle Remus*, and Disney movie.

8 See Morrison's discussion of tar in interview with Thomas LeClair, 'The Language Must Not Sweat: A Conversation With Toni Morrison' [1981], *Conversations*, p. 122.

9 See Susan Willis on the 'beiging' of black models in 'I Shop Therefore I Am: Is There a Place for Afro-American Culture in Commodity Culture', in Cheryl Wall (ed.), *Changing Our Own Words: Essays on Criticism, Theory and Writing* (New Brunswick, Rutgers University Press, 1989), pp. 184–5.

10 Tar Baby in Morrison's *Sula* is named ironically since he looks white.

11 LeClair, 'The Language Must Not Sweat', p. 122.

12 See Marilyn Sanders Mobley, 'Narrative Dilemma: Jadine as Cultural Orphan in *Tar Baby*', in Gates and Appiah, *Toni Morrison: Critical Perspectives Past and Present*, p. 290.

13 We are later told that the hats replay the traumatic scene of her mother's funeral, so that in addition to a sense of confusion about identity, she also suffers from a sense of maternal deprivation and loss.

14 Susan Willis, 'Memory and Mass Culture', in Geneviève Fabre and Robert O'Mealley (eds), *History and Memory in African-American Culture* (Oxford, Oxford University Press, 1994), p. 182. Willis is raising in a different context a question asked by James Clifford in *Predicament of Culture*.

15 Willis, 'Memory and Mass Culture', p. 182.

16 Craig Werner points out that Jadine taps the wisdom of the folktales, giving up struggling in order to survive, but misattributes the wisdom to 'girl scouts' ('The Briar Patch as Modernist Myth', p. 162).

17 See Elliott Butler-Evans, *Race, Gender and Desire: Narrative Strategies in the Fiction of Toni Cade Bambara, Toni Morrison, and Alice Walker* (Philadelphia, Temple University Press, 1989), who usefully suggests that 'Morrison brings to the fore an issue largely marginalized or even suppressed in her earlier works: the contentiousness between the desires of the mythical community and those of Black women' who have different historical and social circumstances than those of the community (p. 162).

18   At the same time, however, the myth of the flying African and the myth of the blind Caribbean horsemen have much in common as responses to domination and enslavement.

Chapter 6

1   Pierre Janet, *Psychological Healing: A Historical and Clinical Study* (New York, 1919), vol. 1, pp. 661–2; cited in Ruth Leys, 'Traumatic Cures: Shell-shock, Janet and the Question of Memory', in Paul Antze and Michael Lambeck (eds), *Tense Past: Cultural Essays in Trauma and Memory* (New York, Routledge, 1996), p. 124.

2   Bonnie Angelo, 'The Pain of Being Black: An Interview with Toni Morrison' [1989] *Conversations*, pp. 256–7.

3   Elsie B. Washington, 'Talk with Toni Morrison' [1987], *Conversations*, p. 235.

4   See Barbara Johnson's '"Aesthetic" and "Rapport" in Toni Morrison's *Sula*' (*Textual Practice* 7:2 (1993), pp. 165–72), which specifically addresses the experience of violation produced by aesthetically beautiful memories.

5   See Mae Henderson's fine reading of the body in *Beloved*: 'Toni Morrison's *Beloved*: Re-Membering the Body as Historical Text', in Hortense J. Spillers (ed.), *Comparative American Identities: Race, Sex, and Nationality in the Modern Text* (New York, Routledge, 1991), pp. 62–86.

6   See Elizabeth A. Waites, *Trauma and Survival: Post-Traumatic and Dissociative Disorders in Women* (New York, Norton, 1993).

7   This point is made by Iyunolu Osagie in her discussion of repetition compulsion in *Beloved*. See 'Is Morrison Also Among the Prophets?: Psychoanalytic Strategies in *Beloved*', *African American Review* 28.3 (1994), 423–40.

8   Cathy Caruth, 'Traumatic Awakenings', in Eve Sedgwick and Andrew Parker (eds), *Performativity and Performance* (London, Routledge, 1995), p. 89.

9   Caruth, 'Traumatic Awakenings', p. 89.

10   Dominick LaCapra, *Representing the Holocaust: History, Theory, Trauma* (Ithaca, Cornell University Press, 1994), p. 200.

11   See Carol Schmudde, 'The Haunting of 124', *African American Review*, 26:3 (1992), 409.

12   Schmudde, 'The Haunting of 124', p. 409.

13   Geraldine Smith-Wright, 'In Spite of the Klan: Ghosts in the Fiction of Black Women Writers', in Lynette Carpenter and Wendy K. Kolmar (eds), *Haunting the House of Fiction: Feminist Perspectives on Ghost Stories by American Women* (Knoxville, University of Tennessee Press, 1991), p. 142.

14   See Robert Holton, 'Bearing Witness: Toni Morrison's *Song of Solomon* and *Beloved*', *English Studies in Canada* 20:1 (1994), 79–90, whose critical reading of these novels depends on the notion that the wrong of loss or damage sustained is compounded by the denial of a right to testify to the damage.

15   According to certain African mythologies, the dead inhabit the bottoms of lakes and seas. Beloved's aquatic associations reinforce her status as ghost. See Sharon P. Holland, 'Bakulu Discourse: The Language of the Margin in *Beloved*', *Literature, Interpretation, Theory* 6:1–2 (1995), 89–100.

16   Many critics have addressed the question of Beloved's identity; see Deborah Horvitz, 'Nameless Ghosts: Possession and Dispossession in *Beloved*', *Studies in American Fiction* 17:2 (1989), 157–68, who argues that the ghost is both Sethe's daughter and her 'African mother', an intergenerational and intercontinental figure who stimulates recollections of the past in various forms (p. 158); see also Linda Krumholz, 'The Ghosts of Slavery: Historical Recovery in Toni Morrison's *Beloved*', *African American Review* 26:3 (1992), 395–408, who argues that while Beloved necessarily provokes the process of healing, undergone by Sethe and the reader, she is also 'a trickster figure who defies narrative closure or categorization, foreclosing the possibility of a complete "clearing" for the reader' (p. 397).

17   See Homi Bhabha, *The Location of Culture* (London, Routledge, 1994), p. 17.

18   See the perceptive and provocative treatment of the epigraph in Robert Broad, 'Giving Blood to the Scraps: Haints, History, and Hosea in *Beloved*', *African American Review* 28:2 (1994), 189–96.

19   For an exposition of the imposter theory see particularly Elizabeth House', Toni Morrison's Ghost: The Beloved Who is Not Beloved', *Studies in American Fiction* 18:1 (1990), 17–26. See also Iyunolu Osagie, 'Is Morrison Also Among the Prophets?: "Psychoanalytic" Strategies in *Beloved*', *African American Review* 28:3 (1994), 423–40, who shows the gaps in House's interpretive strategy.

20   Valerie Smith's suggests that 'pass on' means pass over, as in 'I

pass' when I refuse something. One sense of the line is that this is not a story that can be refused or overlooked. My interpretation, based on Morrison's earlier use of the phrase 'pass on' in the novel emphasises that this is not a story that will die or that we can allow to die or disappear. See Valerie Smith, 'Circling the Subject: History and Narrative in *Beloved*', in Henry Louis Gates Jr and K. Anthony Appiah (eds), *Toni Morrison: Critical Perspectives Past and Present*, p. 353.

Chapter 7

1   Gail Caldwell, 'Author Toni Morrison Discusses Her Latest Novel *Beloved*' [1987], *Conversations*, p. 241.

2   Morrison herself notes in an interview that she intentionally makes her narrator 'without sex, gender or age'. See the interview with Angels Carabi, *Belles Lettres*, 10:2 (1995), 42. On the question of the narrator's ambiguous gender see Katherine Mayberry, 'The Problem of Narrative in Toni Morrison's *Jazz*', in D. Middleton (ed.), *Toni Morrison's Fiction: Contemporary Criticism* (New York, Garland, 1997), p. 303.

3   Carabi, 'Interview', 40–3.

4   Dana Micucci, 'An Inspired Life: Toni Morrison Writes and a Generation Listens' [1992], *Conversations*, p. 275.

5   Leo Ostransky, *The Anatomy of Jazz* (Greenwood, Westport Connecticut, 1960), p. 69.

6   See John Leonard, 'Her Soul's High Song', *The Nation*, 25 May 1992, 706–18, who also sees the narrator as the book itself. I want, however, to emphasise that the narrator is not always to be thought of in this way; in moments of 'concert' and readerly participation, however, the fusion of parts of the narrative enterprise makes narrator and book the same.

7   Camille Billops, James Van Der Zee and Owen Dodson, *The Harlem Book of the Dead* (New York, Morgan and Morgan, 1978), p. 84. Van Der Zee is ninety-one at the time Billops is creating this book. He recalls his youth as a photographer, recording that he took his first pictures of the dead around 1920.

8   *The Harlem Book of the Dead*, p. 52.

9   See Henry Louis Gates, review of *Jazz*, in Gates and Appiah, *Toni Morrison: Critical Perspectives Past and Present*, p. 52.

10 Nathan Irvin Huggins, *Harlem Renaissance* (New York, Oxford University Press, 1971), p. 3.

11 See J. De Jongh, *Vicious Modernism: Black Harlem and the Literary Imagination* (Cambridge, Cambridge University Press), pp. 13–14.

12 Frank Tirro, *Jazz: A History* (London, Dent, 1929), p. 187.

13 This triumphant narrative is part of the blurb on the back cover of Nathan Irvin Huggins (ed.), *Voices from the Harlem Renaissance* (New York, Oxford University Press, 1976).

14 Christine Davis, 'An Interview with Toni Morrison' [1986] *Conversations*, p. 233.

15 Langston Hughes, *The Big Sea: An Autobiography* (New York, Hill and Wang, [1940], 1993), pp. 228–9.

16 Morrison is quoted here in the essay by Carolyn Denard, 'Toni Morrison', in Darlene Clark Hine (ed.), *Black Women in America: An Historical Encyclopedia* (New York, Carlson Publishing Inc., 1993), pp. 816–17.

17 Hughes, *The Big Sea: An Autobiography*, p. 245, p. 244.

18 She possibly means Illinois here.

19 John Hope Franklin, *From Slavery to Freedom: A History of American Negroes*, 2nd edition (New York, Knopf, 1961), p. 434.

20 Alain Locke, 'The New Negro', in Huggins, *Voices from the Harlem Renaissance*, pp. 49–50.

21 Locke, 'The New Negro', pp. 50, 56.

22 See Huggins, *Harlem Renaissance*, p. 14.

23 James Weldon Johnson, *Black Manhattan* (New York, Atheneum, 1968), p. 146.

24 See the discussion in De Jongh, *Vicious Modernism*, p. 9.

25 Cited in Gilbert Osofsky, *Harlem: The Making of a Ghetto, 1890–1930* (New York, Harper, 1966); excerpted in Robert C. Twombly (ed.) *Blacks in White America Since 1865* (New York, McKay, 1971), p. 184.

26 Davis, 'An interview with Toni Morrison', p. 233.

27 See Cary Wintz, *Black Culture and the Harlem Renaissance* (Houston: Rice University Press, 1988), pp. 18–20.

28 E. Franklin Frazier, *The Negro in the United States* (New York, MacMillan, 1940), pp. 408–9.

29 See Jervis Anderson, *Harlem: The Great Black Way* (London, Orbis, 1982), pp. 92–8.

30   See Anderson, *Harlem*, p. 93.

31   On the relation of *Jazz* to jazz, see Alan Rice, 'Jazzing It Up a Storm: The Execution and Meaning of Toni Morrison's Jazzy Prose Style', *Journal of American Studies* 18:3 (1994), 421–32, who argues that *Jazz* is not the only novel so influenced, but that Morrison's entire corpus has been informed by 'the rhythms and cadences of a black musical tradition' (p. 443). See also Craig Werner's recent *Playing the Changes: From Afro-Modernism to the Jazz Impulse* (Urbana, University of Illinois Press, 1994), and the review by Henry Louis Gates, which compares Morrison's orchestration of different narratives within the novel to the mode of composition developed by Duke Ellington around 1926, the time in which *Jazz* is set. His jazz compositions 'were the first that were constructed, or scored, for his individual musicians with their peculiar timbres, their particular *sounds.*' Morrison's jazz is to be found in her manipulation of point of view: arranging the narratives of different voices she has found a way to 'create an ensemble of *improvised* sound out of a *composed* music' (Gates, 'Review', in Gates and Appiah, *Toni Morrison: Critical Perspectives Past and Present*, p. 54).

32   Franklin, *From Slavery to Freedom*, photo caption opp. p. 430.

33   Tirro, *Jazz: A History*, p. 155.

34   Gates, 'Thirteen Ways of Looking at a Black Man', *New Yorker*, 23 October 1995, p. 60.

35   Gloria Naylor, 'A Conversation: Gloria Naylor and Toni Morrison' [1985], *Conversations*, p. 208.

36   Gloria Naylor, *Conversations*, p. 207.

Chapter 8

1   Toni Morrison, *The Nobel Lecture in Literature, 1993* (Knopf, New York, 1994) p. 6.

2   Henry Louis Gates Jr and K. Anthony Appiah (eds), *Toni Morrison: Critical Perspectives Past and Present* (New York, Amistad, 1993), p. xi.

3   The most aggressive assault on her work has been from Stanley Crouch. He has suggested that she is a writer of 'no serious artistic vision or real artistic integrity' (*New Yorker*, 6 November 1995, p. 96). See also 'Aunt Medea', *The New Republic*, 19 October 1987, and *Notes of a Hanging Judge* (Oxford, Oxford University Press, 1990). See also the denigrating review by Bruce Bawer, 'All That

Jazz', *The New Criterion* 10:9 (1992), 10–17.

4   See Valerie Smith, 'Black Feminist Theory and the Representation of the "Other"', in Cheryl Wall (ed.), *Changing Our Own Words: Essays on Criticism, Theory and Writing by Black Women* (New Brunswick, Rutgers University Press, 1989), pp. 38–57; and Katherine Mayberry, 'The Problem of Narrative in Toni Morrison's *Jazz*', in David Middleton (ed.), *Toni Morrison's Fiction: Contemporary Criticism* (New York, Garland, 1997), pp. 297–310.

5   I am indebted to the competent bibliographic assistance provided by Jennifer Andrews and Heidi Tiedemann in the preparation of this critical overview.

6   Trudier Harris, *Fiction and Folklore: The Novels of Toni Morrison* (Knoxville, University of Tennessee Press, 1991), p. 11.

7   Denise Heinze, *The Dilemma of 'Double Consciousness': Toni Morrison's Novels* (Athens, University of Georgia Press, 1993), p. 5.

8   Dorothea Drummond Mbalia, *Toni Morrison's Developing Class Consciousness* (London and Toronto, Associated University Press, 1991), p. 8.

9   Karen Carmean, *Toni Morrison's World of Fiction* (Troy, NY, Whitson, 1993), p. 16.

10 Barbara Hill Rigney, *The Voices of Toni Morrison* (Columbus, Ohio State University Press, 1991), p. 3, p. 1.

11 For example, Melvin Dixon, *Ride Out the Wilderness: Geography and Identity in Afro-American Literature* (Urbana, University of Illinois Press, 1987); Valerie Smith, *Self-Discovery and Authority in Afro-American Narrative* (Cambridge, MA, Harvard University Press, 1987).

12 'Preface' in Gates and Appiah, *Toni Morrison: Critical Perspectives Past and Present*, p. x.

13 See Adam McKible, '"These are the Facts of the Darky's History": Thinking History and Reading Names in Four African American Texts', *African American Review* 28 (1994), 223–35; Madelyn Jablon, 'Rememory, Dream Memory, and Revision in Toni Morrison's *Beloved* and Alice Walker's *Temple of My Familiar*', *CLA Journal* 37:2 (1993), 136–44; Gina Wisker, '"Disremembered and Unaccounted For": Reading Toni Morrison's *Beloved* and Alice Walker's *The Temple of My Familiar*', in Gina Wisker (ed.), *Black Women's Writing* (New York, St. Martin's Press, 1993), pp. 78–95.

14 Elaine Jordan, '"Not My People": Toni Morrison and Identity', Jocelyn Moody, 'Ripping Away the Veil of Slavery: Literacy, Com-

munal love, and Self-Esteem in Three Slave Women's Narratives',
Carol Boyce Davies, 'Mother Right/Write Revisited: *Beloved* and
Dessa Rose and The Construction of Motherhood in Black
Women's Fiction', in Brenda O. Daly and Maureen T. Reddy (eds),
Narrating Mothers: Theorizing Maternal Subjectivities (Knoxville,
University of Tennese Press, 1991) pp. 44–57.

15   See Susan Bowers, '*Beloved* and the New Apocalypse', *The Journal
of Ethnic Studies* 18:1 (1990), 59–77; Sally Keenan, '"Four Hun-
dred Years of Silence": Myth, History, and Motherhood in Toni
Morrison's *Beloved*', in Jonathan White (ed.), *Recasting the
World: Writing after Colonialism* (Baltimore, Johns Hopkins
University Press, 1993), pp. 45–81; Lorraine Liscio, '*Beloved*'s
Narrative: Reading Mother's Milk', *Tulsa Studies in Women's
Literature* 11 1 (1992), 31–46; Josef Pesch, '*Beloved*: Toni
Morrison's Post-Apocalyptic Novel', *Canadian Review of Com-
parative Literature* 20:3/4 (1993), 395–408.

16   Michael Awkward, 'Roadblocks and Relatives: Critical Revision in
Toni Morrison's *The Bluest Eye*', in Nellie McKay (ed.), *Critical
Essays on Toni Morrison* (Boston, G. K. Hall, 1988), pp. 57–67;
Benston, 'Re-Weaving the "Ulysses Scene": Enchantment, Post-
Oedipal Identity, and the Buried Text of Blackness in Toni
Morrison's *Song of Solomon*', in Hortense J. Spillers (ed.), *Com-
parative American Identities: Race, Sex, and Nationality in the
Modern Text* (New York, Routledge, 1991), pp. 87–109; Utelinde
Wedertz-Furtado, 'Historical Dimensions in Toni Morrison's *Song
of Solomon*', in Gunter H. Lenz (ed.), *History and Tradition in Afro-
American Culture* (Frankfurt, Campus Verlag, 1984), pp. 222–41.

17   See Philip M. Weinstein, *What Else But Love? The Ordeal of Race
in Faulkner and Morrison* (New York, Columbia University Press,
1996); Carol Kolmarten *et al.* (eds), *Unflinching Gaze: Morrison
and Faulkner Re-envisioned* (Jackson, University of Mississippi
Press, 1997).

18   David Cowart, 'Faulkner and Joyce in Morrison's *Song of Solomon*',
in Middleton, *Toni Morrison's Fiction: Contemporary Criticism*,
pp. 95–108; Harold Bloom, 'Introduction' *Toni Morrison: Modern
Critical Views* (New York, Chelsea House Publishers, 1990), 1–7;
Eileen Barrett, 'For Books Continue Each Other...': Toni Morrison
and Virginia Woolf', in Mark Hussey and Vara Neverow (eds),
*Virginia Woolf: Emerging Perspectives: Selected Papers from the
Third Annual Conference on Virginia Woolf* (New York, Pace
University Press, 1994), pp. 26–32; Naomi Rand, 'Surviving What
Haunts You: The Art of Invisibility in *Ceremony*, *The Ghost
Writer*, and *Beloved*', *MELUS* 20 (1995), 21–32.

19 See Marianne DeKoven, 'Utopia Limited: Post-Sixties and Postmodern American Fiction', *Modern Fiction Studies* 41 (1995), 75–97; and Gary Daily, 'Toni Morrison's *Beloved*: Rememory, History, and the Fantastic', in Donald E. Morse, Marshall B. Tymn and Csilla Bertha (eds), *The Celebration of the Fantastic* (Westport, Greenwood, 1992), pp. 141–7.

20 See Craig Werner, 'The Briar-Patch as Modernist Myth: Morrison, Barthes, and *Tar Baby* As-Is', in McKay, *Critical Essays on Toni Morrison*, pp. 150–70; Jane Campbell, *Mythic Black Fiction: The Transformation of History* (Knoxville, University of Tennessee Press, 1986); Leslie Harris, 'Myth as Structure in Toni Morrison's *Song of Solomon*', *MELUS* 7.3 (1980), 69–76; Lauren Lepow, 'Paradise Lost and Found: Dualism and Edenic Myth in Toni Morrison's *Tar Baby*', in Middleton, *Toni Morrison's Fiction*, pp. 165–81.

21 See Lynda Koolish, 'Fictive Strategies and Cinematic Representations in Toni Morrison's *Beloved*: Postcolonial Theory/Postcolonial Text', *African American Review* 29 (1995), 421–38.

22 See Susan Willis, *Specifying: Black Women Writing the American Experience* (Madison, University of Wisconsin Press, 1986) and 'I Shop Therefore I Am: Is There a Place for Afro-American Culture in Commodity Culture?', in Wall, *Changing Our Own Words*, 173–95. See also Willis's 'Eruptions of Funk: Historicizing Toni Morrison', reprinted from *Specifying* in Gates and Appiah, *Toni Morrison: Critical Perspectives Past and Present*, pp. 308–29.

23 Willis, 'Eruptions of Funk', p. 309.

24 Willis, 'Eruptions of Funk', p. 325.

25 Susan Willis, 'Memory and Mass Culture', in Geneviève Fabre and Robert O'Meally (eds), *History and Memory in African-American Culture* (Oxford: Oxford University Press, 1994), pp. 178–87.

26 Margaret Bachus, '"Looking for that Dead Girl": Incest, Pornography, and the Capitalist Family Romance in *Nightwood*, *The Years* and *Tar Baby*', *American Imago* 51:4 (1994), 442.

27 See essays by Davies, 'Mother Right/Write Revisited'; Barbara Mathieson, 'Memory and Mother Love in Morrison's *Beloved*', *American Imago* 47:1 (1990), 1–21; Jean Wyatt, 'Giving Body to the Word: The Maternal Symbolic in Toni Morrison's *Beloved*', *PMLA* 108 (1993), 474–88; Peter Erickson, 'Images of Nurturance in Toni Morrison's *Tar Baby*', *CLA Journal* 28:1 (1984), 11–32; and Marianne Hirsch, 'Maternity and Rememory: Toni Morrison's *Beloved*', in Donna Bassin, Margaret Honey, and Meryle Mahrer Kaplan (eds), *Representations of Motherhood* (New Haven, Yale

University Press, 1994), pp. 92–110.

28   Vanessa Dickerson, 'The Naked Father in Toni Morrison's *The Bluest Eye*' in Patricia Yeager and Beth Kowaleski-Wallace (eds), *Refiguring the Father: New Feminist Readings of Patriarchy* (Carbondale, Southern Illinois University Press, 1989), pp. 108–27.

29   William Handley, 'The House a Ghost Built: *Nommo*, Allegory, and the Ethics of Reading in Tony Morrison's *Beloved*', *Contemporary Literature* 36:4 (1995), 676–701, p. 677.

30   Evelyn Hawthorne, 'On Gaining the Double-Vision: *Tar Baby* as Diasporean Novel', *Black American Literature Forum* 22:1 (1988), 97–107.

31   See also Mae G. Henderson, 'Toni Morrison's *Beloved*: Re-Membering the Body as Historical Text', in Spillers, *Comparative American Identities*, pp. 62–86; Patricia Hunt, 'War and Peace: Transfigured Categories and the Politics of *Sula*', *African American Review* 27:3 (1993), 443–59; Keenan, '"Four Hundred Years of Silence"'; Maureen Reddy, 'The Tripled Plot and Center of *Sula*', *Black American Literature Forum* 22:1 (1988), 29–45.

32   Laurie Vickroy, 'The Traumatized Child in Toni Morrison and Marguerite Duras', *Mosaic* 29:2 (1996), 91.

33   For discussion of ghosts and haunting see also Linda Krumholz, 'The Ghosts of Slavery: Historical Recovery in Toni Morrison's *Beloved*', *African American Review* 26.3 (1992), 395–408, and David Lawrence, 'Fleshly Ghosts and Ghostly Flesh: The Word and the Body in *Beloved*', *Studies in American Fiction* 19:2 (1991), 189–201.

34   Bowers, '*Beloved* and the New Apocalypse', 60.

35   Alan Rice, 'Jazzing it up in a Storm: The Execution and Meaning of Toni Morrison's Jazzy Prose Style', *Journal of American Studies* 18:3 (1994), 421–32, p. 425, p. 426.

36   Joyce Irene Middleton, 'From Orality to Literacy: Oral Memory in Toni Morrison's *Song of Solomon*', in Valerie Smith (ed.) *New Essays on Song of Solomon* (Cambridge, Cambridge University Press, 1995), p. 22.

37   Toni Morrison, 'Rootedness: The Ancestor as Foundation', in Mari Evans (ed.), *Black Women Writers (1950–1980)* (New York, Anchor/Doubleday, 1984), p. 341. Reader response is addressed in essays by Brian Finney, 'Temporal Defamiliarization in Toni Morrison's *Beloved*', *Obsidian II* 5:1 (1990), 20–36; Jablon, 'Rememory, Dream Memory, and Revision in Toni Morrison's *Beloved* and

Alice Walker's *Temple of My Familiar*', 136–44; Rigney, 'A Story to Pass On'; Linda Krumholz, 'The Ghosts of Slavery: Historical Recovery in Toni Morrison's *Beloved*', *African American Review* 26:3 (1992), 395–408; Marilyn Mobley Saunders, 'Call and Response: Voice, Community and Dialogic Structures in Toni Morrison's *Song of Solomon*', in Smith, *New Essays on Song of Solomon*, pp. 41–68.

Chapter 9

1   Toni Morrison, *Paradise* (New York, Knopf, 1998), p. 306; subsequent references are given parenthetically in the text.

2   Angels Carabi, 'Interview', *Belles Lettres* 10:2 (1995), 40.

3   Carabi, 'Interview', 40.

4   Marsha Darling, 'In the Realm of Responsibility: A Conversation with Toni Morrison', [1988] *Conversations*, p. 254.

5   See Danille Taylor-Guthrie, *Conversations*, p. xiii.

6   Donna Nurse, Oral Conversation with Toni Morrison (6 January 1998).

7   The title, *Paradise*, recalls Milton's *Paradise Lost* and *Paradise Regained*, as well as Dante's *The Divine Comedy*. 'Paradiso' is the third part of this famous trilogy of which the first two parts are 'Inferno' and 'Purgatorio' – *not* correlatives of *Beloved* and *Jazz*.

8   Dinitia Smith, 'Mixing Tragedy and Folklore', *The New York Times*, 8 January 1998, B2.

9   Morrison has noted that she was looking through a book of photographs, *Ghost Towns of Oklahoma*, and found that 'it scarcely mention[ed] any of the black ones, but it did include one that was all-female. I think it lasted about eight months at the turn of the century.' See Christopher Hitchens, 'Morrison's True West', *Vanity Fair*, February 1998, p. 144. Another source for her idea of an all-female community was a trip to Brazil in the 1980s, where she heard a story (which she subsequently learned was untrue) about 'a convent of black nuns who took in abandoned children and practised *candomblé*, an Afro-Brazilian religion. The local populace considered them an outrage and they were murdered by a posse of men.'' Morrison nevertheless liked the story for what it had to say about the closeness of institutional and uninstitutional religion. See Dinitia Smith, 'Mixing Tragedy and Folklore', *The New York*

Times, 8 January 1998, B2–B3.

10   Piedade is the name of an area of Rio de Janeiro. The word also produces the anagram 'epi dead'.

11   Dinitia Smith, 'Mixing Tragedy and Folklore', B2.

Select bibliography

Works by Toni Morrison

FICTION

The Bluest Eye, London, Picador, 1970.

Sula, London, Picador, 1973.

Song of Solomon, London, Picador, 1977.

Tar Baby, London, Picador, 1981.

Beloved, London, Picador, 1987.

Jazz, London, Picador, 1992.

Paradise, New York, Knopf, 1998

NON-FICTION

Playing in the Dark: Whiteness and the Literary Imagination, New York, Vintage Books, 1992.

(ed.), *Race-ing Justice, En-gendering Power: Essays on Anita Hill, Clarence Thomas, and the Construction of Social Reality*, New York, Pantheon, 1992.

(ed.) with Claudia Brodsky Lacour, *Birth of a Nation'hood: Gaze, Script, and Spectacle in the O. J. Simpson Case*, New York, Pantheon, 1997.

ARTICLES, ESSAYS, INTRODUCTIONS, PUBLISHED SPEECHES

'Rootedness: The Ancestor as Foundation', in Mari Evans (ed.), *Black Women Writers (1950–1980)*, New York, Anchor/Doubleday, 1984.

'Memory, Creation, and Writing', *Thought: A Review of Culture and Idea*, 59 (1984), 385–90.

'The Site of Memory', in William Zinsser (ed.), *Inventing the Truth: The Art and Craft of the Memoir*, Boston, Houghton Mifflin, 1987, pp. 103–24.

'Unspeakable Things Unspoken: The Afro-American Presence in American Literature', *Michigan Quarterly Review*, 28 (1989), 1–34.

'A Bench by the Road', *The World*, 3:1 (1989), 4–5, 37–41.

'On the Backs of Blacks', in Nicolaus Mills (ed.), *Arguing Immigration: The Debate Over the Changing Face of America*, New York, Touchstone Books, 1994.

Lecture and Speech of Acceptance, Upon the Award of the Nobel Prize for Literature, *The Nobel Lecture in Literature*, New York, Alfred Knopf, 1994.

Criticism

BOOKS

Awkward, Michael, *Inspiriting Influences: Tradition, Revision and Afro-American Women's Novels*, New York, Columbia University Press, 1989.

Bhabha, Homi K., *The Location of Culture*, London, Routledge, 1994.

Bjork, Patrick Bryce, *The Novels of Toni Morrison*, New York, Peter Lang, 1992.

Bloom, Harold (ed.), *Toni Morrison: Modern Critical Views*, New York, Chelsea House Publishers, 1990.

Butler-Evans, Elliott, *Race, Gender, and Desire: Narrative Strategies in the Fiction of Toni Cade Bambara, Toni Morrison, and Alice Walker*, Philadelphia, Temple University Press, 1989.

Campbell, Jane, *Mythic Black Fiction: The Transformation of History*, Knoxville, University of Tennessee Press, 1986.

Carmean, Karen, *Toni Morrison's World of Fiction*, Troy, NY, Whitson, 1993.

Coser, Stelamaris, *Bridging the Americas: The Literature of Toni Morrison, Paule Marshall, and Gayle Jones*, Philadelphia, Temple University Press, 1994.

Dubey, M., *Black Women Novelists and the Nationalist Aesthetic*, Bloomington, Indiana University Press, 1994.

Furman, Jan, *Toni Morrison's Fiction*, Columbia, SC, University of South Carolina Press, 1996.

Gates, Henry Louis, Jr and K. Anthony Appiah (eds), *Toni Morrison: Critical Perspectives Past and Present*, New York, Amistad, 1993.

Guthrie-Taylor, Danielle (ed.), *Conversations with Toni Morrison*, Jackson, University Press of Mississippi, 1994.

Harris, Trudier, *Fiction and Folklore: The Novels of Toni Morrison*, Knoxville, University of Tennessee Press, 1991.

Heinze, Denise, *The Dilemma of 'Double-Consciousness': Toni Morrison's Novels*, Athens, University of Georgia Press, 1993.

Mckay, Nellie (ed.), *Critical Essays on Toni Morrison*, Boston, G. K. Hall, 1998.

Middleton, David, L., *Toni Morrison: An Annotated Bibliography*, New York, Garland, 1987.

— (ed.), *Toni Morrison's Fiction: Contemporary Criticism*, New York, Garland, 1997.

Otten, Terry, *The Crime of Innocence in Toni Morrison's Fiction*, Columbia, University of Missouri Press, 1989.

Page, Philip, *Dangerous Freedom: Fusion and Fragmentation in Toni Morrison's Novels*, Jackson, University of Mississippi Press, 1995.

Pryse, Majorie, and Hortense J. Spillers (eds), *Conjuring: Black Women, Fiction, and Literary Tradition*, Bloomington, Indiana University Press, 1985, pp. 192–202.

Rigney, Barbara, *The Voices of Toni Morrison*, Columbus, Ohio State University Press, 1991.

Samuels, Wilfred D. and Clenora Hudson-Weems, *Toni Morrison*, Boston, Twayne Publishers, 1990.

Smith, Valerie (ed.), *New Essays on Song of Solomon*, Cambridge, Cambridge University Press, 1995.

Walker, Melissa, *Down from the Mountaintop: Black Women's Novels in the Wake of the Civil Rights Movement, 1966–1989*, New Haven, Yale University Press, 1991.

Willis, Susan, *Specifying: Black Women Writing the American Experience*, Madison, University of Wisconsin Press, 1986.

ARTICLES AND ESSAYS

Anderson, Linda, 'The Re-imagining of History in Contemporary Women's Fiction', in Linda Anderson (ed.), *Plotting Change: Contemporary Women's Fiction*, London, Edward Arnold, 1990, pp. 129–41.

Backus, Margot Gayle, '"Looking for That Dead Girl": Incest, Pornography, and the Capitalist Family Romance in *Nightwood*, *The Years* and *Tar Baby*', *American Imago*, 51:4 (1994), 421–45.

Bakerman, Jane S., 'Failures of Love: Female Initiation in the Novels of Toni Morrison', *American Literature*, 52:4 (1981), 541–63.

Barrett, Eileen, '"For Books Continue Each Other…": Toni Morrison and Virginia Woolf', in Mark Hussey and Vara Neverow (eds), *Virginia Woolf: Emerging Perspectives: Selected Papers from the Third Annual Conference on Virginia Woolf*, New York, Pace University Press, 1994, pp. 26–32.

Bennett, Paula, 'The Mother's Part: Incest and Maternal Deprivation in Woolf and Morrison', in Brenda O. Daly and Maureen T. Reddy (eds), *Narrating Mothers: Theorizing Maternal Subjectivities*, Knoxville, University of Tennessee Press, 1991, pp. 125–38.

Benston, Kimberly W., 'Re-weaving the "Ulysses Scene": Enchantment, Post-Oedipal Identity, and the Buried Text of Blackness in Toni Morrison's *Song of Solomon*', in Hortense J. Spillers (ed.), *Comparative American Identities: Race, Sex, and Nationality in the Modern Text*, New York, Routledge, 1991, pp. 87–109.

Berger, James, 'Ghosts of liberalism: Morrison's *Beloved* and the Moynihan report', *PMLA*, 111:3 (May 1996), 408–20.

Berret, Anthony J., 'Toni Morrison's Literary Jazz', *CLA Journal*, 32:3 (1989), 267–83.

Boudreau, Kristin, 'Pain and the Unmaking of Self in Toni Morrison's *Beloved*', *Contemporary Literature*, 36:3 (1995), 447–65.

Bowers, Susan, '*Beloved* and the New Apocalypse', *The Journal of Ethnic Studies*, 18:1 (1990), 59–77.

Broad, Robert L., 'Giving Blood to the Scraps: Haints, History, and Hosea in *Beloved*', *African American Review*, 28:2 (1994), 189–96.

Bryant, Cedric Gael, 'The Orderliness of Disorder: Madness and Evil in Toni Morrison's *Sula*', *Black American Literature Forum*, 24:4 (1990), 731–45.

Byerman, Keith E., 'Intense Behaviours: The Use of the Grotesque in *The Bluest Eye* and *Eva's Man*', *CLA Journal*, 25:4 (1982), 447–57.

Coleman, Alisha R., 'One and One Makes One: A Metacritical and Psychoanalytic Reading of Friendship in Toni Morrison's *Sula*', *CLA Journal*, 37:2 (1993), 145–55.

Comfort, Susan, 'Counter-Memory, Mourning and History in Toni Morrison's *Beloved*', *Literature, Interpretation, Theory*, 6:1–2 (1995), 121–32.

Daily, Gary W., 'Toni Morrison's *Beloved*: Rememory, History, and the Fantastic', in Donald E. Morse, Marshall B. Tymn and Csilla Bertha (eds), *The Celebration of the Fantastic*, Westport, CN, Greenwood, 1992, pp. 141–7.

Davies, Carol Boyce, 'Mother Right/Write Revisited: *Beloved* and *Dessa Rose* and the Construction of Motherhood in Black Women's Fiction', in Brenda O. Daly and Maureen T. Reddy, (eds), *Narrating Mothers: Theorizing Maternal Subjectivities*, Knoxville, University of Tennessee Press, 1991, pp. 44–57.

Denard, Carolyn, 'Toni Morrison', in Darlene Clark Hine (ed.), *Black Women in America: An Historical Encyclopedia*, New York, Carlson Publishing Inc., 1993.

Dickerson, Vanessa D., 'The Naked Father in Toni Morrison's *The Bluest Eye*', in Patricia Yeager and Beth Kowaleski-Wallace (eds), *Refiguring the Father: New Feminist Readings of Patriarchy*, Carbondale, Southern Illinois University Press, 1989, pp. 108–27.

Eckard, Paula Gallant, 'The Interplay of Music, Language, and Narrative in Toni Morrison's *Jazz*', *CLA Journal*, 38:1 (1994), 11–19.

Epstein, Grace A., 'Out of Blue Water: Dream Flight and Narrative Construction in the Novels of Toni Morrison', in Nicholas Ruddick (ed.), *State of the Fantastic: Studies in the Theory and Practice of Fantastic Literature and Film*, Westport, CT, Greenwood, 1992, pp. 141–7.

Erickson, Peter B., 'Images of Nuturance in Toni Morrison's *Tar Baby*', *CLA Journal*, 28:1 (1984), 11–32.

Ferguson, Rebecca, 'History, Memory, and Language in Toni Morrison's *Beloved*', in Susan Sellers (ed.), *Feminist Criticism: Theory and Practice*, Toronto, University of Toronto Press, 1991, pp. 109–27.

Finney, Brian, 'Temporal Defamiliarization in Toni Morrison's *Beloved*', *Obsidian II*, 5:1 (1990), 20–36.

Fitzgerald, Jennifer, 'Selfhood and Community: Psychoanalysis and Discourse in *Beloved*', *Modern Fiction Studies*, 39:3/4 (1993), 669–87.

Gates, Henry Louis, Jr and K. Anthony Appiah, Review of *Jazz*, in *Critical Perspectives Past and Present: Toni Morrison*, New York, Amistad, 1993, pp. 52–5.

—, 'Thirteen Ways of Looking at a Black Man', *The New Yorker*, 23 October 1995.

Gillespie, Diane, and Missy Dehn Kubitschek, 'Who Cares? Women-Centered Psychology in *Sula*', *Black American Literature Forum*, 24:1 (1990), 21–48.

Grant, Robert, 'Absence into Presence: The Thematics of Memory and "Missing" Subjects in Toni Morrison's *Sula*', in Nellie McKay (ed.), *Critical Essays on Toni Morrison*, Boston, G. K. Hall, 1988, pp. 90–103.

Grewal, Gurleen, 'Memory and the Matrix of History: The Poetics of Loss and Recovery in Joy Kogawa's *Obasan* and Toni Morrison's *Beloved*', in Amritjit Singh *et al.* (eds), *Memory and Cultural Politics: New Approaches to American Ethnic Literatures*, Boston, Northeastern University Press, 1996, pp. 140–74.

Guth, Deborah, 'A Blessing and a Burden: The Relation to the Past in *Sula, Song of Solomon*, and *Beloved*', *Modern Fiction Studies*, 39:3/4 (1993), 575–96.

Handley, 'The House a Ghost Built: *Nommo*, Allegory, and the Ethics of Reading in Toni Morrison's *Beloved*', *Contemporary Literature*, 36.4 (1995): 676–701.

Harris, A. Leslie, 'Myth as Structure in Toni Morrison's *Song of Solomon*', *MELUS*, 7:3 (1980), 69–76.

Hawthorne, Evelyn, 'On Gaining the Double-Vision: *Tar Baby* as Diasporean Novel', *Black American Literature Forum*, 22:1 (1988), 97–107.

Henderson, Mae G., 'Toni Morrison's *Beloved*: Re-Membering the Body as Historical Text', in Hortense J. Spillers (ed.), *Comparative American Identities: Race, Sex, and Nationality in the Modern Text*, New York, Routledge, 1991, pp. 62–86.

Hirsch, Marianne, 'Maternity and Rememory: Toni Morrison's *Beloved*', in Donna Bassin, Margaret Honey and Meryle Mahrer Kaplan (eds), *Representations of Motherhood*, New Haven, Yale University Press, 1994, pp. 92–110.

—, 'Knowing Their Names: Toni Morrison's *Song of Solomon*', in Valerie Smith (ed.), *New Essays on Song of Solomon*, Cambridge, Cambridge University Press, 1995.

Holton, Robert, 'Bearing Witness: Toni Morrison's *Song of Solomon* and *Beloved*', *English Studies in Canada*, 20:1 (1994), 79–90.

Horvitz, Deborah, 'Nameless Ghosts: Possession and Dispossession in *Beloved*', *Studies in American Fiction*, 17:2 (1989), 157–68.

House, Elizabeth B., 'Toni Morrison's Ghost: The Beloved Who is Not Beloved', *Studies in American Fiction*, 18:1 (1990), 17–26.

Hunt, Patricia, 'War and Peace: Transfigured Categories and the Politics of *Sula*', *African American Review*, 27:3 (1993), 443–59.

Johnson, Barbara, '"Aesthetic" and "Rapport" in Toni Morrison's *Sula*', *Textual Practice*, 7:2 (1993), 165–72.

Jones, Carolyn M., '*Sula* and *Beloved*: Images of Cain in the Novels of Toni Morrison', *African American Review*, 27:4 (1993), 615–26.

Jordan, Elaine, '"Not My People": Toni Morrison and Identity', in Gina Wisker (ed.), *Black Women's Writing*, London, Macmillan, 1993, pp. 111–26.

Keenan, Sally, '"Four Hundred Years of Silence": Myth, History, and Motherhood in Toni Morrison's *Beloved*', in Jonathan White (ed.), *Recasting the World: Writing after Colonialism*, Baltimore, Johns Hopkins University Press, 1993, pp. 45–81.

Krumholz, Linda, 'The Ghosts of Slavery: Historical Recovery in Toni Morrison's *Beloved*', *African American Review*, 26:3 (1992), 395–408.

Kuenz, Jane, '*The Bluest Eye*: Notes on History, Community, and Black Female Subjectivity', *African American Review*, 27:3 (1993), 421–31.

Lawrence, David, 'Fleshly Ghosts and Ghostly Flesh: The Word and the Body in *Beloved*', *Studies in American Fiction*, 19:2 (1991), 189–201.

Ledbetter, T. Mark, 'An Apocalypse of Race and Gender: Body Violence and Forming Identity in Toni Morrison's *Beloved*', David Jasper (ed.), *Postmodernism, Literature and the Future of Theology*, London, St. Martin's Press, 1993, pp. 78–90.

Lewis, Barbara Williams, 'The Function of Jazz in Toni Morrison's *Jazz*', in David Middleton (ed.), *Toni Morrison's Fiction: Contemporary Criticism*, New York, Garland, 1997, pp. 271–81.

Levy, Andrew, 'Telling *Beloved*', *Texas Studies in Literature and Languages*, 331:1 (1991), 115–23.

Liscio, Lorraine, '*Beloved*'s Narrative: Reading Mother's Milk', *Tulsa Studies in Women's Literature*, 11:1 (1992), 31–46.

Mathieson, Barbara Offutt, 'Memory and Mother Love in Morrison's *Beloved*', *American Imago*, 47:1 (1990), 1–21.

Mayberry, Katherine, 'The Problem of Narrative in Toni Morrison's *Jazz*', in David Middleton (ed.), *Toni Morrison's Fiction: Contemporary Criticism*, New York, Garland, 1997, 297–309.

Miller Budick, Emily, 'Absence, Loss, and the Space of History in Toni Morrison's *Beloved*', *Arizona Quarterly*, 48:2 (1992), 117–38.

Moody, Jocelyn K., 'Ripping Away the Veil of Slavery: Literacy, Communal Love, and Self-Esteem in Three Slave Women's Narratives', *Black American Literature Forum*, 24:4 (1990), 633–48.

Osagie, Iyunolu, 'Is Morrison Also Among the Prophets?: "Psychoanalytic" Strategies in *Beloved*', *African American Review*, 28:3 (1994), 423–40.

Reddy, Maureen T., 'The Tripled Plot and Center of *Sula*', *Black American Literature Forum*, 22:1 (1988), 29–45.

Rice, Alan, 'Jazzing it up a Storm: The Execution and Meaning of Toni Morrison's Jazzy Prose Style', *Journal of American Studies*, 18:3 (1994), 421–32.

Rigney, Barbara Hill, '"A Story to Pass On": Ghosts and the Significance of History in Toni Morrison's *Beloved*', in Lynette Carpenter and Wendy K. Kolmar (eds), *Haunting the House of Fiction: Feminist Perspectives on Ghost Stories by American Women*, Knoxville, University of Tennessee Press, 1991, pp. 229–35.

Rody, Caroline, 'Toni Morrison's *Beloved*: History, "Rememory", and a "Clamor for a Kiss"', *American Literary History*, 7 (1995), 92–119.

Rushdy, Ashraf H. A., '"Rememory": Primal Scenes and Constructions in Toni Morrison's Novels', *Contemporary Literature*, 31:3 (1990), 300–23.

Schapiro, Barbara, 'The Bonds of Love and the Boundaries of Self in Toni Morrison's *Beloved*', *Contemporary Literature*, 32:2 (1991), 194–210.

Schmudde, Carol E., 'The Haunting of 124', *African American Review*, 26:3 (1992), 409–16.

Skerrett Jr, Joseph T., 'Recitation to the *Griot*: Storytelling and Learning in *Song of Solomon*', in Marjorie Pryse and Hortense J. Spillers (eds), *Conjuring: Black Women, Fiction, and Literary Tradition*, Bloomington, Indiana University Press, 1985, pp. 192–202.

Smith-Wright, Geraldine, 'In Spite of the Klan: Ghosts in the Fiction of Black Women Writers', in Lynette Carpenter and Wendy K. Kolmar (eds), *Haunting the House of Fiction: Feminist Perspectives on Ghost Stories by American Women*, Knoxville, University of Tennessee Press, 1991, pp. 142–65.

Vickroy, Laurie, 'The Politics of Abuse: The Traumatized Child in Toni Morrison and Marguerite Duras', *Mosaic*, 29:2 (1996), 91–109.

Wedertz-Furtado, Utelinde, 'Historical Dimensions in Toni Morrison's *Song of Solomon*', in Gunter H. Lenz (ed.), *History and Tradition in Afro-American Culture*, Frankfurt, Campus Verlag, 1984, pp. 222–41.

Willis, Susan, 'Eruptions of Funk: Historicizing Toni Morrison', in Henry Louis Gates Jr (ed.), *Black Literature and Literary Theory*, London, Routledge, 1984, pp. 262–83.

Wisker, Gina, '"Disremembered and Unaccounted For": Reading Toni Morrison's *Beloved* and Alice Walker's *The Temple of My Familiar*', in Gina Wisker (ed.), *Black Women's Writing*, New York, St. Martin's Press, 1993, pp. 78–95.

Wolff, Cynthia Griffin, '"Margaret Garner": A Cinncinnati Story', in Christopher K. Lohmann (ed.), *Discovering Difference: Contemporary Essays in American Culture*, Bloomington, Indiana University Press, 1993, pp. 105–22.

Wyatt, Jean, 'Giving Body to the Word: The Maternal Symbolic in Toni Morrison's *Beloved*', *PMLA* 108 (1993), 474–88.

General Works

TRAUMA AND MEMORY

Antze, Paul and Michael Lambek (eds), *Tense Past: Cultural Essays in Trauma and Memory*, New York, Routledge, 1996.

Aberbach, David, *Surviving Trauma: Loss, Literature and Psychoanalysis*, New Haven, Yale University Press, 1989.

Caruth, C. (ed.), *Trauma: Explorations in Memory*, Baltimore, Johns Hopkins University Press, 1995.

—, *Unclaimed Experience: Trauma, Narrative, and History*, Baltimore, Johns Hopkins University Press, 1996.

Felman, Shoshana, and Dori Laub, *Testimony: Crises of Witnessing in Literature, Psychoanalysis, and History*, London, Routledge, 1992.

Fentress, James, and Christopher Wickham, *Social Memory*, Oxford, Blackwell, 1992.

Granofsky, Ronald, *The Trauma Novel: Contemporary Symbolic Depictions of Collective Disaster*, New York, Peter Lang, 1995.

Hartman, Geoffrey H., 'On Traumatic Knowledge and Literary Studies', *New Literary History*, 26:3 (1995), 537–63.

Herman, Judith Lewis, *Trauma and Recovery*, New York, Basic Books, 1992.

LaCapra, Dominick, *Representing the Holocaust: History, Theory, Trauma*, Ithaca, Cornell University Press, 1994.

Tal, Kali, *Worlds of Hurt: Reading the Literatures of Trauma*, Cambridge, Cambridge University Press, 1996.

Waites, Elizabeth A., *Trauma and Survival: Post-Traumatic and Dissociative Disorders in Women*, New York, Norton, 1993.

AFRICAN AMERICAN CULTURE AND POLITICS

Anderson, Jervis, *Harlem: The Great Black Way*, London, Orbis, 1982.

De Jongh, J., *Vicious Modernism: Black Harlem and the Literary Imagination*, Cambridge, Cambridge University Press, 1990.

Fabre, Geneviève, and Robert O'Meally (eds), *History and Memory in African-American Culture*, Oxford, Oxford University Press, 1994.

Franklin, John Hope, *From Slavery to Freedom: A History of American Negroes*, 2nd edition, New York, Knopf, 1961.

hooks, bell, *Yearning: Race, Gender and Cultural Politics*, Boston, South End Press, 1990.

—, *Killing Rage: Ending Racism*, London, Penguin Books, 1996.

Huggins, Nathan Irvin, *Harlem Renaissance*, New York, Oxford University Press, 1971.

—, (ed.), *Voices from the Harlem Renaissance*, New York, Oxford University Press, 1976.

Vandeburg, William L., *New Day in Babylon: The Black Power Movement and American Culture, 1965–1975*, Chicago, University of Chicago Press, 1992.

Werner, Craig Hansen, *Playing the Changes: From Afro-Modernism to the Jazz Impulse*, Urbana, University of Illinois Press, 1994.

Wintz, Cary D., *Black Culture and the Harlem Renaissance*, Houston, Rice University Press, 1988.

Index